ANDREW WYETH AT KUERNER FARM: THE EYE OF THE EARTH

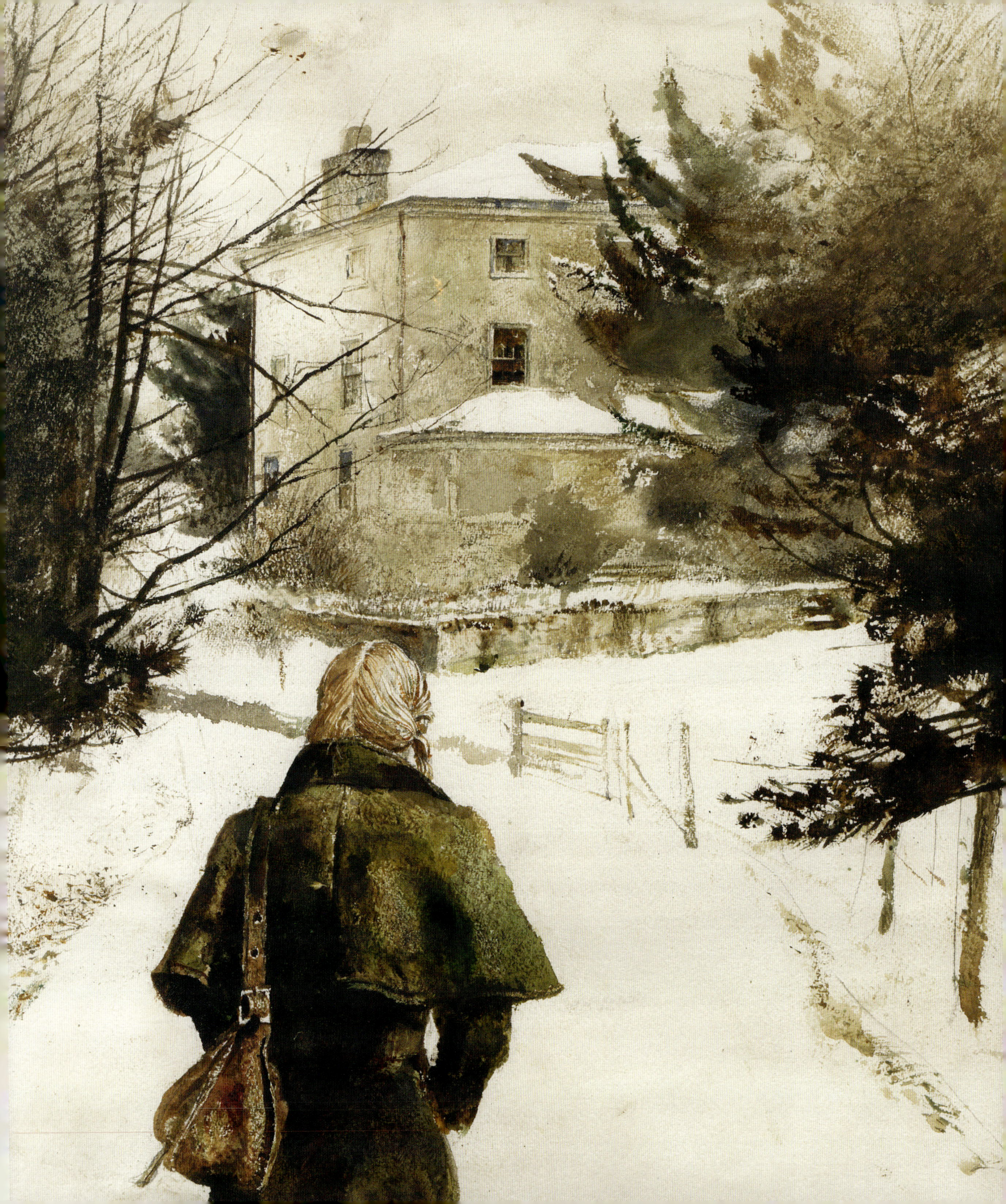

ANDREW WYETH
AT KUERNER FARM: THE EYE OF THE EARTH

TEXTS BY WILLIAM L. COLEMAN, ALLISON C. SLABY,
JAMES WELLING, AND KAREN BAUMGARTNER

FOREWORD BY THOMAS PADON AND ALLISON PERKINS

PHOTOGRAPHY BY JOSHUA MCHUGH

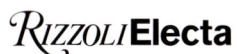 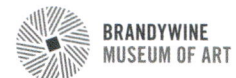 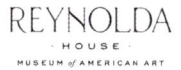

IN ASSOCIATION WITH THE WYETH FOUNDATION FOR AMERICAN ART

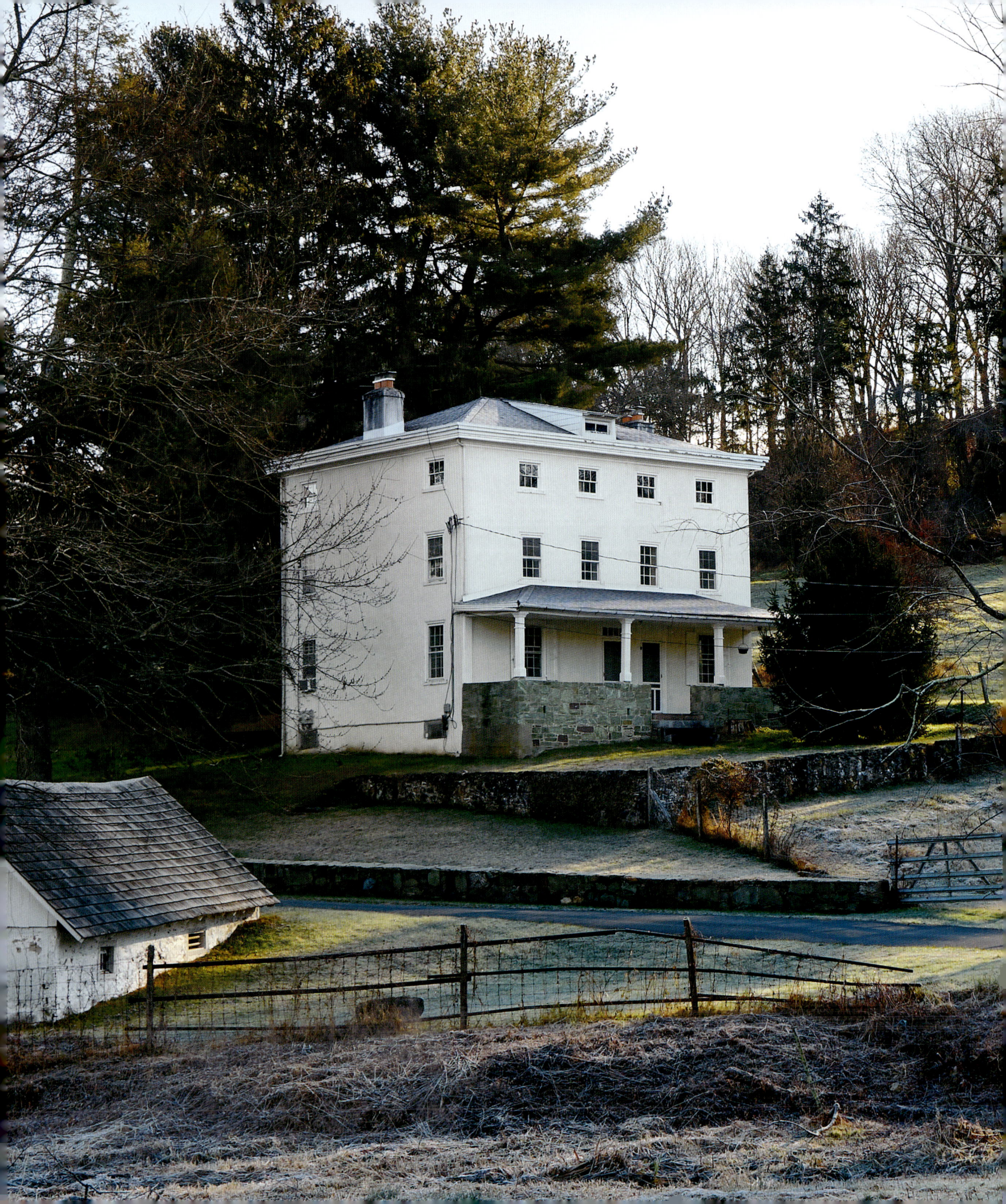

CONTENTS

7   **Directors' Foreword**
Thomas Padon and Allison Perkins

13   **Nothing Simple: Unpacking the Kuerner Myth**
William L. Coleman

25   **"Kuerners Is a Tough Place": Andrew Wyeth's *Farm Pond* and Its Place in His Dark Oeuvre**
Allison C. Slaby

35   **Wyeth's Vibe**
James Welling

41   **The People behind the Paintings: Karl and Anna Kuerner**
Karen Baumgartner

49   **Plates**

154   List of Illustrations

156   Contributors

158   Photography Credits

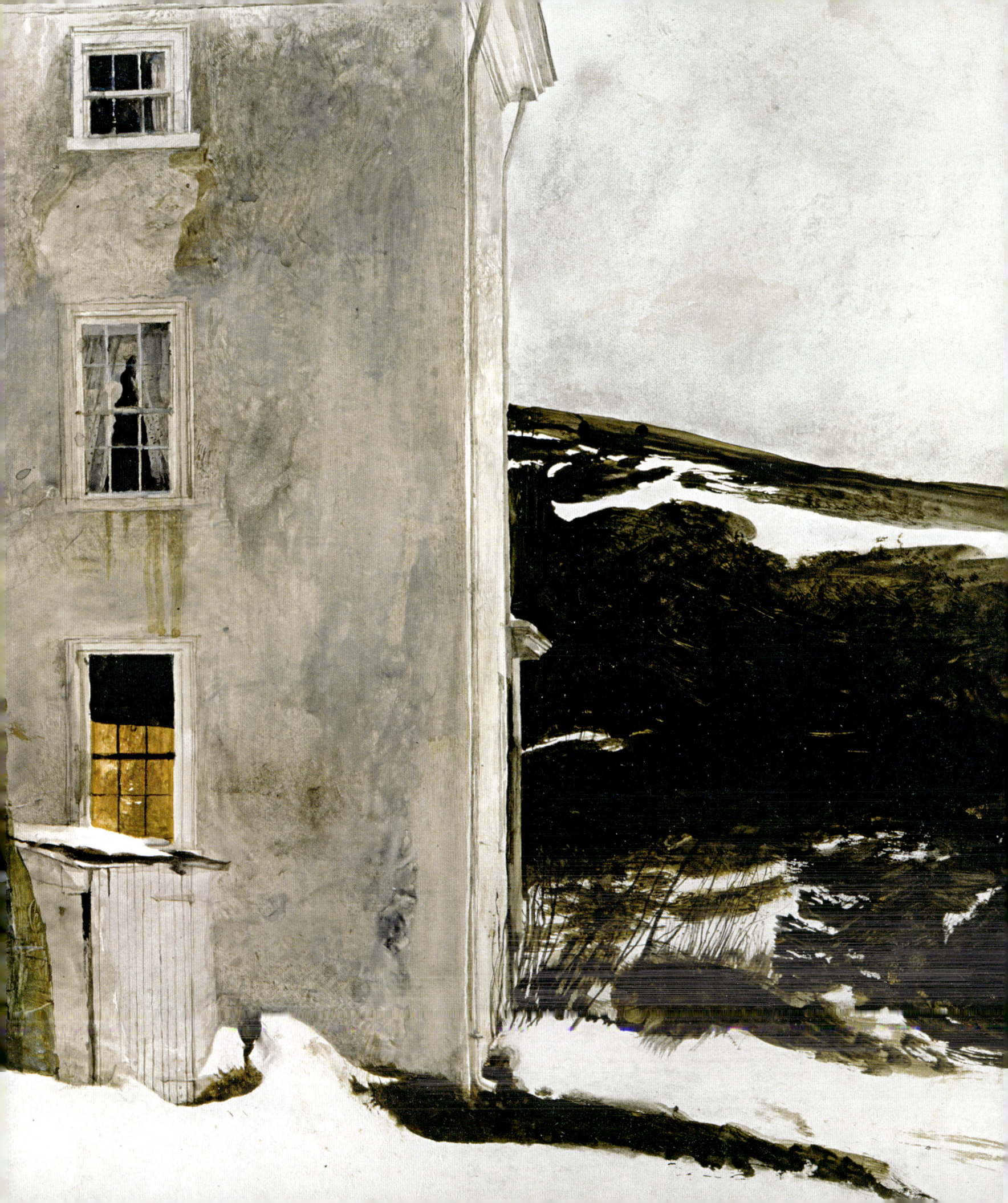

DIRECTORS' FOREWORD

THOMAS PADON
James H. Duff Director, Brandywine Museum of Art

ALLISON PERKINS
Executive Director, Reynolda House
Wake Forest University Associate Provost
for Reynolda House Museum of American Art
and Reynolda Gardens

The works of art Andrew Wyeth created depicting Kuerner Farm are the legacy of a remarkable creative practice with few close parallels in the history of art. Over the course of seven decades, the hundreds of temperas, oils, and works on paper he produced in relation to this agrarian and domestic environment constitute a lasting statement of the possibilities of a rigorously place-based practice. In landscape, figure painting, architectural studies, and intimate interiors, Wyeth partnered with the people of this place to produce some of his most enigmatic and, simultaneously, best-loved paintings. While this story is important to both our institutions through the related objects in our permanent collections that we share with our publics, there has never been a national exhibition solely focused on Wyeth's Kuerner Farm works. The last project that seriously examined this theme was *Two Worlds of Andrew Wyeth: Kuerners and Olsons* (1976), organized by the Metropolitan Museum of Art, yet that exhibition was fifty years ago, after which Wyeth continued depictions of the farm. The twenty-fifth anniversary of the gift of Kuerner Farm to the Brandywine Museum of Art by Karl Kuerner Jr. and his son, artist Karl J. Kuerner, in 1999 is a fitting occasion for a reappraisal of this rich chapter of American art.

So widely admired is Wyeth's Kuerner work that a significant amount of baggage has accrued to these paintings and drawings. The subject matter is often interpreted as archetypal and unidimensional: a site of darkness and harshness peopled by individuals who stand in for generic, broad-brush ideas. *Andrew Wyeth at Kuerner Farm: The Eye of the Earth* has been co-organized by our institutions to challenge this received narrative and to bring fresh nuance to the unique creative chapter that this place inspired and to the living, breathing individuals who were central to the encounter and who had their own perspectives on it. The project was first proposed by Reynolda's curator, Allison C. Slaby, who found an eager

Andrew Wyeth, *Dusk*, 1978 (detail, p. 119)

collaborator in the Brandywine's William L. Coleman shortly after the start of a new era of Brandywine management of the Andrew & Betsy Wyeth Collection of the Wyeth Foundation for American Art. This important group of some seven thousand works of art provides the essential core of the exhibition's checklist, with key loans from private and public collections nationwide. The core members of the project team, including Karen Baumgartner and Bethany Engel at the Brandywine and Katie Womack at Reynolda, tracked down rarely exhibited objects and ensured that this rich project would be seen also at a third venue, the Cummer Museum of Art and Gardens, which has been an excellent partner. Essays from Coleman, Slaby, and Baumgartner as well as by artist James Welling have fundamentally changed our understanding of the abiding inspiration of Kuerner Farm. We extend our thanks to all these individuals, as well as to the publication team: the Brandywine's Head of Creative Services, Joshua Schnapf, catalogue production coordinator Todd Bradway, editor Sheri Walter, and designer Robin Brunelle, in addition to Rizzoli's Margaret Chace, associate publisher, and editor Jason Best. Not least, we are grateful for the generous cooperation of the museums and individuals who allowed us to share highlights of their collections in a new context and to the Wyeth Foundation for American Art for their thoughtful partnership and for their support of this project's national tour. We are delighted to celebrate and honor the generosity of the Wells Fargo Foundation, our national sponsor of *Andrew Wyeth at Kuerner Farm: The Eye of the Earth*. We extend our deep appreciation to the foundation for its recognition of the important impact that this exhibition will have in three distinct and diverse American art museums and communities on its national tour.

At the Brandywine, we add thanks to Virginia A. Logan, the Frolic Weymouth Executive Director and CEO of the museum's parent organization, the Brandywine Conservancy & Museum of Art, for her enthusiastic support of this project from the start, as well as to Cuyler H. Walker, Chair of the Brandywine's Board of Trustees, and D. D. Matz, Vice Chair, for their generous support of all aspects of our work. Michelle Moskal, Carolanne Deal, Daniel Krull, Abigail Peterman, and Mary Cronin all made important contributions to the execution of this exhibition at the Brandywine.

At Reynolda House Museum of American Art, we are indebted to Barbara Babcock Millhouse, Founding President of the museum, who in 1984 generously purchased *Farm Pond* by Andrew Wyeth (p. 71), the inspiration for this exhibition. We extend our sincere appreciation to Dr. Susan R. Wente, President of Wake Forest University, the museum's affiliated partner, for her unwavering support of the museum and this project. Phil Archer, Kim Hampton, Sarah Blackwell, Brittany Norton, Katie Wolf, Caroline Gallagher, and Shane Carrico have been instrumental in the successful implementation of this exhibition at Reynolda House.

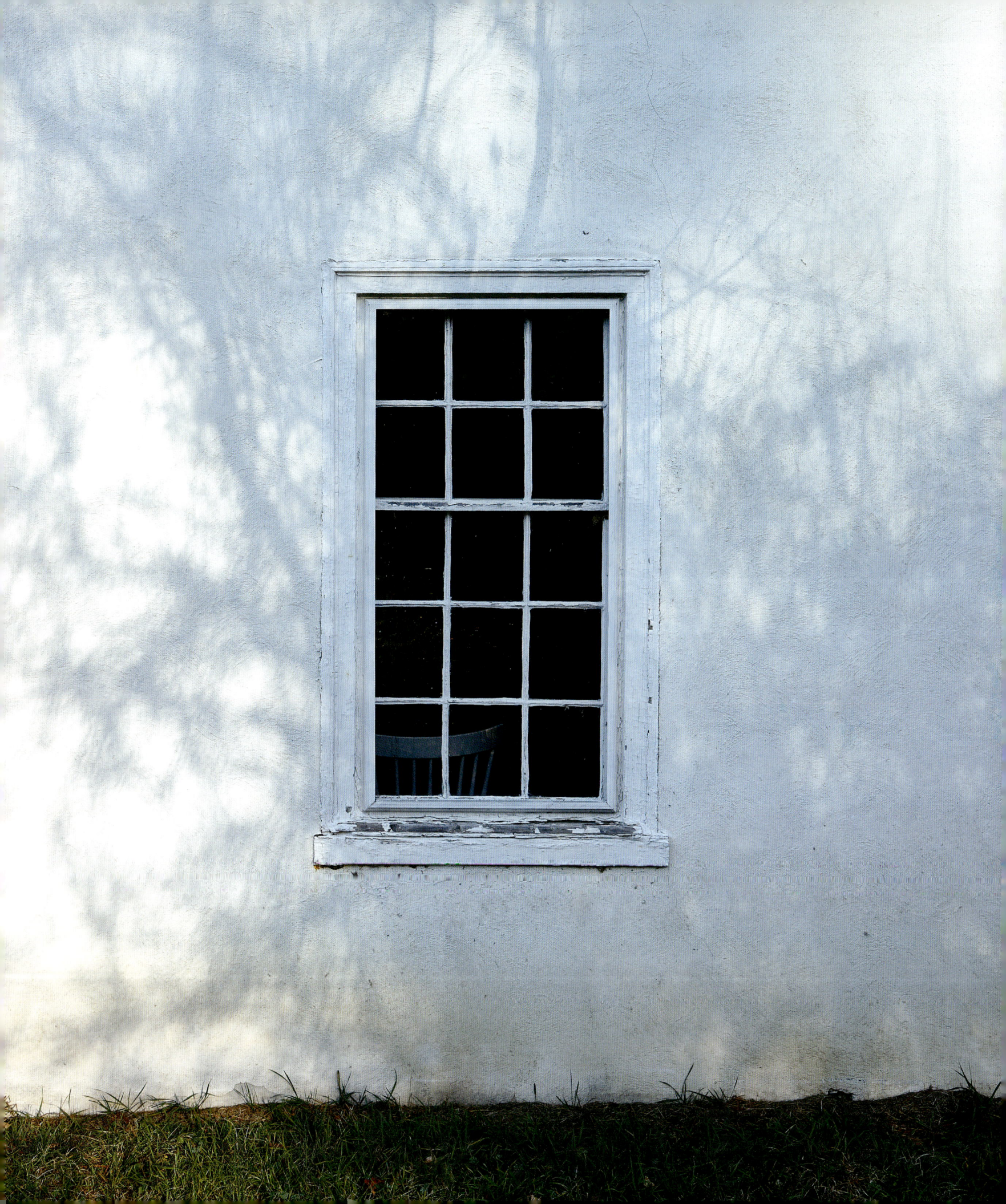

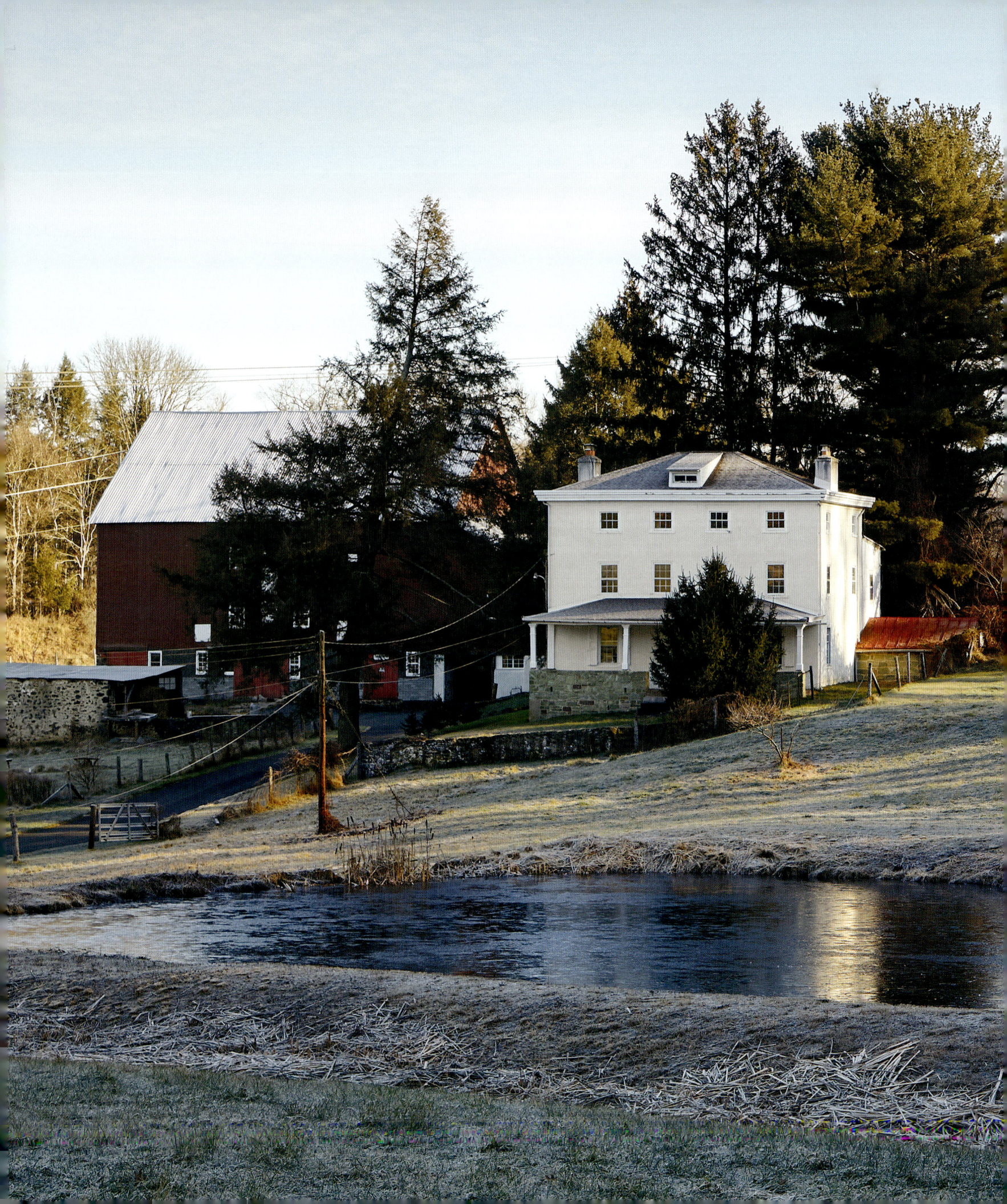

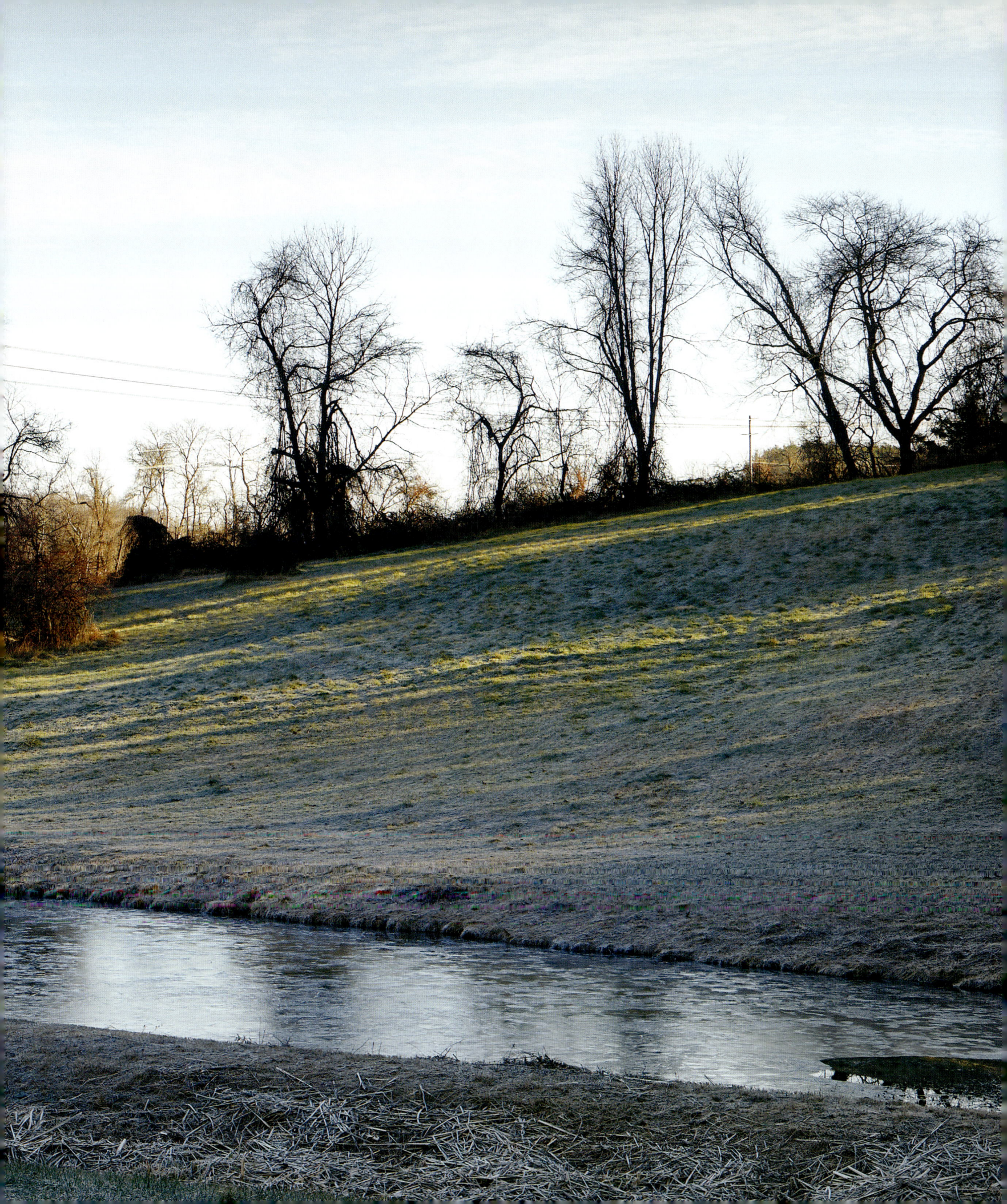

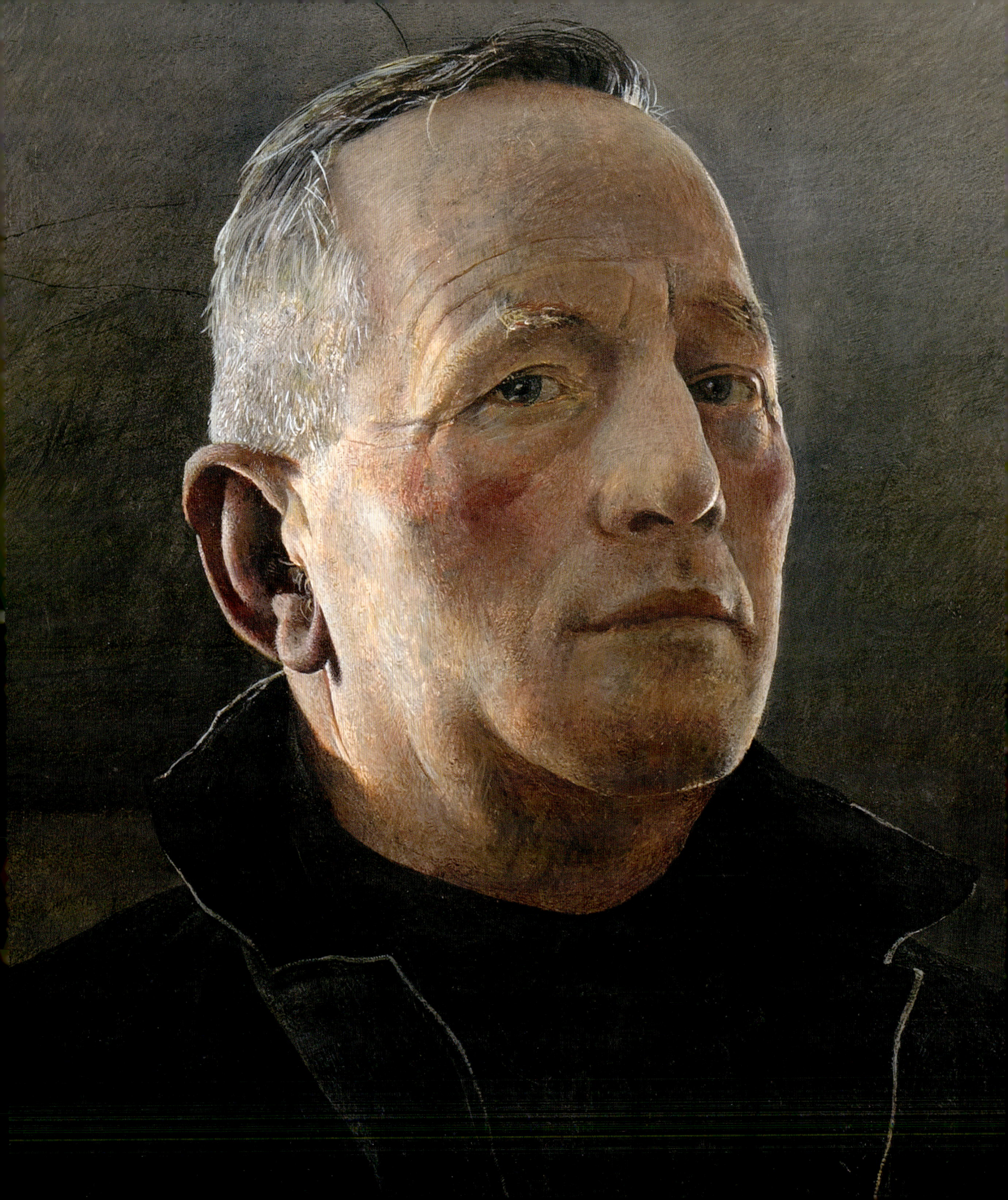

NOTHING SIMPLE: UNPACKING THE KUERNER MYTH

WILLIAM L. COLEMAN

Andrew Wyeth's decades-long commitment to the subject of Kuerner Farm is one of the most remarkable stories of creative focus in the history of art. Among the hundreds of works he produced over about seven decades in response to the landscape, buildings, and people of this place, there are some of his major achievements in the mediums of watercolor and egg tempera, like *Wolf Moon* (1975; p. 115) and *Karl* (1948; p. 67), and works that have been given canonical status by their inclusion on US postage stamps and in the first solo exhibition at the White House of a living artist (fig. 1).[1] With this lofty public reputation comes an unspoken question: Why Kuerner Farm? What was it about this hard-edged agricultural site with few of the trappings of conventional picturesque subject matter that called out for this kind of visionary investment, resulting in some of the most influential paintings of Wyeth's career?

The widespread love of Wyeth's Kuerner works has spawned a cottage industry of attempts to explain the fascination with and associations of the place. No book on Wyeth would be complete without some attention to the problem of Kuerners, and a sizable edifice of mythology has grown up around it as a result. According to the folklore, Kuerners is a place of brutal archetypes. It is a landscape irrevocably imbued with violence: echoes of the musket fire of the Revolutionary War's Battle of Brandywine mingling with the memory of Karl Kuerner's lethal work with a German Maxim 08/15 light machine gun in the Battle of Verdun, the sudden death of N. C. Wyeth after a train struck the automobile he was in nearby, and the everyday brutalities of hunting and farming.[2] The people of the place have similarly come to embody stock romantic values. We are told that Karl Kuerner is the cruel one, his wife, Anna Faulhaber Kuerner, is the troubled one, and Karl's sometimes caretaker, Helga Testorf, is the breath of fresh air. In

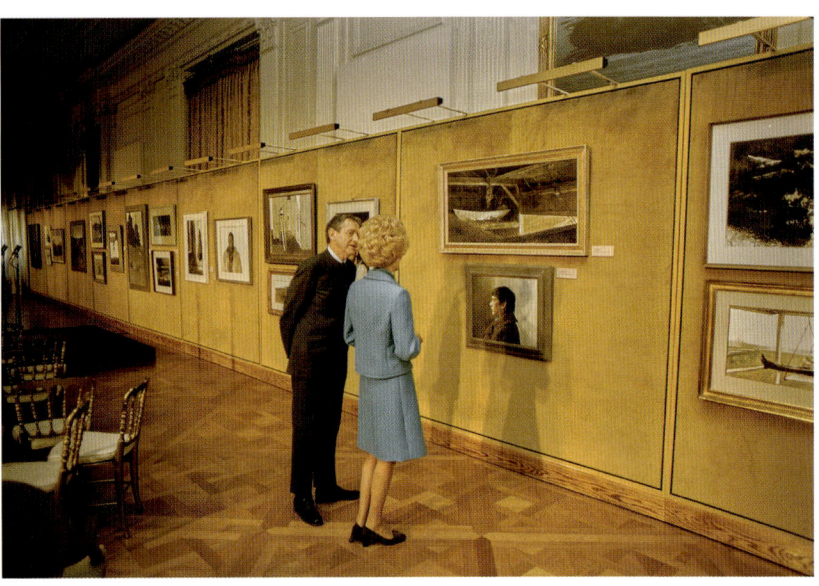

Fig. 1. Andrew Wyeth and First Lady Pat Nixon at the opening of the artist's solo exhibition at the White House, 1970

the mythmaking, the tall, white vernacular farmhouse at the heart of this world is accorded an emotional register of its own. According to one account: "Cold and grim [it] hunkers against the hillside. Full of secrets, it echoes with shouts, sobs, and the sound of children laughing."[3]

There is a kernel of truth at the heart of the Kuerner mythology, and certainly Andrew and Betsy Wyeth contributed to the spread of engaging stories about this subject matter through the couple's rich creative collaboration around all aspects of Andrew Wyeth's work and the way it reached an audience. Just as the stories have become a collective veil that governs how we perceive Kuerner Farm today, the paintings themselves have been steeped in the received narrative, making it difficult indeed to speak precisely about the choices and motivations that went into their making. The multiyear research project on which this exhibition and accompanying catalogue are based, which builds on the preceding decades of rigorous curatorial work overseen by Betsy Wyeth herself, seeks to offer some clarity.

Andrew Wyeth at Kuerner Farm: The Eye of the Earth enters into this ongoing dialogue with the benefit of a perspective rooted in twenty-five years of stewardship of Kuerner Farm as a public site by the Brandywine Conservancy & Museum of Art; the insights gained from the Andrew & Betsy Wyeth Collection of seven thousand artworks, managed by the museum as a public resource since 2022; and the salutary distance our thoughtful colleagues at Reynolda bring to the project. In their respective essays, cocurator Allison C. Slaby delves into the nature of Wyeth's darkness, while Karen Baumgartner, a longtime Wyeth family employee who now shares her expertise as collection manager of the museum's Andrew & Betsy Wyeth Study Center, explores the historical record to foreground the lived experience of Anna and Karl Kuerner. The insights and work of artist James Welling serve as a compelling example of the ways in which Wyeth's oeuvre in general and his Kuerner project in particular continue to inspire new work in a variety of media. In this good company, I turn our gaze to 1976, a key moment in the historiography of Kuerner Farm. At that time, when Wyeth was still actively painting the site, two linked projects established some of the aforementioned tropes of the reception history and left behind important and previously unexplored evidence of a key value at work in Wyeth's Kuerner paintings that is deserving of further investigation: simplicity.

The two projects in question were each distinctly different, yet together they singled out what was happening at Kuerners as discrete and significant: The first was Betsy James Wyeth's book *Wyeth at Kuerners* (fig. 2); the second, the exhibition and book *Two Worlds of Andrew Wyeth: Kuerners and Olsons* by Thomas Hoving, director of the Metropolitan Museum of Art.[4] *Wyeth at Kuerners* was innovative for publishing an extensive group of previously unseen studies alongside the finished watercolors and temperas to which they relate, allowing a broad audience a glimpse into the artist's decision-making process and the value he placed on reduction and abstraction. *Two Worlds* established in the popular imagination the now seemingly inevitable dichotomy between Kuerner Farm and its equivalent in Maine, the Olson House, whose austere domestic context also occupied the artist's attentions for decades. Betsy

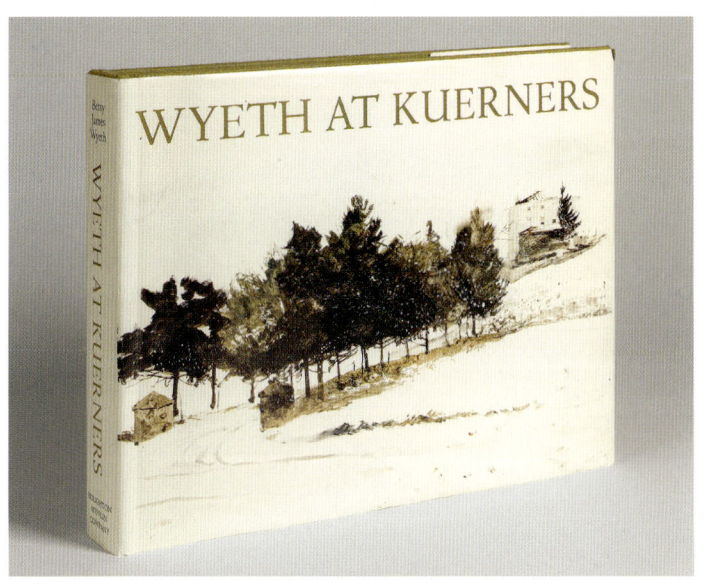

Fig. 2. Betsy James Wyeth, *Wyeth at Kuerners*, published by Houghton Mifflin, New York, 1976

Wyeth's commentaries on the images in *Wyeth at Kuerners* reflect the couple's cultivation of dramatic narrative to engage the attention of the public, and the art market.[5] Hoving's interviews with the artist that make up the body of his book are some of the most extensive surviving instances of Wyeth speaking about his own work and include key revelations that have inspired *The Eye of the Earth*, which constitutes the first sustained approach to Wyeth's engagement with Kuerner Farm since 1976.

The precise details of how these pioneering, and overlapping, Kuerner projects came about nearly fifty years ago have long been murky, even to Wyeth insiders. Hoving credited Betsy Wyeth as the source of the idea of his exhibition in his memoir, but not how it related to her book.[6] Previously unpublished materials in the Thomas Hoving Papers at the Metropolitan Museum confirm that *Wyeth at Kuerners* was already in the works when the exhibition prospect took shape. Early planning documents from the second half of 1974 for the Met's show indicate the intention to include specific artworks that would have represented a broader array of Wyeth's Maine subjects to date.[7] As late as a formal exhibition agreement between the museum and the Wyeths dated December 18, 1974, there is only a concept of focusing in general on the two towns between which the couple divided each year—Chadds Ford, Pennsylvania, and Cushing, Maine—nowhere singling out the Kuerner and Olson properties.[8] This agreement also states, "The Museum will contact the Houghton Mifflin Company in order to coordinate the sale of their Wyeth book authored by Mrs. Wyeth, which will appear almost at the same time as the show."[9] From this confirmation that her project was already under contract with a publisher by this date, we know that the self-sufficiency of Kuerners as a subject representative of the full range of Andrew Wyeth's practice, as well as the parallel between Kuerners and Olsons, had already crystallized independently for Betsy Wyeth.

Just as the annus mirabilis of 1976 established that a substantial and representative Wyeth story could be told through the lens of Kuerners, and in dialogue with Olsons, thanks to Betsy Wyeth's good offices, so did this moment produce a major body of reflection in the artist's own words on what the subject meant to him, through the efforts of Hoving. As an editor at Houghton Mifflin phrased it in a letter to Hoving, "In *Wyeth at Kuerners*, Betsey [*sic*] makes the pictures talk and in *The Two Worlds of Andrew Wyeth* you make the artist talk."[10] Hoving's interviews are known primarily via excerpts that appeared in *Two Worlds* and in the 1995 Hoving–Wyeth collaboration, *Andrew Wyeth: Autobiography*. However, for *The Eye of the Earth*, we returned to the original interview transcripts and to the handwritten annotations Hoving made to them in preparation for both *Two Worlds* and the autobiography. Wyeth was a notoriously elusive interviewee who nevertheless enjoyed spinning a good story, in the service of which he was known to bend the truth, so his comments must not be taken as the final word on his work at Kuerners. Yet the unedited conversations remain richly suggestive.

In Hoving's interviews, the artist evokes the recursive and almost meditative nature of his practice, as well as the gulf that separates the plainness of a subject like Kuerners from the complexity of the work that emerged from it. His own language about the place, across several interviews, reveals some important patterns of thought:

In Pennsylvania, there's a substantial foundation underneath, of depths of dirt, earth, breathing of the earth.[11]

I am constantly shocked by the fact that I have just scraped the surface, the depth.[12]

A change of subject is really very unimportant to me. Because there's always new revelations coming out of that same object.[13]

I was fascinated by the place and all of its associations, the strange ivory white, discolored white of the plastered wall and how the steps curve up to the attic, and the cool air that comes out of that door when you open it. Every section of that house is full of strange feelings to me. I often thought I would like to paint the house transparently and look into each room as if it were a series of thin membranes like the insides of a human being.[14]

I didn't go to that farm because it was bucolic. . . . It was an abstract, almost military quality of that farm that originally appealed to me and still does. . . . Everything is made to be useful.[15]

I'm limited if I travel. That is the strange effect it has on me. I feel more free in the surroundings that I don't have to be conscious of. I'll say that I love the object, or I love the hill. But that hill sets me free. I can wander over timeless hills. This one hill becomes thousands of hills to me. In finding this one object, I found a world.[16]

I feel that the simpler the thing the more complex it is bound to be. I've found that some of the simplest people (I'm talking about country people) are elemental. Very profound and actually very complex. . . . Just because you have a simple subject of a hill, doesn't mean that it isn't complex as hell.[17]

From these enigmatic reflections, two conclusions emerge. First, Wyeth found in Kuerners the basis of a highly individual, almost iconoclastic discipline. For centuries, artists had felt called to travel widely to broaden their perspective and skills, and Wyeth knew their journeys well through his extensive library of books on historical and contemporary art.[18] In decided contrast, he articulates a concept of inward travel, and of the ways in which a represented subject, no matter how humble, approached in the right spirit of openness and reflection, can reveal startling depths, even seeming to be "the eye of the earth," as Wyeth described the Kuerner Farm pond.[19] Second, Wyeth was an active participant in a contemporary creative environment that cultivated the value of simplicity, which in turn was a fertile source of a kind of modernism that formed an alternative to the Abstract Expressionism of the New York School. Latent in both threads—the inward journey and the twentieth-century art world's cultivation of simplicity—is Wyeth's well-documented fascination with the values and design legacies of the historic peace churches, especially Quakerism and its offshoot, Shakerism. A brief foray into the writings of these sects will clarify the resonance of Wyeth's language with theirs, and some discussion of Wyeth's contemporaries in the creative pathways commonly known as Precisionism and Regionalism will similarly reflect that while Wyeth's specific set of artistic preoccupations were unique, they were anything but anomalous.

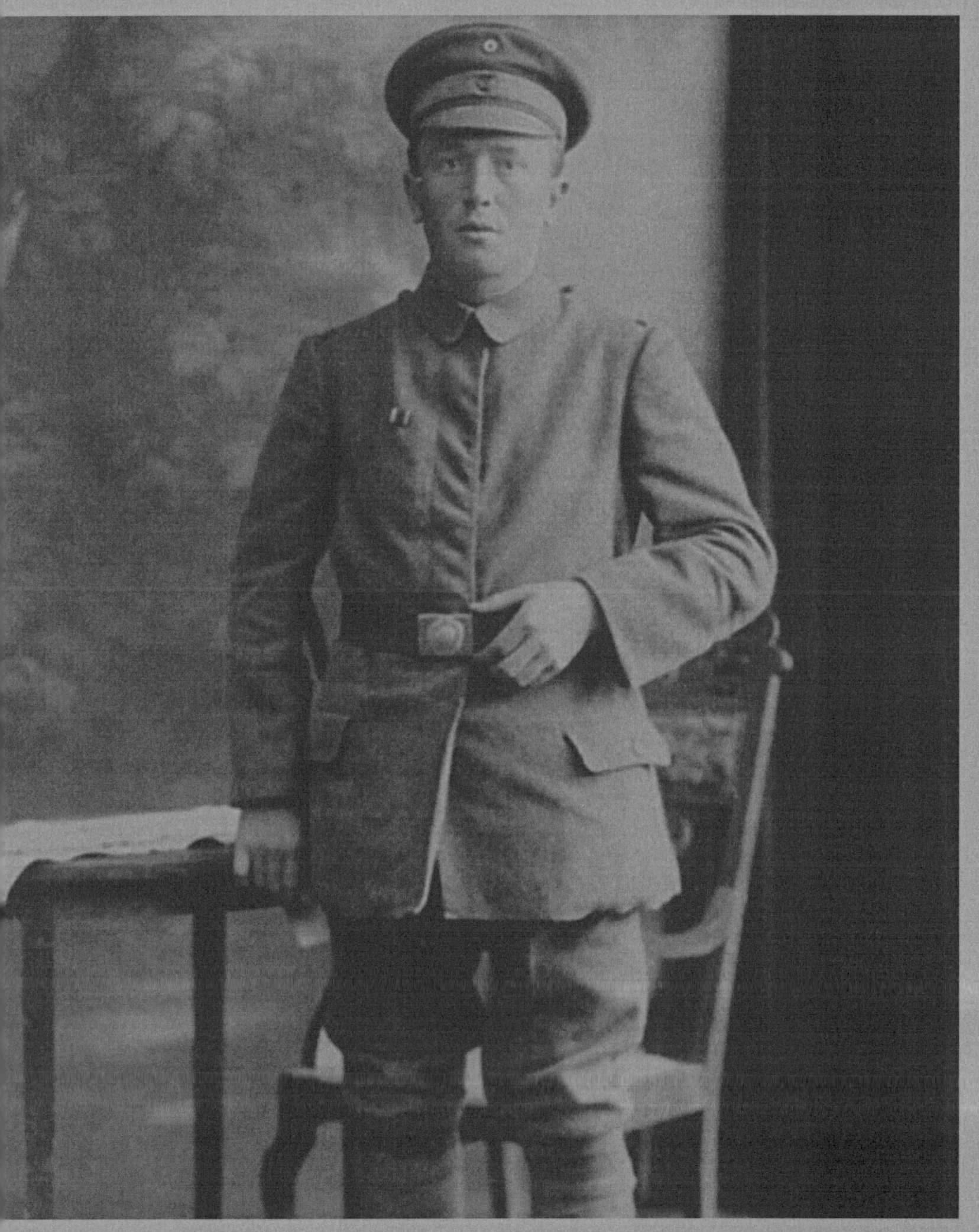

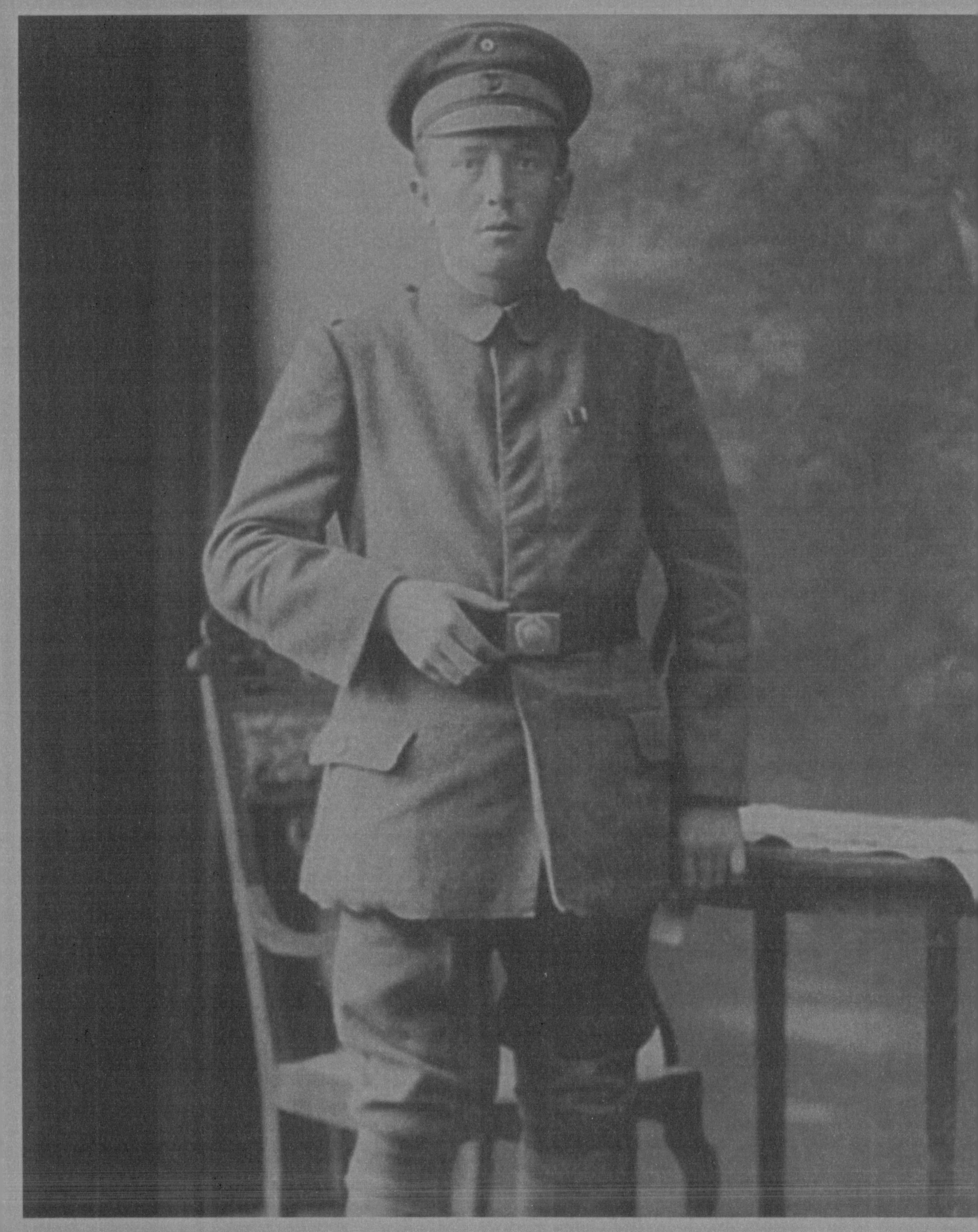

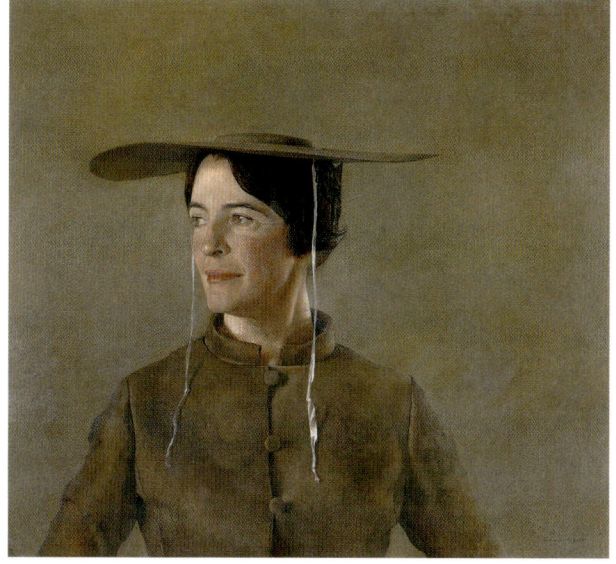

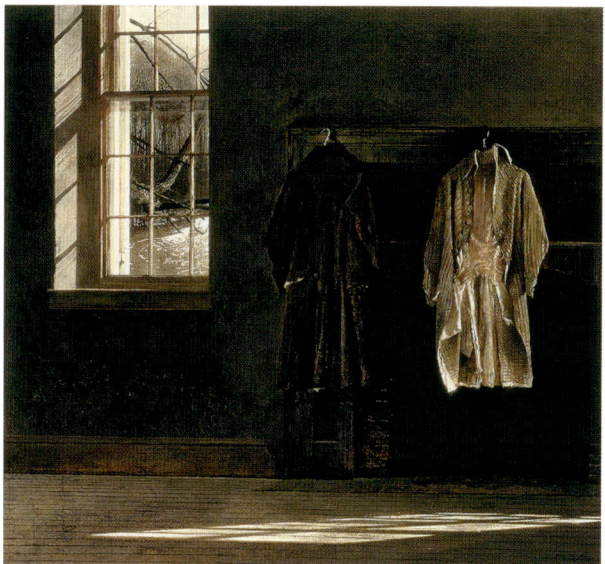

Fig. 3 (left). Andrew Wyeth, *Maga's Daughter*, 1966. Egg tempera on panel, 26½ × 30¼ in. Wyeth Foundation for American Art

Fig. 4 (right). Andrew Wyeth, *The Quaker*, 1975. Egg tempera on panel, 36½ × 40 in. Private collection

The reflections Wyeth shared with Hoving surrounding what he found at Kuerner Farm bear a strong resemblance to many key Quaker and Shaker tenets, which is hardly surprising. The Wyeths owned numerous books on both sects and lived with examples of furniture produced or inspired by both faith communities. Andrew Wyeth referenced both traditions in the content of his paintings, as did Betsy Wyeth in the titles she selected for them (figs. 3 and 4).[20] Quakerism in particular was in the water in Chadds Ford, the early Euro-American settlers of which were largely members of the denomination, and the Kuerner farmhouse itself was built in 1814 by one such Quaker inhabitant, Caleb Brinton Ring Sr.; Quaker ownership of the land dates to at least 1753.[21] For these reasons, the Wyeths can be assumed to have been more than passingly aware of the practices of Friends, as Quakers are known. These include a concept of continual revelation of the divine, silent worship broken by moments of spontaneously inspired ministry, and the core tenet of simplicity, with the closely related principle of plainness. According to *Quaker Faith and Practice*, "The heart of Quaker ethics is summed up in the word 'simplicity.' Simplicity is forgetfulness of self and remembrance of our humble status as waiting servants of God. Outwardly, simplicity is shunning superfluities of dress, speech, behaviour, and possessions, which tend to obscure our vision of reality."[22] Quaker mystic and Haverford College professor Rufus M. Jones adds a nuance that echoes Wyeth's words: "Simplicity does not mean shallowness. It is not the same thing as superficiality. A life can be very simple without being either thin or narrow. . . . I have often noticed the most unusual dimensions of life in quiet, simple Friends."[23] Likewise, Shakers believed that "immediate revelations and charismatic gifts were available to anyone possessing spiritual powers of discernment" and sang hymns with lyrics like

I'll be simple, I'll be lowly
In it flows such heav'nly mirth
To be humble, to be holy
Is the prettiest thing on earth.[24]

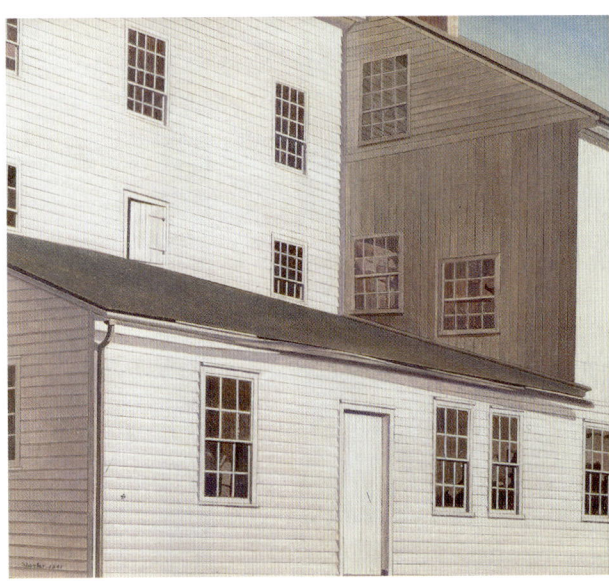

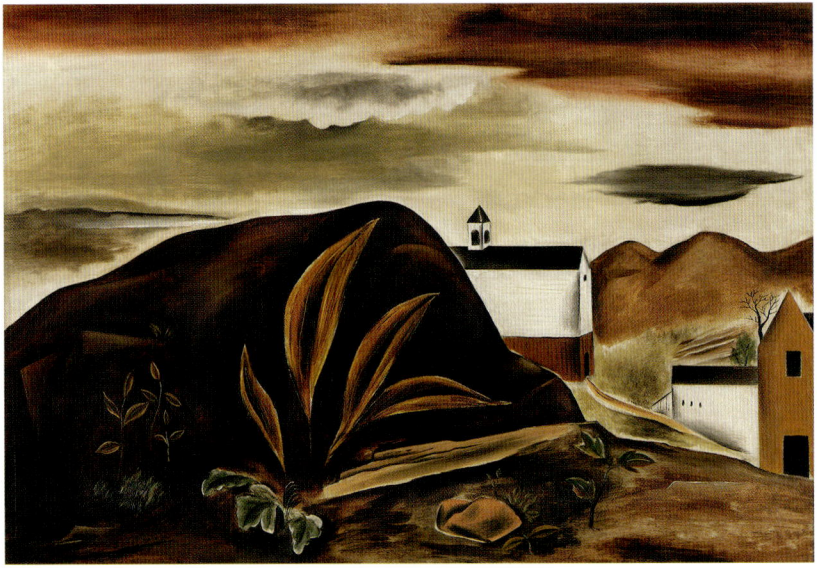

Fig. 5 (left). Charles Sheeler, *Shaker Detail*, 1941. Oil and tempera on Masonite, 13¼ × 14¼ in. Newark Museum of Art, New Jersey

Fig. 6 (right). Yasuo Kuniyoshi, *Landscape*, 1924. Oil on linen, 20¼ × 30⅛ in. Whitney Museum of American Art, New York

Wyeth's accounts of "new revelations" from continued openness to inspiration by Kuerner Farm, his expressions of admiration for the unadorned, practical nature of the place, and his description of the meaning of simplicity to his practice all resonate strongly with these faith traditions.

Even as Wyeth found kinship with abstract painters such as Franz Kline and Kenneth Noland through the common formal values of their work, the ideas and aesthetics of the historic peace churches provided him a rich source of inspiration for making a modern American art for the twentieth century, and Wyeth was not alone.[25] This subject matter brought him into dialogue with numerous other visual, performing, and musical artists. Charles Sheeler is the best known of these; Precisionist works like *Shaker Detail* (fig. 5) recognize a latent geometric abstraction in the hard edges of Shaker plainness. Yasuo Kuniyoshi's sophisticated counter-Regionalism is less commonly associated with the peace church aesthetic (fig. 6), but art historian Gail Levin has shown the important role that American folk culture played in his experience of immigration. This included serious collecting of material culture, such as the trip he took "to a Quaker village" with fellow artists from the art colony in Ogunquit, Maine. "They claimed to have been gone for two or three days, spent approximately twenty-seven dollars between them, and had to hire a truck to bring back their early American treasures."[26] There is a distinct possibility the "Quaker village" in question could have been the village of South China, Maine, where the "weighty Friend" Rufus M. Jones was from, bringing the story full circle.[27] Perhaps the ultimate example of the wider cultural fascination with the historic peace churches in Wyeth's lifetime is *Appalachian Spring*, the collaboration between choreographer Martha Graham and composer Aaron Copland, with original sets by artist Isamu Noguchi (fig. 7). Edythe Gilfond's costume designs pay tribute to plain dress, recalling Wyeth's *Maga's Daughter* and *The Quaker*, and Copland's score famously incorporated variations on the theme of the Shaker hymn *Simple Gifts*.

Wyeth was part of a wider Regionalist turn to the simplicity associated with the historic peace churches in the mid-twentieth century through his selections of subjects and the language he used in describing the driving forces of his practice, but his engagement with this source of inspiration was not always so overt.

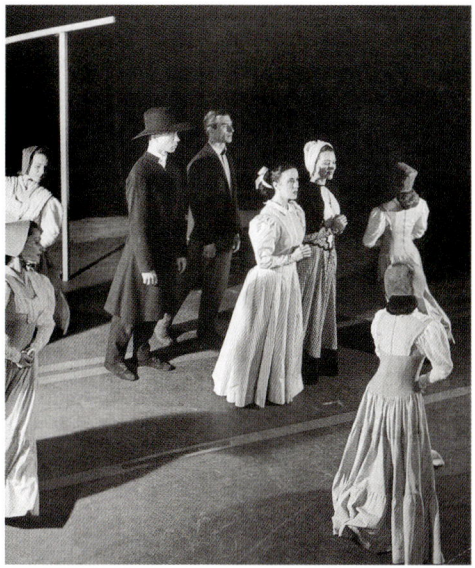

Fig. 7. Martha Graham, *Appalachian Spring*, 1944. Composed by Aaron Copland. Costumes by Edythe Gilfond and sets by Isamu Noguchi.

Simplicity, both as a core pictorial value across a lifetime's work and as a lived practice, crystallized for the artist when he "found a world" at Kuerner Farm. Around this encounter with one key site coalesced a rigorous creative focus, manifest in his decision to reject broader travels; to adopt a severely restricted palette of muted earth tones for his mature work; and to cultivate a characteristic mood of expectant stillness. As such, Kuerners can be understood as the place that clarified and cemented many of the fundamental components of his project. By looking beyond the received stories and archetypes of this place, we rediscover a much richer story: not of an isolated enigma but, rather, a fascinating moment in the history of art in which Wyeth and many others elected to constrain their materials, styles, and subject matter, and found an alternate modernism in simple places.

Notes

1. *Spring Fed* (1967; p. 93) and *Young Bull* (1960; p. 86) were among the twelve works included in the 2017 Andrew Wyeth First-Class Forever stamp set. The 1970 Wyeth exhibition at the White House included the Kuerner works *Snow Flurries* (1953; p. 69), *Winter, 1946* (1946; p. 64), and *Young Bull*.

2. An 1848 map of Delaware County indicates that there was an American gun emplacement during the Battle of Brandywine at the northern tip of the property and another on Kuerner Hill to the west. Robert Wise Consulting, *The Kuerner Farm: Historic Structures Report* (Chadds Ford, PA: Brandywine Conservancy, 2000), 11.

3. LuLynne Streeter, *Frozen Lives: Karl and Anna Kuerner, Andrew Wyeth's Iconic Couple* (Atglen, PA: Schiffer, 2017), 9. Another key contributor to this narrative is Richard Meryman, *Andrew Wyeth: A Secret Life* (New York: HarperCollins, 1996).

4. Betsy James Wyeth, *Wyeth at Kuerners* (Boston: Houghton Mifflin, 1976); Thomas Hoving, *Two Worlds of Andrew Wyeth: Kuerners and Olsons* (New York: Metropolitan Museum of Art, 1976). The latter can be downloaded in full at https://www.metmuseum.org/art/metpublications.

5. Examples of Betsy Wyeth's cultivation of dramatic narrative in her interpretation of the Kuerner studies that she included in *Wyeth at Kuerners*: her discussion of N. C. Wyeth's violent death nearby in relation to *Downgrade* (1968; private collection) and her evocation of "the hunting lodges [Karl Kuerner] knew as a shepherd in his youth back in the Black Forest of Germany" in relation to studies for *The Kuerners* (1971; p. 103). B. Wyeth, *Wyeth at Kuerners*, 60, 276.

6. Thomas Hoving, *Making the Mummies Dance: Inside the Metropolitan Museum of Art* (New York: Touchstone, 1993), 397. As this paraphrased comment indicates, Betsy Wyeth's skillful management of her husband's career extended to hands-on involvement not only in the marketing and reproduction of his art but also in the content of exhibitions and publications by outside entities. This consolidated communication strategy would be difficult to replicate today and was not without its drawbacks, but it did have a justification based on his complex critical reception.

7. For example, the Broad Cove Farm works *Distant Thunder* (1961; private collection) and *Her Room* (1963; Farnsworth Art Museum) were pegged for inclusion, as well as *Teels Island* (1954; private collection), a subject off Port Clyde that was indeed included in a separate section of the final *Two Worlds* exhibition that featured other Wyeth holdings of the exhibition's sponsors, Mr. and Mrs. Joseph E. Levine. See Hoving, *Two Worlds*, 188.

8. It was under this more vague mid-career retrospective approach that the Met's curator for twentieth-century art first requested to serve as the curator of the project, in an internal memo dated December 20, 1974. The memo is preserved in box 46, folder 6, Thomas Hoving Papers, Watson Library, Metropolitan Museum of Art, New York. As Hoving recalls in his memoir, curator Henry Geldzahler would later back out: "My clique wouldn't like having me associated with Andrew Wyeth." *Making the Mummies Dance*, 398.

9. Exhibition Agreement between Andrew Wyeth and the Metropolitan Museum of Art, December 18, 1974, box 46, folder 6, Hoving Papers.

10. Austin Olney to Thomas Hoving, October 14, 1976, box 46, folder 5, Hoving Papers.

11. Box 46, folder 2, reel XI, 29, Hoving Papers.

12. Box 46, folder 1, reel VII, 4, Hoving Papers.

13. Box 46, folder 1, reel 2, 2, Hoving Papers.

14. Box 46, folder 1, reel 4, 3, Hoving Papers.

15. Box 46, folder 1, reel 2, 2, Hoving Papers. These were among the lines that appeared in *Two Worlds*, but the change they underwent is representative of what is gained by accessing the source material. The Met's publication rendered "Everything is made to be useful" as "Everything is utilized." Hoving, *Two Worlds*, 40.

16. Box 46, folder 1, reel 2, 13–14, Hoving Papers.

17. Hoving, *Two Worlds*, 101.

18. Wyeth's personal art-reference library is preserved across the Andrew Wyeth Studio and the Andrew & Betsy Wyeth Study Center, both part of the Brandywine Museum of Art.

19. Hoving, *Two Worlds*, 48.

20. Pertinent books in the Wyeths' library include William Sewel, *The History of the Rise, Increase, and Progress of the Christian People Called Quakers, Intermixed with Several Remarkable Occurrences* (London: Dalton and Harvey, 1834); Albert Myers Cook, *Immigration of the Irish Quakers into Pennsylvania, 1682–1750, with Their Early History in Ireland* (Swarthmore, PA: Albert Myers Cook, 1902); Timothy D. Rieman et al., *Shaker: The Art of Craftsmanship* (Alexandria, VA: Art Services International/Chrysler Museum); and Paul Rocheleau and June Sprigg, *Shaker Built: The Form and Function of Shaker Architecture* (New York: The Monacelli Press, 1994). Among other Shaker references at the various properties designed by Betsy Wyeth are Shaker pegboards in the buildings known as the Schoolhouse in Chadds Ford and the Oar House on Benner Island, Maine. Among the Wyeths' extensive collections of early American furniture, it is very likely that some items have Quaker provenance, but this has not yet been documented. Wyeth depicted Quaker "plain dress" in works such as those reproduced here and Quaker religious sites in more than a dozen works, including *Birmingham Meeting House* (1933; Wyeth Foundation for American Art) and *Kennett Meeting* (1980; Menard Art Museum, Japan). A cataloguing note on the latter, which seems to be the words of Wyeth himself, describes this work as depicting "the solidity of the Quaker religion." Betsy James Wyeth, "Black Books," Andrew & Betsy Wyeth Study Center, Brandywine Museum of Art, Chadds Ford, PA.

21. Wise, *Historic Structures Report*, 10, 13.

22. *Quaker Faith and Practice: The Book of Christian Discipline of the Yearly Meeting of the Religious Society of Friends (Quakers) in Britain* (London: The Yearly Meeting of the Religious Society of Friends [Quakers] in Britain, 1995), 20, 27, quoted in Peter J. Collins, "Quaker Plaining as Critical Aesthetic," *Quaker Studies* 5, no. 2 (2001): 122.

23. Rufus M. Jones, *The Faith and Practice of the Quakers* [1927] (Richmond, IN: Friends United Press, 2002), 100–101.

24. Douglas L. Winiarski, "Souls Filled with Ravishing Transport: Heavenly Visions and the Radical Awakening in New England," *The William and Mary Quarterly* 61, no. 1 (January 2004): 11; Julia Neal, *The Kentucky Shakers* (Lexington: University Press of Kentucky, 1982), 51.

25. For more on Wyeth's relationship with abstraction and abstract artists, see Karen Baumgartner et al., *Abstract Flash: Unseen Andrew Wyeth* (Chadds Ford, PA: Brandywine Museum of Art, 2023).

26. Wanda Corn, *The Great American Thing: Modern Art and National Identity, 1915–1935* (Berkeley: University of California Press, 1999), 394, n57; cited in Gail Levin, "Between Two Worlds: Folk Culture, Identity, and the American Art of Yasuo Kuniyoshi," *Archives of American Art Journal* 43, no. 3/4 (2003): 4.

27. Jones is frequently cited as an example of a weighty Friend, a consensus term in common use in unprogrammed meetings for worship to designate those whose ministry holds extra weight despite the lack of ordained clergy. An example can be found in Christy Randazzo, "Affirmation Mysticism: The Activist Theology of Rufus Jones," *Quaker Religious Thought* 133 (2019): 14.

Karl Kuerner's German army helmet from World War I

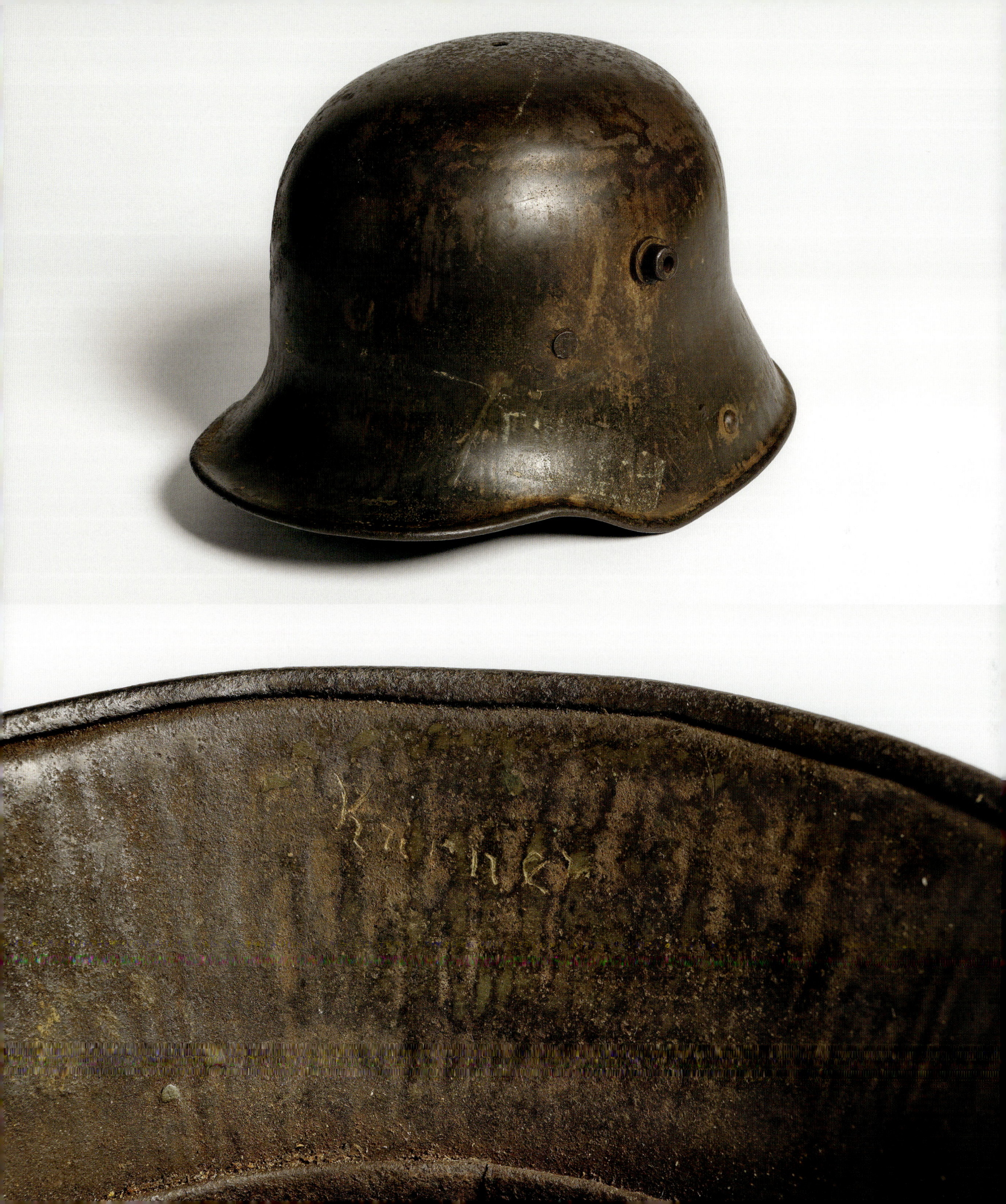

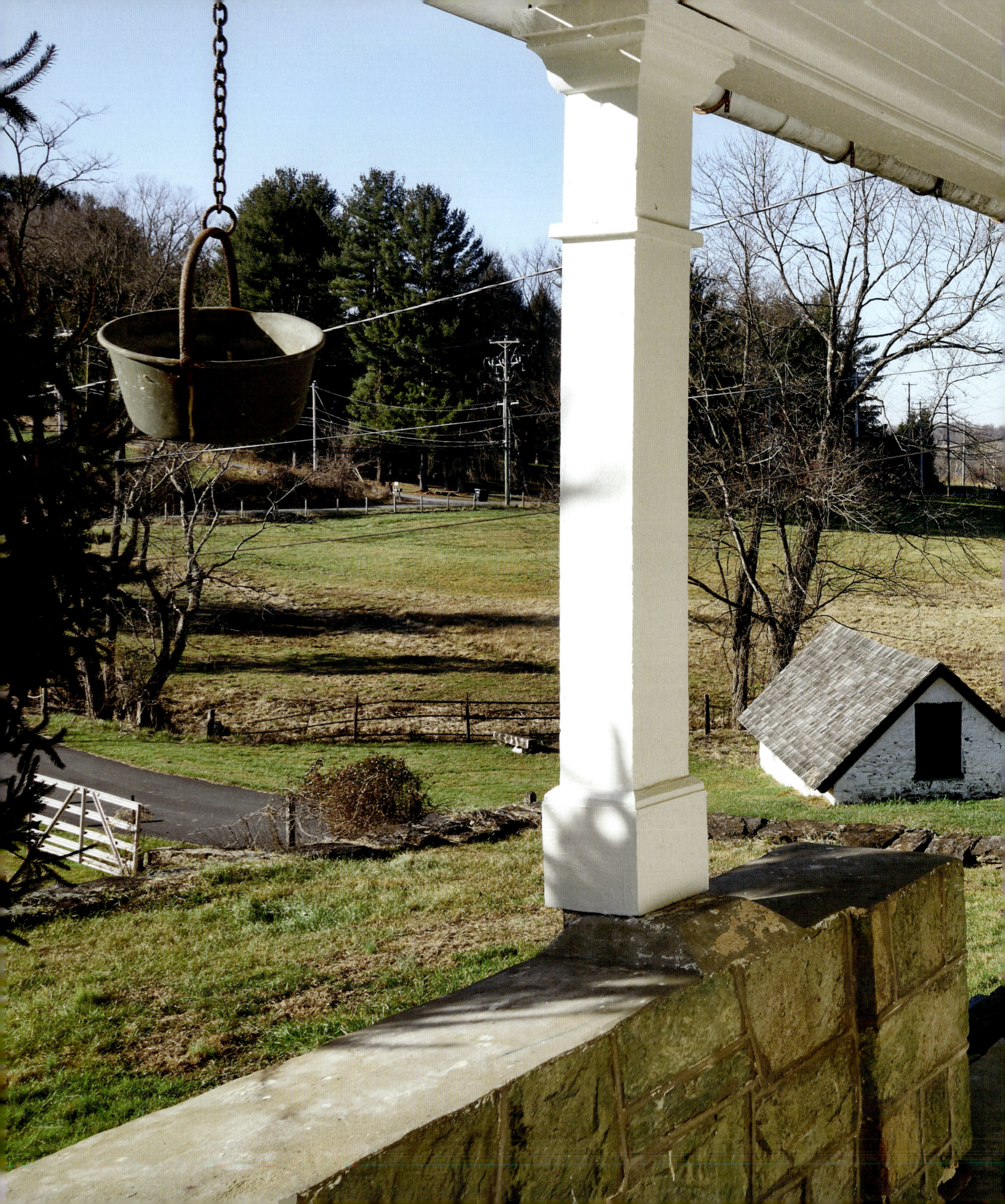

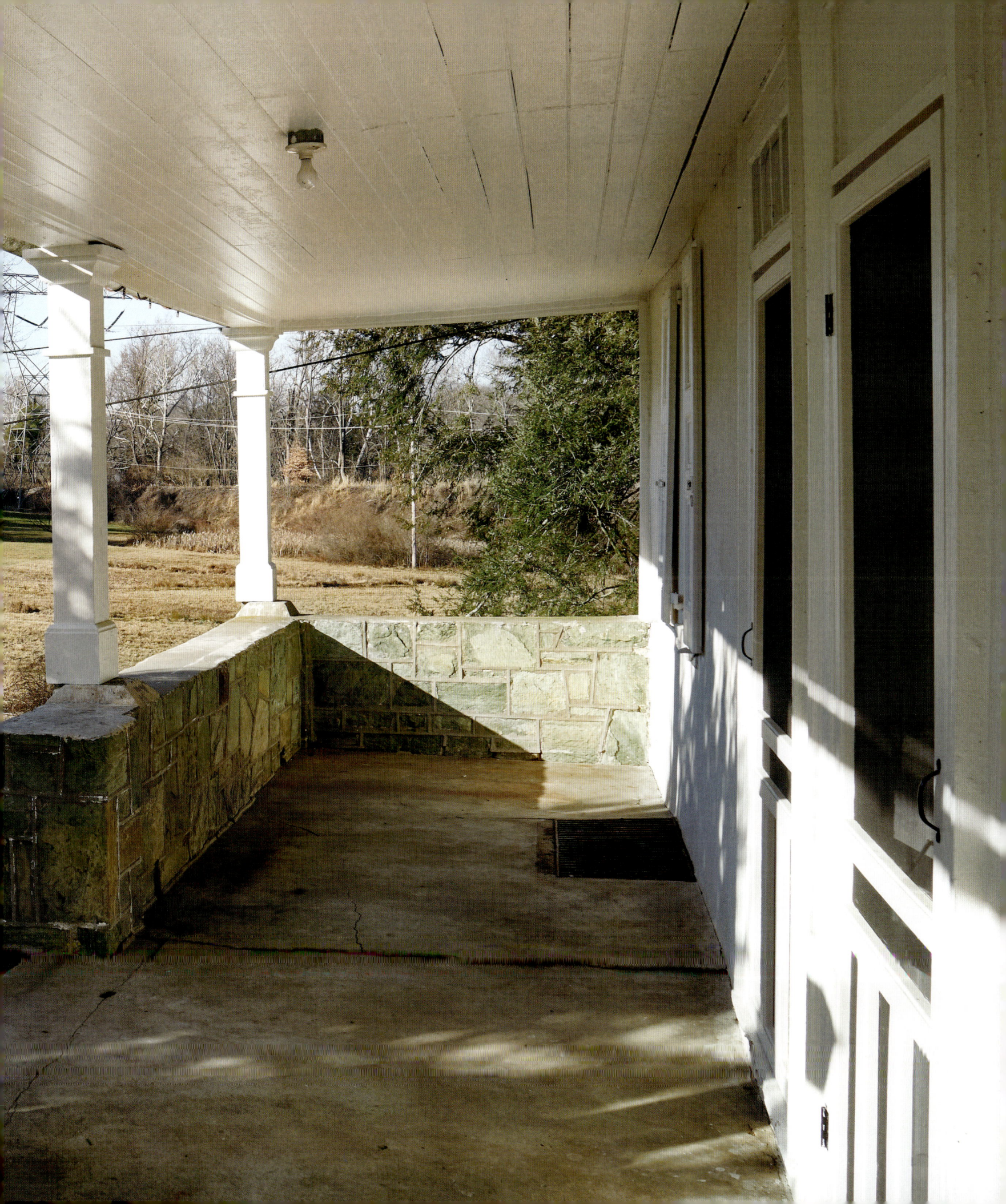

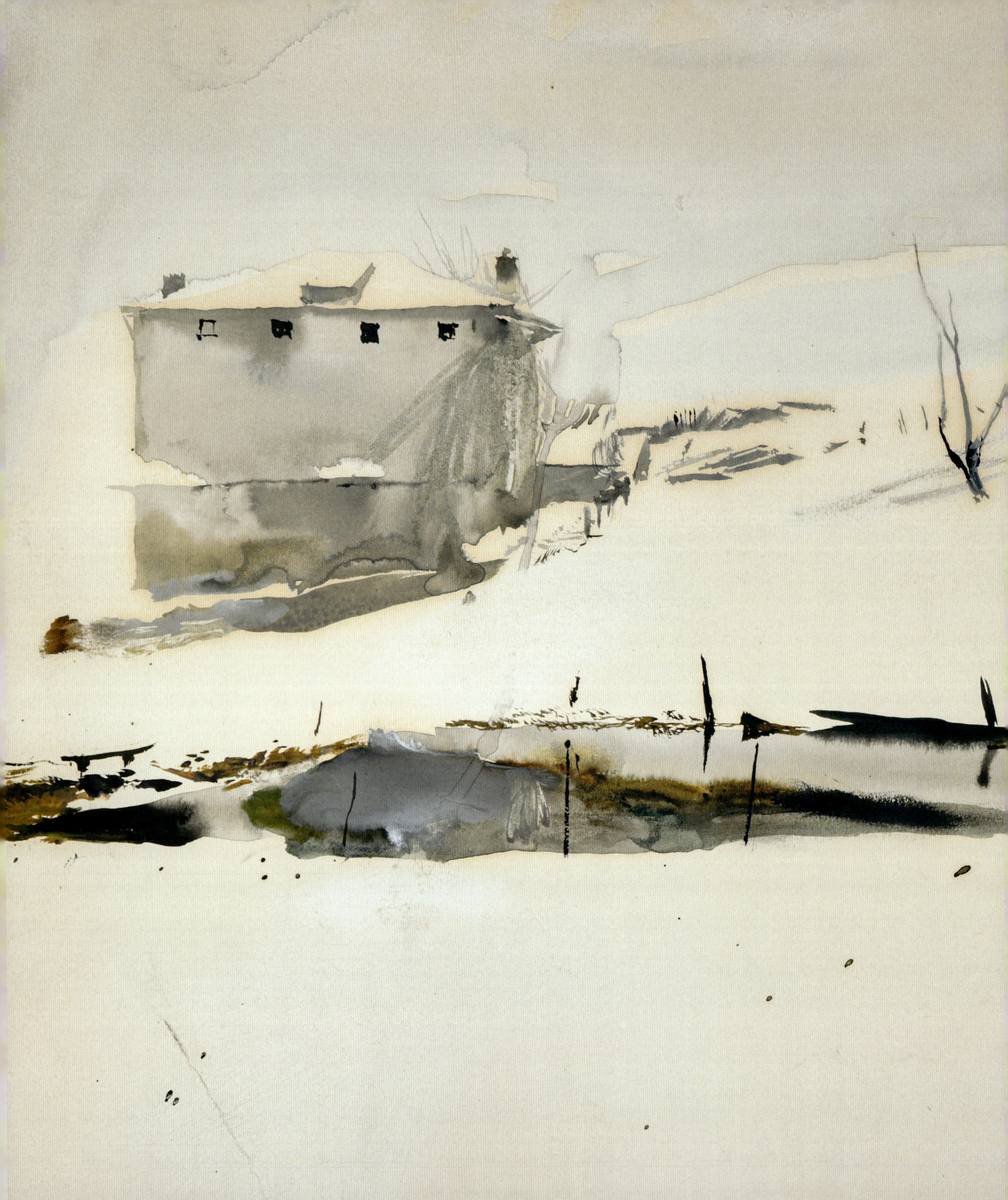

"KUERNERS IS A TOUGH PLACE": ANDREW WYETH'S FARM POND AND ITS PLACE IN HIS DARK OEUVRE

ALLISON C. SLABY

In 1935, a teenage Andrew Wyeth painted *Spring Landscape at Kuerners* (1935; p. 54). Executed in oil paint, the piece is a picturesque depiction of the farm of his neighbor Karl Kuerner. It bears the hallmarks of the illustration work of the artist's father: bright colors, a sunny atmosphere, and nostalgic subject matter. It was a style that Wyeth had absorbed quickly—and just as quickly abandoned.

Fewer than ten years later, Wyeth completed *Winter Corn Fields* (fig. 1), a study of a farm adjacent to Kuerners. The painting shares its agrarian setting with *Spring Landscape at Kuerners*, but the works diverge sharply in both medium and mood. The sunlit landscape has been replaced by muted tones of brown and tan. Rather than focusing on a wide expanse of rolling hills, Wyeth brings his viewer's attention down to earth, homing in on a wild tangle of corn shocks left in a barren field. By this point, Wyeth had largely forsaken the medium of oil in favor of watercolor and tempera.

Even starker than *Winter Corn Fields* is the brutal drybrush and watercolor study *Crows* (fig. 2), which Wyeth eventually worked up into the tempera painting

Andrew Wyeth, *Farm Pond, Study for Brown Swiss*, 1957 (detail, p. 71)

25

Woodshed (1944; p. 59). As Wyeth later recalled, "I saw these crows hanging on the fence. Karl Kuerner's son had shot them. Sad, but farmers do shoot these marvelous birds. It was a March day, and they were there with their black feathers blowing."[1] The painting reflects what Wyeth perceived as the brutality at Kuerner Farm.

Wyeth himself attributed the change in his artistic temperament, from sunny to dark, to his father's violent death in a train accident in 1945, but as *Winter Corn Fields*, *Crows*, and *Woodshed* illustrate, this shift occurred before, rather than after, that shocking event.[2] Instead, I contend that it was Wyeth's enduring fixation on Kuerner Farm and its inhabitants that engendered this bleak turn in his work, a view shared by art historian Patricia Junker, who has noted that Wyeth found in this place "something in its character that suited a very dark temperament."[3]

Wyeth perhaps found precedent for such a distinct shift in tone in the work of an artist he admired. In the 1870s and the aftermath of the Civil War, Winslow Homer made picturesque watercolors of pretty farm girls and dynamic oil paintings of boys in sailing boats. During a trip to England in 1881–82, however, both his subject matter and palette changed abruptly. Settling in the fishing village of Cullercoats, Homer trained his eye on the stark confrontations between the fishermen who relied on the sometimes violent sea for their livelihoods and the women and children who awaited them on shore. For the rest of his life, he explored man's elemental struggles against the sublime forces of nature and the threat of death, in muted tones that mirror those Wyeth employed for his paintings of Kuerner Farm.

The watercolor *Farm Pond* (1957; p. 71), in the collection of Reynolda House Museum of American Art, perfectly encapsulates Wyeth's complex feelings about the property. In the artist's own words, "Kuerners is a tough place."[4] Seen from a distance, across the rolling road, the farmhouse appears as a "great block of ice, cut out of Europe, out of Germany, a world of his own," in the words of Wyeth's model and muse Helga Testorf.[5] In the painting, the artist pushes the farmhouse to the extreme left side, giving the piece an unbalanced quality. He also eliminates several windows from the house, stripping it down to essential forms. Emphasizing the chilly, barren landscape and the sunless day, Wyeth executed *Farm Pond* in a limited range of gray, blue, and brown hues. For the snow, he simply left large areas of the white paper unpainted. The pond itself is a nearly abstract swath of icy blue watercolor outlined in ink. Wyeth once described this small dammed stream as a "lucid pond looking almost like the eye of the earth, reflecting everything in creation."[6]

Farm Pond, a study for the tempera painting *Brown Swiss* (p. 72) of the same year, is one of a series of works that Wyeth created from this vantage point. The first, an inky-black drawing on paper, he dashed off quickly one day and then abandoned. Later, he re-created the composition in more refined versions. The ultimate product is *Brown Swiss*, a masterpiece of his work in the 1950s. Rather than choosing a snowy landscape for *Brown Swiss* in the dead of winter, Wyeth opted for a muted palette of brown, gray, and white. He said that he wanted it to be "almost like the tawny brown pelt of a Brown Swiss bull."[7]

Wyeth intended *Brown Swiss* to be a portrait (not a landscape) of everything that is going on in the house and on the farm. One of the activities taking place here is slaughter. *Young Buck* (1944; p. 60), created, like *Woodshed*, before the death of the artist's father, captures one such severe moment he witnessed. "I came around the corner of Karl Kuerner's barn and saw this young buck and I went into the shed. And the snow was blowing, spitting around it," Wyeth later

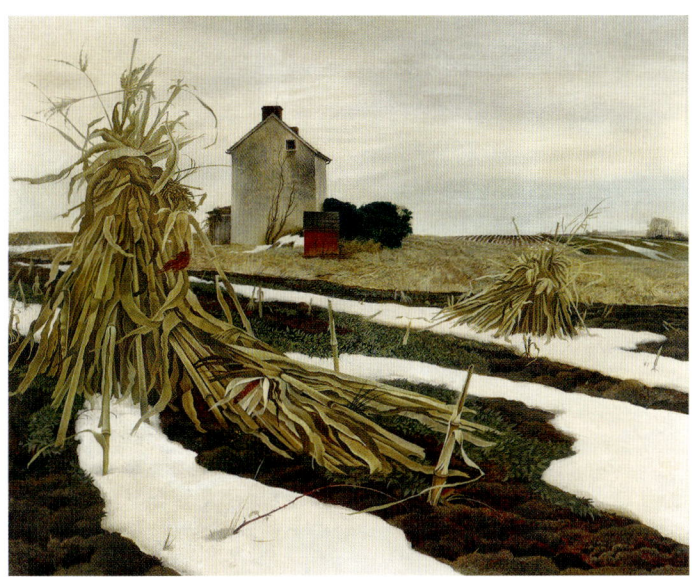

Fig. 1. Andrew Wyeth, *Winter Corn Fields*, 1942. Egg tempera on panel, 31⅜ × 39½ in. Private collection

recalled. "I was struck by the delicacy of the legs, the sort of tragic weakness of them—against the brutality of the whole thing. I kept thinking of the deer alive, running in the country behind it, and the man who shot it."[8]

Like *Farm Pond*, the delicate pencil drawing *Rope and Chains* (1957; p. 74) is a study for *Brown Swiss*. "The tree and chain was where Karl Kuerner had been slaughtering a pig," the artist remembered. "Under the chain are some child's bells—don't know how they got there—which to me give a childlike innocence to the brutality that goes with everyday farm life."[9] Again and again, Wyeth refers to the butchery that he encountered at Kuerner Farm.

In addition to the regular slaughter of livestock, Wyeth also found evidence of more carnage: Kuerner's penchant for hunting. In *The Trophy* (1963; p. 88), Wyeth captures an enormous rack of bull moose antlers; Kuerner had shot the animal on a trip into the northeastern woods. As striking as the antlers themselves are the spiky shadows that project on the wall behind them. Created by bright beams of sunshine, they are sharp and dangerous, almost lethal in appearance. The window at left denies the viewer a glimpse into the dark and shrouded house.

The farm was not just a site of killing animals but a place that Wyeth associated with death and loss in his own life. On October 19, 1945, the artist's father, famed illustrator N. C. Wyeth, was killed when the car he was driving was struck by a train on a track that bordered Kuerner Farm. Andrew's three-year-old nephew was also killed. Forever after, Andrew Wyeth associated the farm with not just brutality but death. Months later, he painted *Winter, 1946* (p. 64), which shows a young Chadds Ford boy, Allan Lynch, running down Kuerner Hill. To Wyeth, "the hill seemed to be breathing—rising and falling—almost as though it was my father's chest."[10]

After the accident, Wyeth's interest in Karl Kuerner deepened. In 1948, the artist created one of the most striking portraits of his career when he captured Kuerner in the farmhouse (p. 67). The perspective of the portrait is unusual: Kuerner is shown close and slightly above the viewer, so that he is visible only from the shoulders up. Above him, talon-like hooks are embedded in the steeply pitched ceiling. Used to dry sausage, they are prosaic yet also threatening, providing a foreboding note. Cracks in the ceiling, ending at Kuerner's head, underscore the age of the house.

As an immigrant who had served in the army of his native Germany during World War I, Kuerner undoubtedly struck a menacing figure, and Wyeth notes the man's violent nature in his autobiography. In this portrait, Kuerner is unsmiling. He makes eye contact with the viewer, but he is turned slightly away. Art historian Wanda Corn has suggested that his head is cocked upon hearing his wife moving around downstairs.[11] Whether this anecdote is true, the gesture gives Kuerner a guarded and untrusting expression, which contributes to the unnerving nature of the portrait. Wyeth's wife, Betsy, described Karl's wife, Anna, arguing with and threatening the image in the painting as if she were speaking to her husband himself.[12]

Anna Faulhaber Kuerner is an enigmatic figure in the story of Kuerner Farm. Wyeth found her no less fascinating than he did her husband and drew and painted her several times, here in watercolor (fig. 3). Whether Anna may have had some

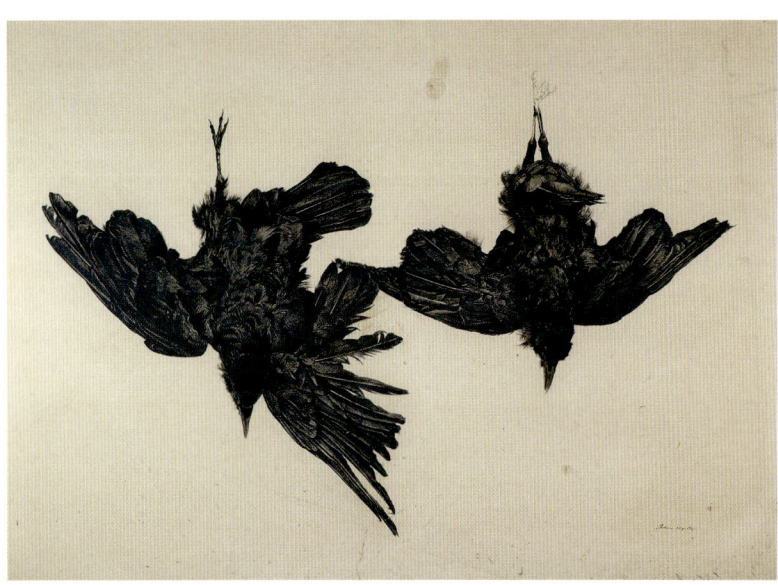

form of mental illness is unclear. Certainly, she was isolated and spoke little English. Betsy Wyeth recalled that Anna suffered from terrible headaches and almost always wore a cap or a kerchief tied tightly around her head to treat the malady.[13] She was constantly cooking and cleaning; Wyeth depicted her at work in the kitchen and out in the yard.

Anna's farm duties were grueling and kept her up into the middle of the night, as Wyeth himself witnessed. "About one o'clock in the morning I was up in back of the Kuerner house. The moon was full and illuminated the melted patches of snow on the hill in a mysterious way. Then I heard this soft, regular sound from the woodshed where there was a light, and I knew it was Anna chopping wood. . . . Finally she stopped. The light in the woodshed went out, and I watched as the other lights went on and off as she went upstairs."[14] Wyeth re-created this memory in *Wolf Moon* (1975; p. 115). The artist contrasts the stark white of the patches of moonlit snow with the yellow lamplight glowing from the woodshed window in the lower left. "The sounds of the wolves are there," Wyeth later recalled of the wintry scene. "You can almost hear them howling."[15]

In *The Kuerners* (1971; p. 103), Wyeth brought the couple together in one of his most iconic and unsettling paintings. In a spare, whitewashed room, Karl stands bundled in a thick brown coat. He holds a long rifle, the barrel bisecting his body and projecting into the space behind him. The shaft is dark and menacing against the stark white wall, and it points directly at Anna, a severe figure standing in a shabby dress and her customary kerchief. Her expression, in profile, is inscrutable. Wyeth recalled that she had come upstairs to scold Karl, in German, for not having come down to dinner.[16]

Wyeth reworked the painting over a period of a few years. Initially, he included one of Karl's antler racks on the wall between the two figures, but he scrubbed the impressions out with sandpaper.[17] The resulting empty white space, "an appalling stretch of blank wall," as critic Brian O'Doherty has asserted, suggests a gulf between Karl and Anna.[18] Wyeth referred to suppressed violence in symbolic objects at the farm.[19] Thus, the gun barrel may hint at violent acts that he perceived within the house, whether real or imagined. Wyeth biographer Richard Meryman has written that the Kuerner home evoked "death and madness beneath a thin skin of domesticity."[20]

Indeed, Karl had committed acts of violence as a German soldier. "He's very cruel, you know," Wyeth commented. "He told me how he mowed down a line of Americans in the First Word War, then lowered the sights of the machine gun and went over them again."[21] For *The German* (1975; p. 112), Wyeth had Karl pose in his old army uniform and helmet. Executed mostly in gray, black, and white, the painting has but two flashes of brilliant color: Karl's cold, icy-blue eyes and his uniform's blood-red collar and trim. As he did in his 1948 portrait, Wyeth depicts Karl unsmiling, his grim expression paired with his severe uniform. Black trees behind him contrast with the bleak, snow-covered ground. In *The German*, Wyeth creates an austere portrait evocative of a brutal past, brought into the present at Kuerner Farm.

Beyond the fearsome man of the house and his lonely, withdrawn wife, there were other occupants of the farm who displayed dramatic behavior. Karl kept several

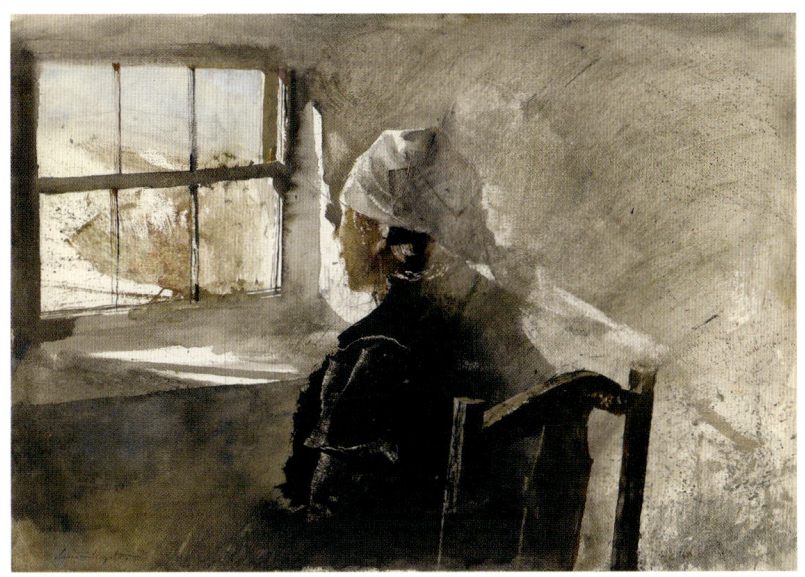

Fig. 3. Andrew Wyeth, *Mrs. Kuerner*, 1958. Watercolor and pencil on paper, mounted on a strainer, 14⅞ × 21½ in. Hirshhorn Museum and Sculpture Garden, Washington, D.C. Gift of the Joseph H. Hirshhorn Foundation, 1966

generations of German Shepherds, all named Nellie. In *Wild Dog* (1959; p. 79), Wyeth captures a wraithlike form prowling around the house. Sparingly painted, with just a few rangy strokes of black watercolor, the dog is featureless yet menacing, her form suggesting motion as if she is sprinting after prey. "That dog is nasty," Wyeth told an interviewer. "You have to watch her."[22] Wyeth utilized his customary muted tones here—just black, white, and brown, evoking a midwinter scene. The log in the background, having been dragged up the hill by a tractor, would eventually become firewood; for now, it is stuck in the snowy mud, still bearing a chain around it.[23] The chain alludes to Nellie, too, who was often chained in the yard. In Wyeth's mind, the dog and the log were inextricably linked. He painted them repeatedly in studies for his iconic *Groundhog Day* (1959; pp. 80, 77–79); this watercolor is the only study in which they occupy the farmyard together.

In later years, strangers entered the farm and brought new life and light to the work Wyeth created there. Karl was diagnosed with cancer in 1970, so the Kuerners hired a neighbor, Helga Testorf, to be his nurse. Born in Germany, Helga had immigrated to America with her husband in the early 1960s. Wyeth was struck by her red hair, pale eyes, and strong Germanic features, and he began drawing and painting her in the privacy of Kuerner Farm. The works of art—more than two hundred of them, created over fifteen years—caused a sensation when they were revealed in 1986. Both the art world and the public were stunned that Wyeth had kept them a secret, even from his wife.

In *Loden Coat* (1978; p. 107), Wyeth sets Helga in a snowy landscape, marching up the hill to the farmhouse. With her green wool coat, red braids, and boots, she embodies the quintessential German peasant woman. There is a jauntiness to her step—her long stride, the satchel swinging behind her—that suggests that Wyeth has been revitalized by her youth and freshness. In the house in the distance, Wyeth has restored the windows to their rightful places, literally opening the structure to the wintry light.

Karl's illness lingered for years. Often, he lay on a bed on the first floor of the house, where Wyeth began to sketch him. This once virile man, who had always been represented as emphatically vertical, was now supine and weakened. Late in his career, Wyeth embraced a strong strain of magic realism, and it was in this vein that he captured Karl in *Spring* (1978; p. 122). In a strange imaginative twist, he covered Karl's nude, recumbent form with a snowdrift on Kuerner Hill, a type of painting in Wyeth's oeuvre that art historian John Wilmerding has called "portrait still lifes, or 'stilled lives.'"[24] It is an eerie yet fitting farewell from Wyeth to the subject who had intrigued and haunted him for decades.

Wyeth painted Karl and Anna Kuerner for the final time in *Snow Hill* (1989; p. 140). The painting is simultaneously one of his strangest and most enchanting. At the top of snowy Kuerner Hill, a group of people has gathered incongruously around a Maypole. They grasp colored ribbons and dance in a circle, holding hands. Karl, dressed in his uniform and helmet, is at left. Next to him is Anna, recognizable by the kerchief tied around her head. Helga in her loden coat and boots swings out to the right. Across from Helga is Allan Lynch, the boy running down the hill in *Winter, 1946*. Other figures from Wyeth's paintings round out the party. Here, he has gathered both the living and the dead in a bizarre yet merry celebration. Could the artist himself be the unseen figure holding the white ribbon across from Anna?

Ultimately for Wyeth, Kuerner Farm and its inhabitants evoked the darkness he associated with this singular, ghostly place. In his 1957 watercolor *Farm Pond*, he renders the farmhouse and surrounding land in a stark, muted, and stripped-down mode. For decades, Wyeth had free rein in this humble landscape, at once "a world of his own" and one that he made iconic.

Notes

1. Andrew Wyeth, *Andrew Wyeth: Autobiography* (Boston: Little, Brown and Co., 1995), 26.
2. Cécile Whiting, "Andrew Wyeth and Birds of War," *Panorama: Journal of the Association of Historians of American Art* 7, no. 2 (Fall 2021), https://doi.org/10.24926/24716839.12367.
3. Patricia Junker, "Andrew Wyeth, Rebel," in David Cateforis, ed., *Rethinking Andrew Wyeth* (Berkeley: University of California Press, 2014), 161.
4. Andrew Wyeth, quoted in Richard Meryman, *Andrew Wyeth: A Secret Life* (New York: HarperCollins, 1996), 232.
5. Helga Testorf, quoted in Kathleen A. Foster, "Meaning and Medium in Wyeth's Art: Revisiting *Groundhog Day*," in Anne Classen Knutson et al., *Andrew Wyeth: Memory & Magic* (New York: Rizzoli, 2005), 87.
6. Wyeth, *Autobiography*, 46.
7. Ibid.
8. Andrew Wyeth, quoted in Brian O'Doherty, "A Visit to Wyeth Country," in Wanda Corn, ed., *The Art of Andrew Wyeth* (Greenwich, CT: New York Graphic Society, 1973), 26.
9. Wyeth, *Autobiography*, 45.
10. Wyeth, quoted in Meryman, *Secret Life*, 231.
11. Corn, *The Art of Andrew Wyeth*, 144.
12. Betsy James Wyeth, *Wyeth at Kuerners* (Boston: Houghton Mifflin, 1976), 255.
13. Ibid., 115.
14. Wyeth, *Autobiography*, 105.
15. Ibid.
16. Ibid., 91.
17. Ibid.
18. O'Doherty, "A Visit to Wyeth Country," 24.
19. Wyeth, quoted in Foster, "Meaning and Medium in Wyeth's Art," 85.
20. Meryman, *Secret Life*, 288.
21. Wyeth, quoted in O'Doherty, "A Visit to Wyeth Country," 26.
22. Andrew Wyeth, quoted in Thomas Hoving, *Two Worlds of Andrew Wyeth: Kuerners and Olsons* (New York: Metropolitan Museum of Art, 1976), 82.
23. Foster, "Meaning and Medium in Wyeth's Art," 96.
24. John Wilmerding, "Introduction," in Knutson, *Memory & Magic*, 24.

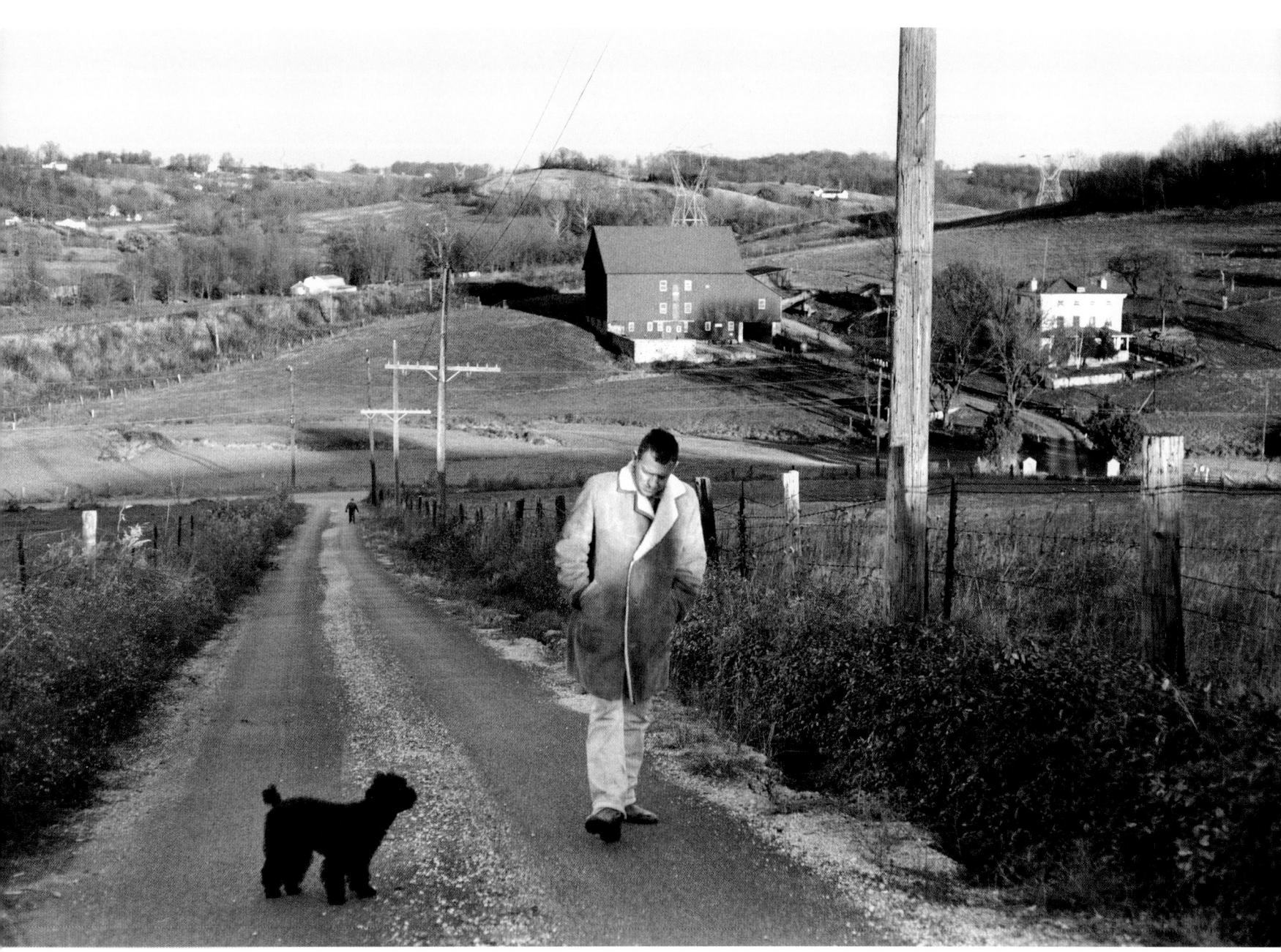

Andrew Wyeth at Kuerner Farm, 1959

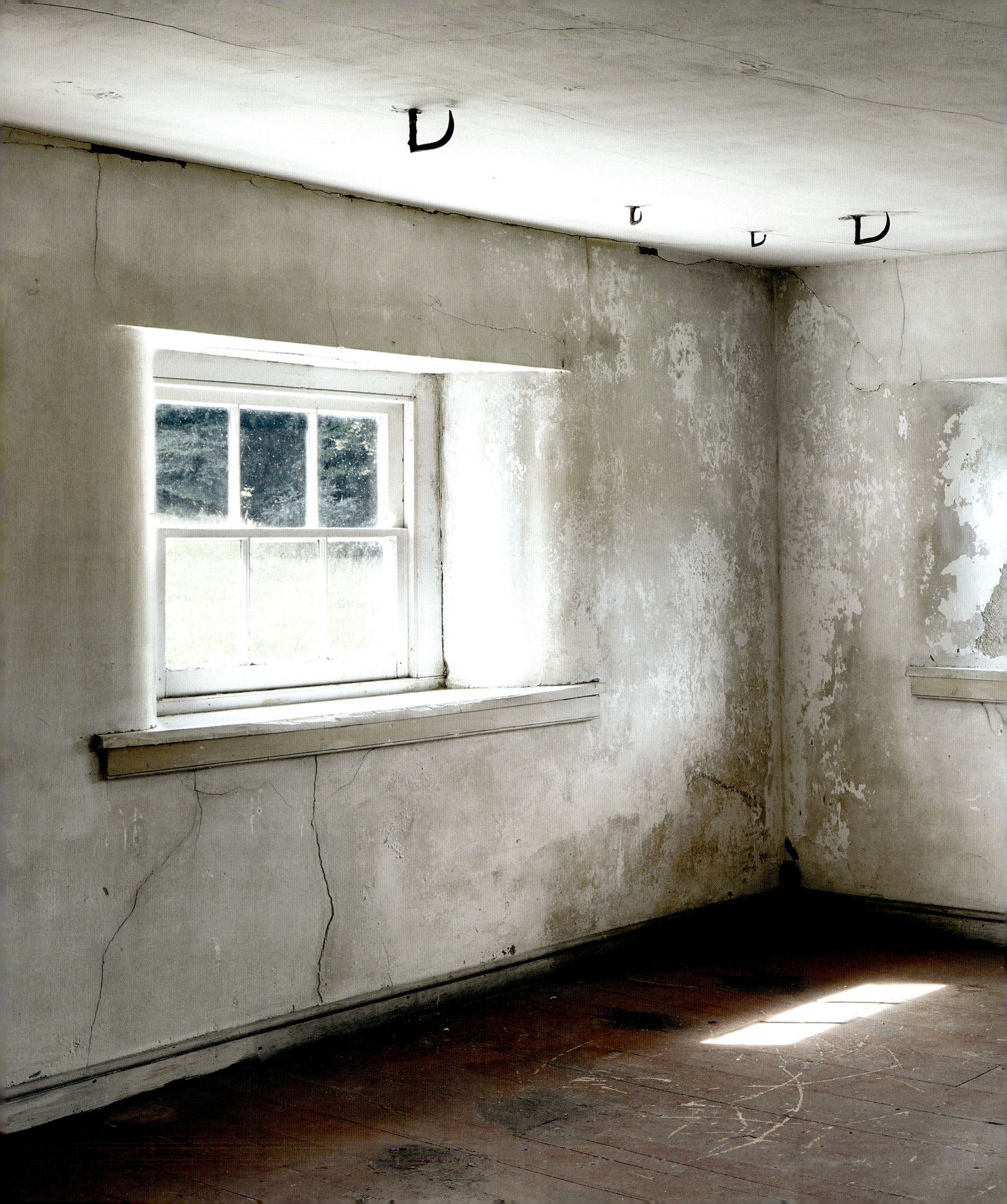

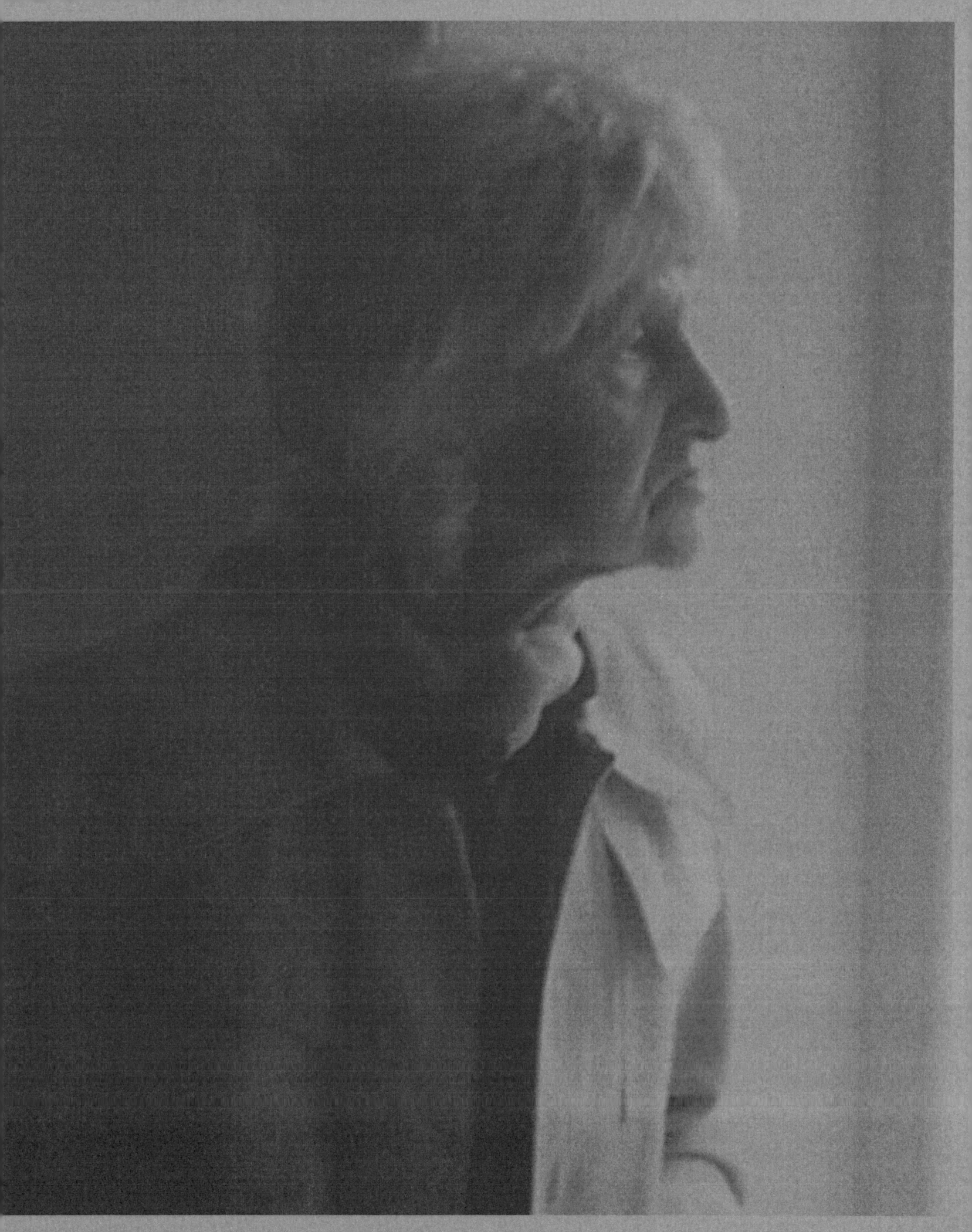

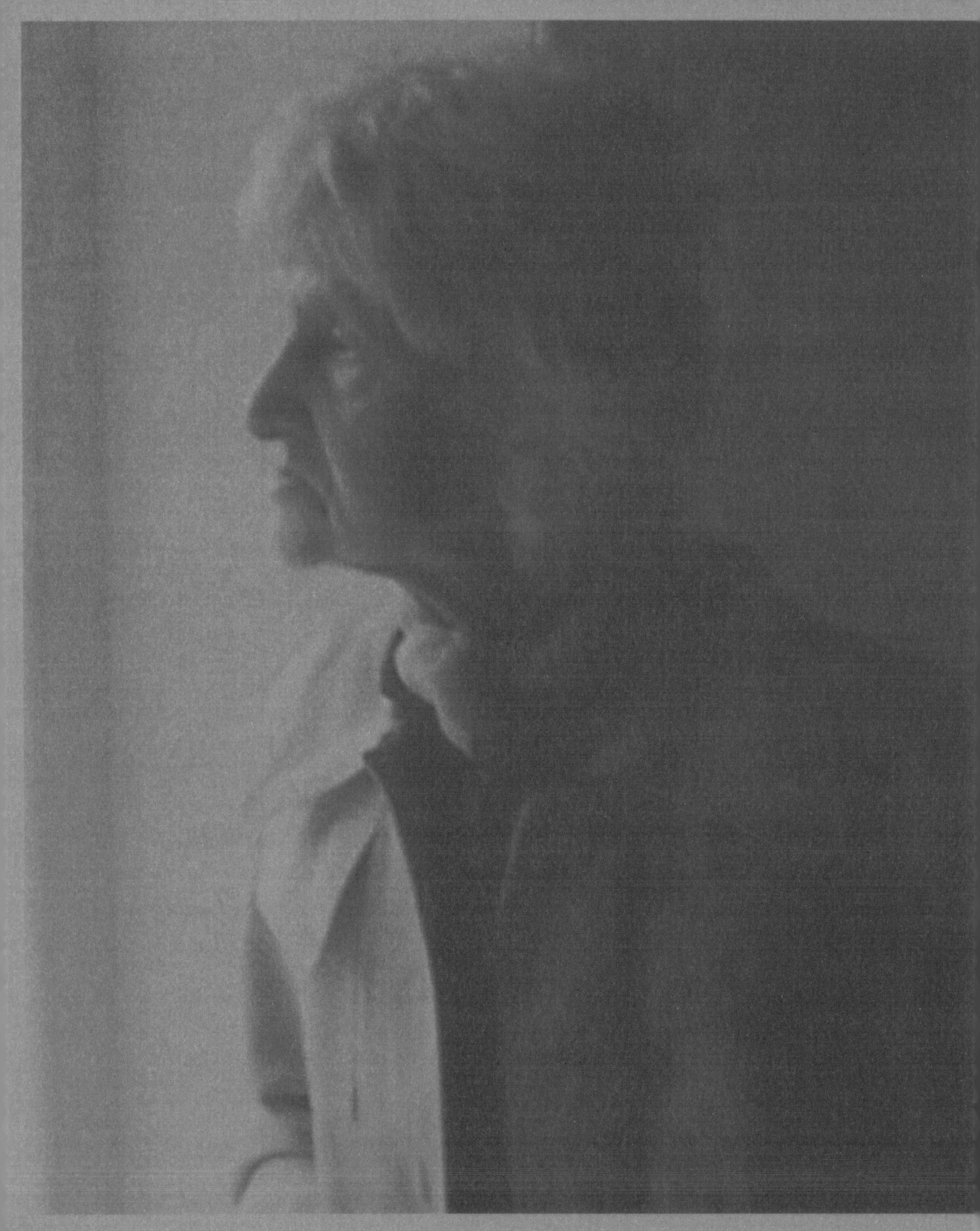

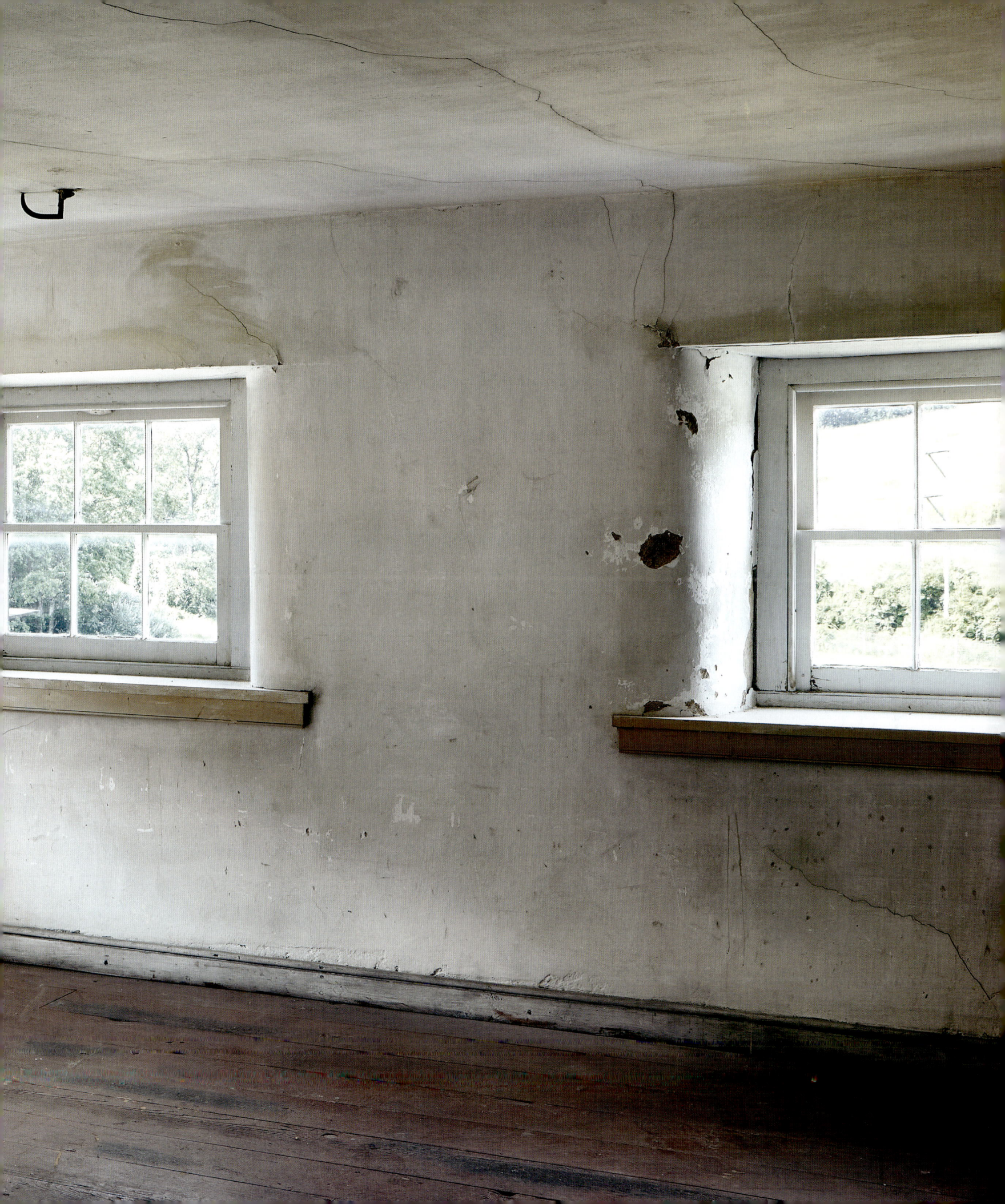

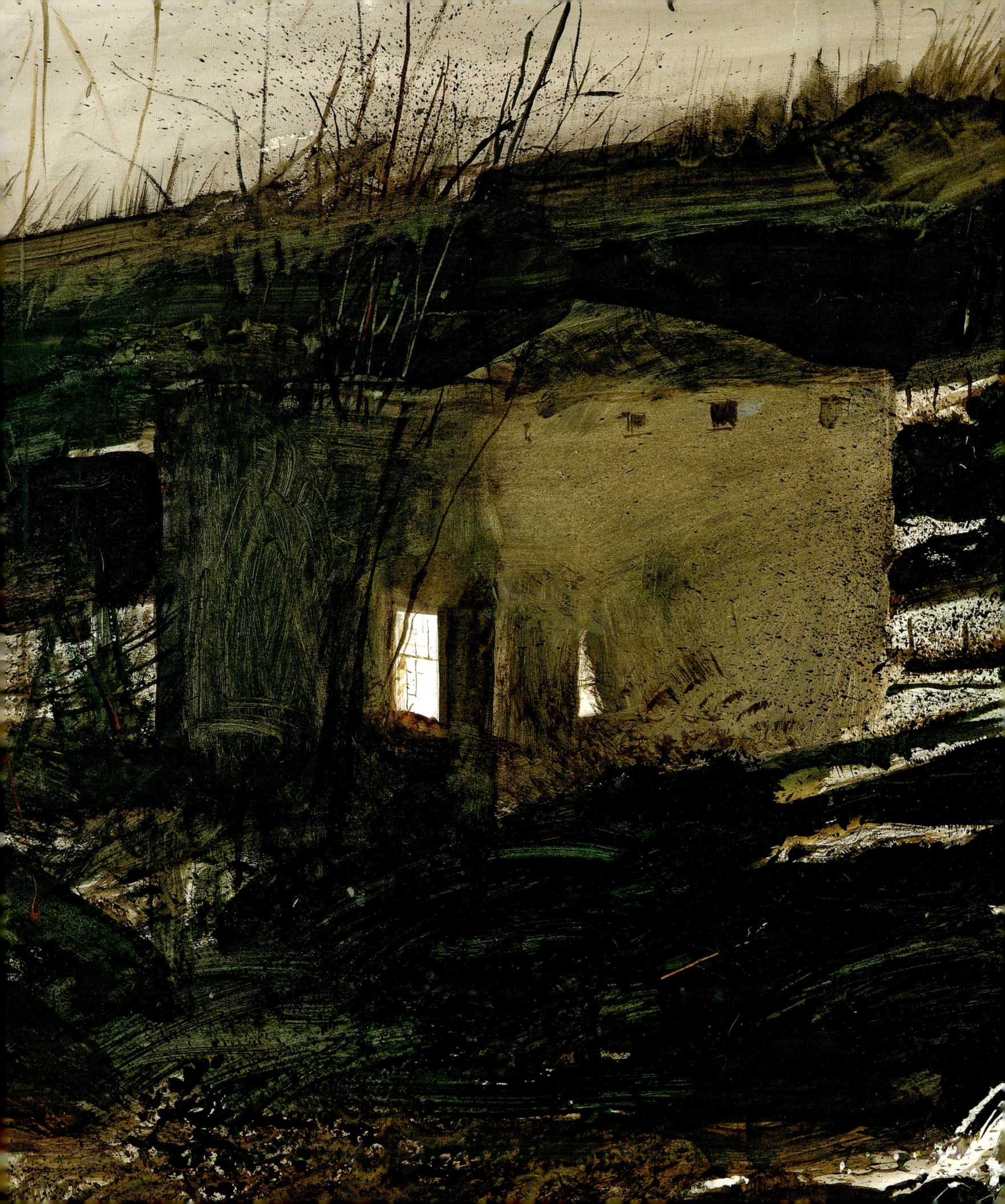

WYETH'S VIBE

JAMES WELLING

In December 2010, I arrived at Kuerner Farm on a bitterly cold morning to photograph the property and its buildings. The sky was overcast, and the temperature was below zero. Mary Cronin from the Brandywine Museum of Art escorted me to the farmhouse. We walked through the frosty front room, down a passageway, and into the kitchen. My first location was to be the window and sparse table depicted in Andrew Wyeth's 1959 tempera *Groundhog Day* (p. 80). As I moved around the room with my camera, I became aware of a chilly, musty odor. This distinct smell instantly reminded me of houses I had visited in Belgium and Germany in the 1990s. How uncanny, I thought, that the closeted air in this farmhouse could transport me to other houses and to other winters.

After I had finished in the kitchen, I asked Mary to show me the rest of the house. We walked through the empty rooms on each floor, finally arriving at the low-ceilinged attic where Wyeth painted his 1948 portrait of Karl Kuerner (p. 67). Above the subject's impassive head Wyeth depicts the metal hooks that Kuerner had inserted into the ceiling to dry sausages. After having photographed the hooks from different positions, I looked through the garret windows on two sides of the room. From this vantage I could see the gently rolling pastures and farmland that encircle the house.

A jumble of empty suitcases and broken wicker chairs was at the far end of the attic. As I approached, I was stunned to see drops of dried watercolor and tendril-like paint splatters on the rough floor planks. These forensic traces are evidence of Wyeth's robust watercolor practice.

We then went to the barn to locate the sink that figures in Wyeth's *Spring Fed* (1967; p. 93), the title of which refers to the invisible source of water that still flows into the blocky stone sink. The painted scene is illuminated by an incandescent

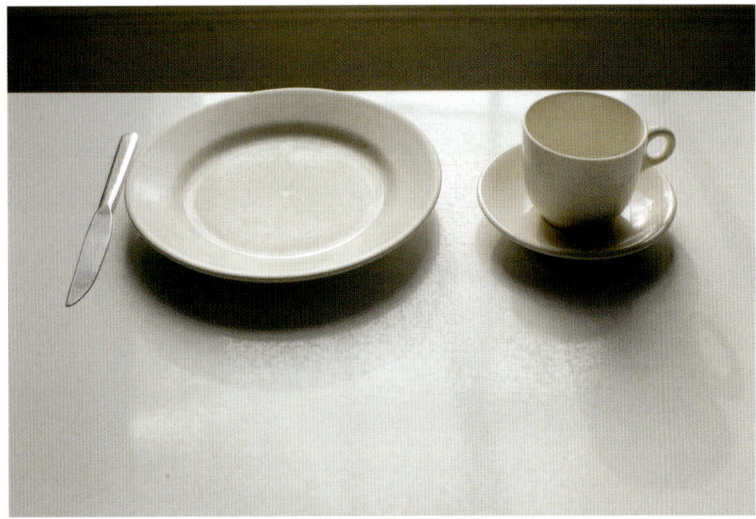

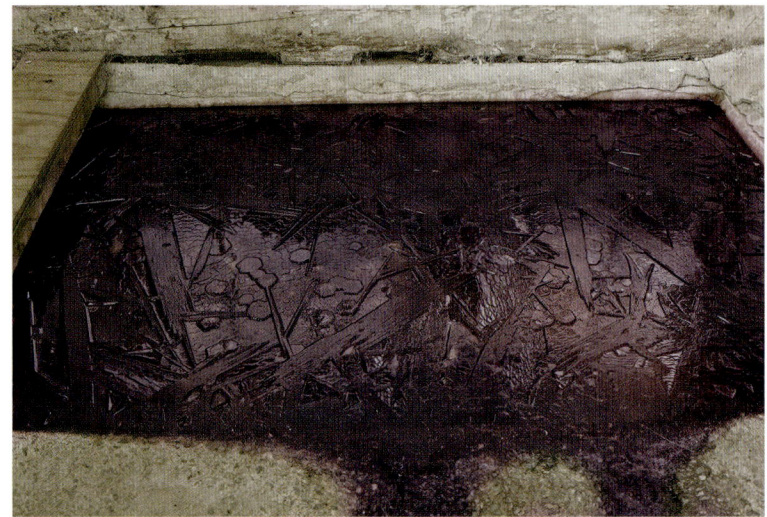

light above the sink and by a pair of double-hung windows that face a fenced-in yard. Inside the present-day barn, the interior is very dark, so we found our way to the sink by following the repetitive drip of water from the metal faucet. After my eyes had adjusted to the darkness, I set my camera on a tripod to make a long exposure. The paper-thin layer of ice atop the water in the sink had created extraordinary floral patterns. It was as if clusters of hexagonal "flowers" had bloomed amid a tangle of spiky "weeds."

Outside the barn, Mary pointed to a forest adjacent to the Kuerner property. These trees now cover the low hills depicted in Wyeth's 1953 tempera *Snow Flurries* (p. 69). After I said goodbye to Mary, I walked up the long driveway to the other side of Ring Road and climbed the hill there, known as Kuerner Hill. From that vantage point, I was able to get a clearer view of the woods that Mary had indicated. The trees were characteristic of a second-growth forest, one that propagates on previously farmed land. Formed over the past seventy-odd years, this new forest now provides privacy for the suburban development beyond it. I looked at the woods and tried unsuccessfully to imagine the painting's rolling hills without trees.

As if on cue, light snow began to fall as I walked down Kuerner Hill toward my car. I stopped and took my camera from my knapsack. Shielding the lens from the precipitation, I framed an image of the forest that now obscures the vista in *Snow Flurries*, but then I decided to leave that photograph untaken.

I have returned several times to photograph Chadds Ford, and on every visit, I have encountered Wyeth in unexpected ways. I like to attribute my heightened sensitivity to Wyeth's vibe, which still courses through the farm.

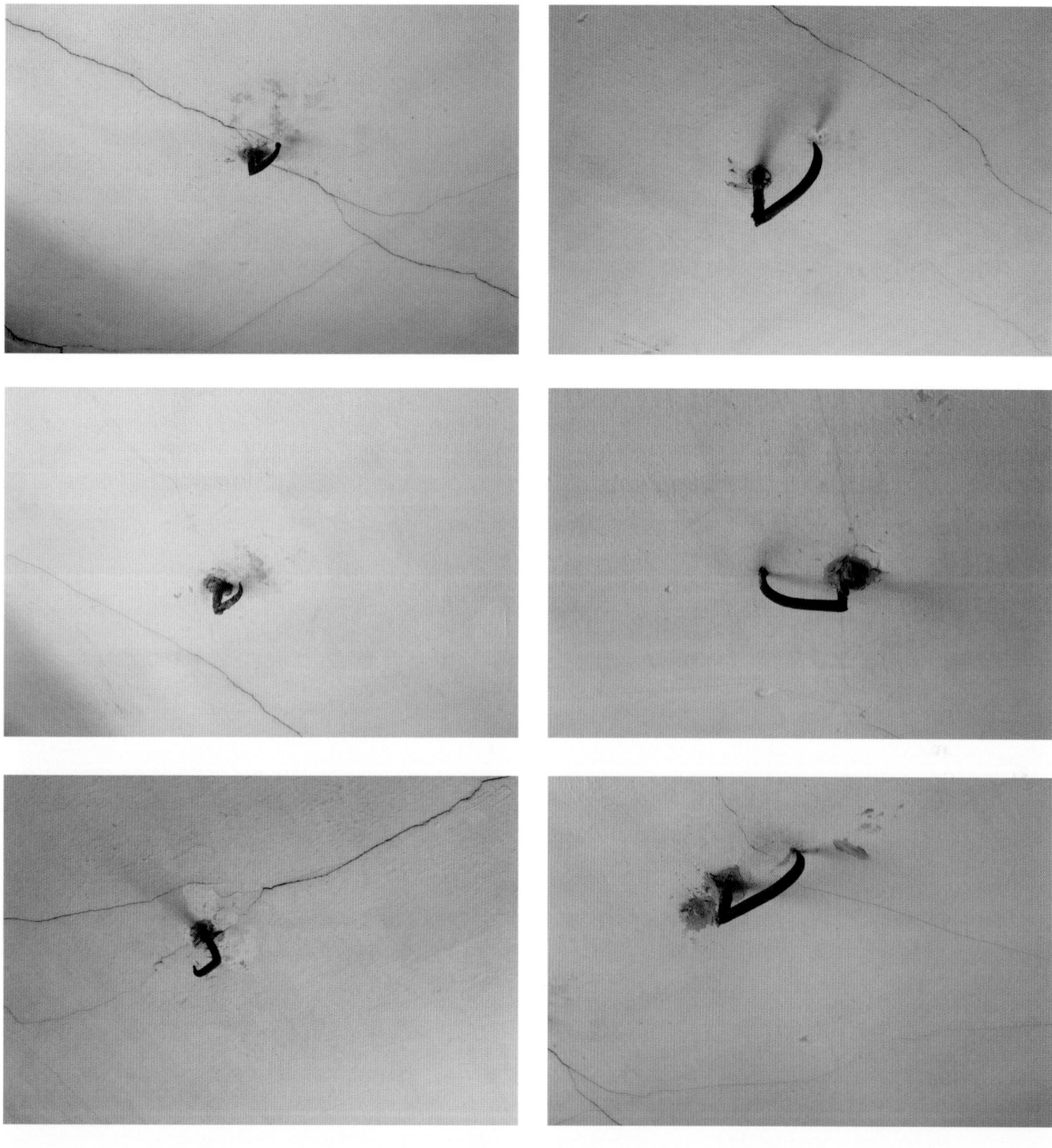

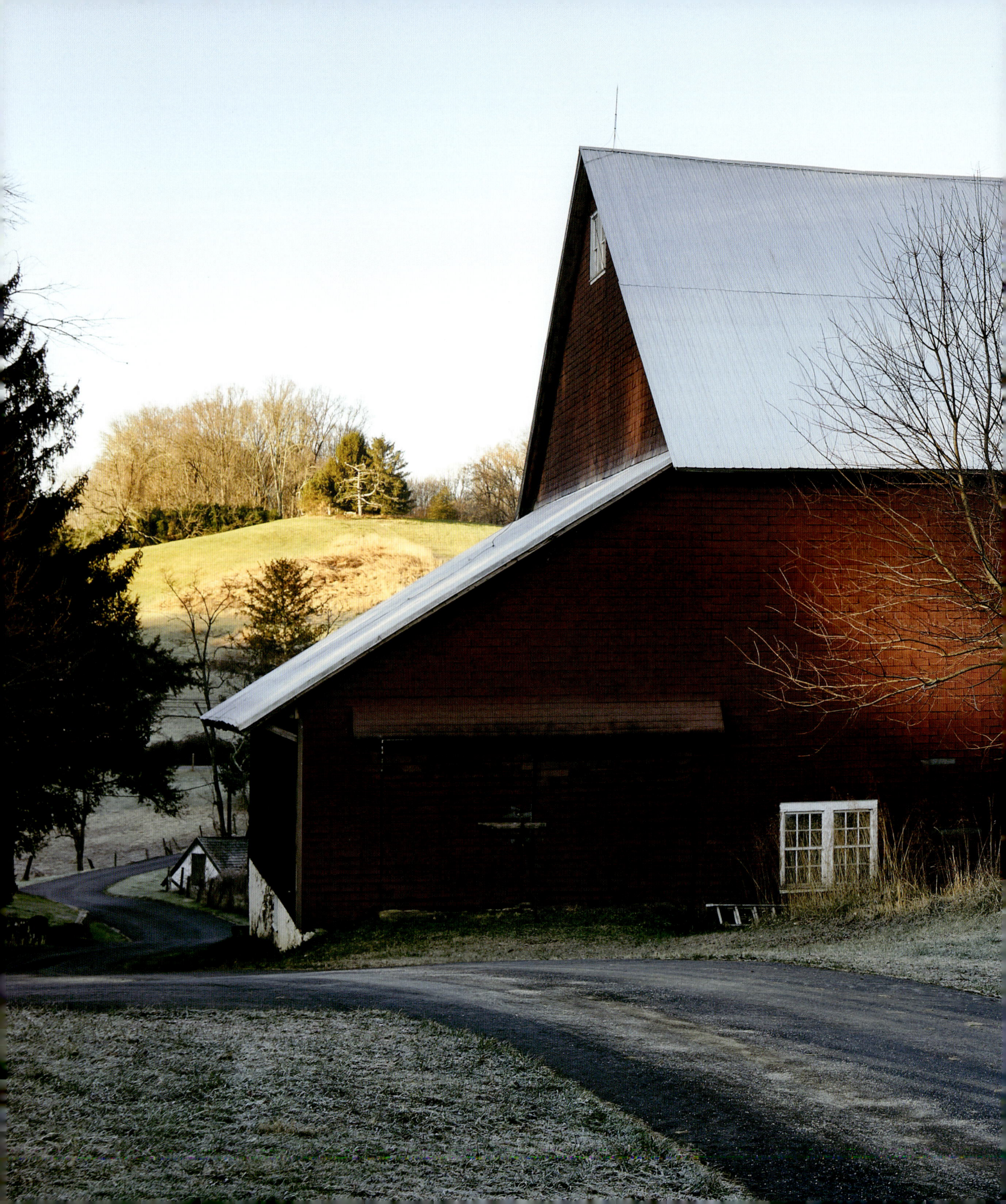

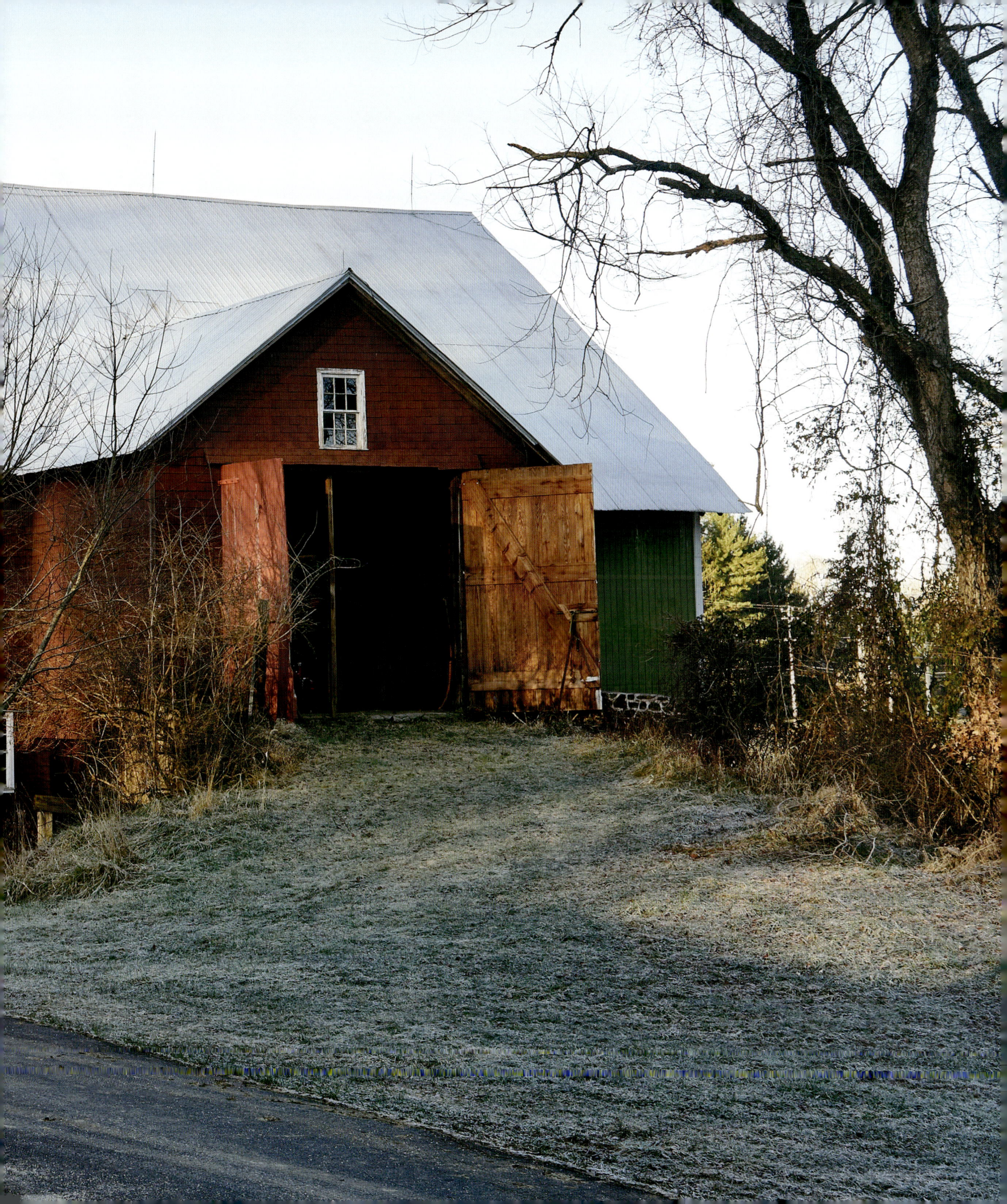

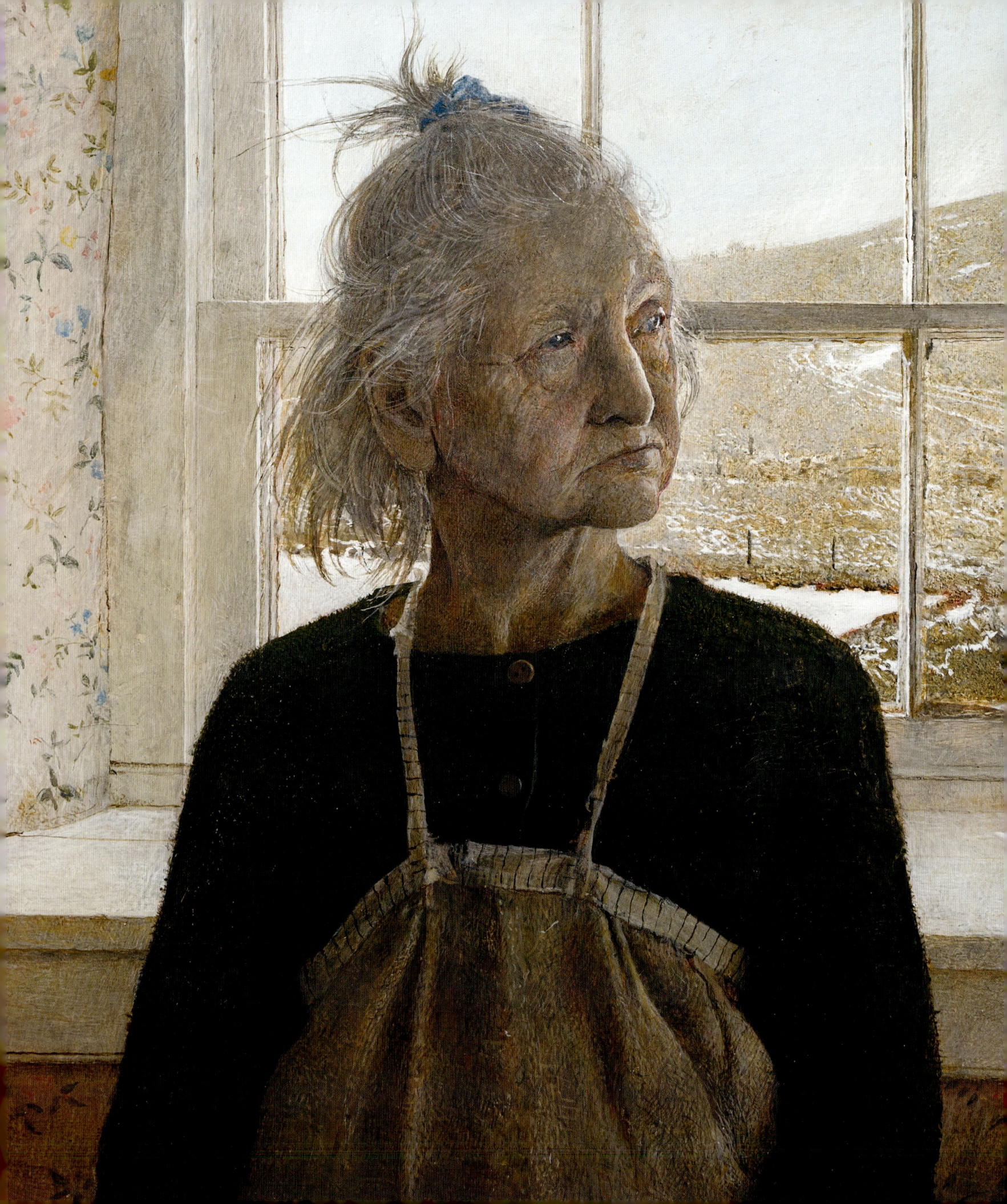

THE PEOPLE BEHIND THE PAINTINGS: KARL AND ANNA KUERNER

KAREN BAUMGARTNER

Karl and Anna Kuerner were made famous by their association with Andrew Wyeth. Art lovers around the world recognize their faces, their house, their landscape. Their much-reproduced depictions, such as the artist's now classic 1971 portrait of them (p. 103), have made them almost as iconic as the couple in Grant Wood's *American Gothic* (fig. 1). The result of this treatment, however, has been a public image of the Kuerners shaped almost exclusively by Wyeth's view of them, and while that perspective was undoubtedly formed over decades of close connection, it nevertheless reflects the artist's vision rather than the story that the family themselves might have told. This exhibition and its accompanying catalogue present an opportunity to go beyond the popular lore assigned to the Kuerners and to learn what we can of their story of immigration, loss, and resilience.

Karl Wilhelm Kuerner was born on April 17, 1898, in Neuffen, a small village in southwest Germany near the Black Forest. He had four brothers and one sister.[1] Little is known of his childhood, but he came from an era and a place that would see great political upheaval during his youth. As a teenager, Kuerner was a shepherd before he enlisted in the German military to serve in World War I, following in the steps of two brothers.[2] A severe injury to his arm took him from the front, but he refused amputation. After months of rehabilitation, Kuerner returned to combat in the Battle of Verdun, the lengthy campaign that would see some 700,000 casualties.[3] He was a distinguished machine gunner, earning the Iron Cross, first class.[4] Kuerner returned to civilian life and to sheepherding at the war's end.[5] His brothers also survived the conflict, one becoming an amateur painter, an association that may have contributed to Kuerner's future willingness to allow another artist access to his property, a decision that would eventually bring him into the public eye.[6]

Andrew Wyeth, *Anna Kuerner*, 1971
(detail, p. 101)

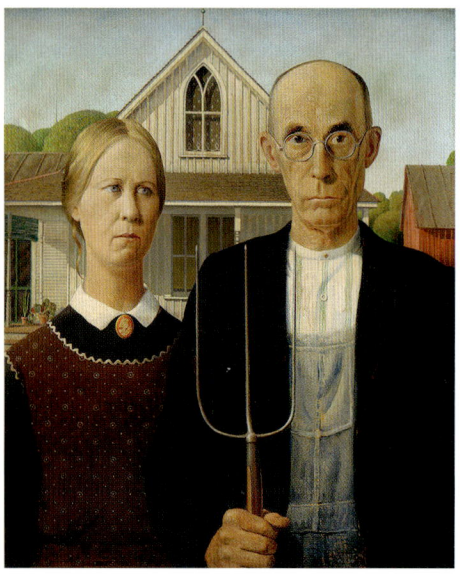

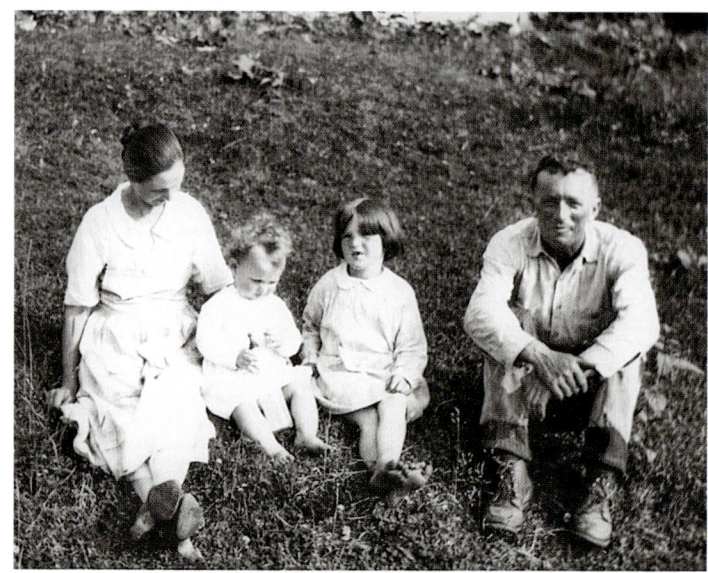

Fig. I (left). Grant Wood, *American Gothic*, 1930. Oil on beaverboard, 30¾ × 25¾ in. The Art Institute of Chicago. Friends of American Art Collection, 1930.934

Fig. 2 (right). Anna, Karl Jr., Louise, and Karl Kuerner Sr. at Ring Farm, c. 1928

The young veteran met Anna Faulhaber while driving his flock through Göllsdorf, another small town in the state of Baden-Württemberg. Born November 18, 1899, Faulhaber was one of twelve children and worked on her family's farm. During the couple's courtship, she joined Kuerner and his sheep in the hills. The date of their wedding is unclear,[7] but their first child, Louise, was born in 1922; a son followed shortly after, though he died in infancy.

With the backdrop of a defeated country struggling with postwar food shortages and skyrocketing inflation, Kuerner was encouraged by paternal uncles who had successfully resettled near Philadelphia to immigrate to America, where he could enjoy the stability they had found and receive further medical care for his war injury.[8] A passenger manifest documents Kuerner's arrival on United American Lines's SS *Resolute* in 1923. With support from his uncles, he established himself by working in a slaughterhouse to earn enough so that Anna and Louise could join him.[9] The two crossed unaccompanied on the Cunard Line's SS *Andania* in 1925. Separated from her family and away from her home for the first time in her life, Anna could not bear the noise of the city.[10] Both for her comfort and because he much preferred farming to work in the slaughterhouse, Karl found a farm to rent in Chadds Ford, a small town that better resembled the rural fields of the couple's childhoods overseas.[11]

The site of this farm about thirty miles west of Philadelphia was originally inhabited by the Lenni Lenape people, who had lived in the region for hundreds of years before the appearance of European settlers. Beginning in the eighteenth century, the Indigenous nation traveled westward. They had been forced from their ancestral land as settlers introduced the concept of land ownership and produced duplicitous agreements such as the Walking Treaty and the Treaty of Easton.[12] The first known recorded history of the property was in 1777, when the fighting of the American Revolution's Battle of Brandywine came within a half mile of the house. The owner then was a Quaker farmer and mill operator, Benjamin Ring. His descendants lived there until 1899, and so the place came to be known as Ring Farm. For the Kuerners, the Ring name stayed with the farm; they did not yet know that their own name would one day become just as firmly attached to it—if not more so.

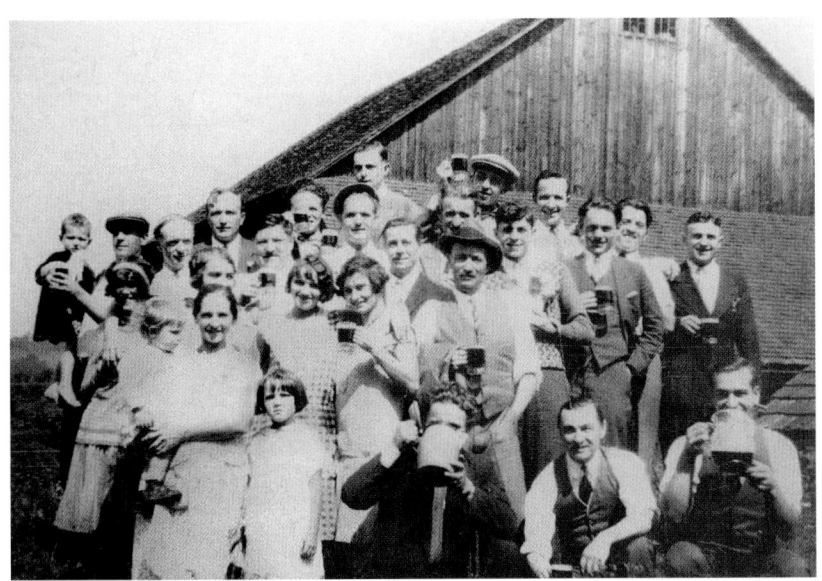

Fig. 3. The Kuerners' extended family and friends gather at Kuerner Farm, c. 1930. Anna holds Karl Jr. in the foreground, lower left, with Louise on the right.

With the rental of this Chadds Ford property from Arthur Cleveland, a prominent local citizen, the Kuerners established a new family home (fig. 2). Karl and Anna worked long hours with the goal of one day owning the property themselves. More Kuerner children were born there: Karl Jr. in 1927, Clara in 1928, Lydia in 1930, and Elizabeth in 1932. Friends and members of the Kuerners' extended family frequently visited from the Philadelphia area and occasionally from overseas to enjoy dinner, dancing, music, and beer (fig. 3).[13] Anna, however, is remembered as less sociable during these gatherings than her husband, keeping mostly to her work in the kitchen and participating little in the conversation.

In 1933, the youngest son of a prosperous and artistic family living about a half mile away asked for permission to paint on the property.[14] Andrew Wyeth was welcomed to such a degree that eventually he was given access to the buildings and fields as if he were a member of the family. A strong work ethic was a mark of pride among the Kuerners, and Karl may have recognized the artist's dedication to his art as similar to his own to the farm.[15] Not only did the children have their own farm chores, their father instructed them to assist Wyeth, such as constructing a nest of burlap to keep the artist warm when he worked in the snow.[16] Other members of the Wyeth clan also visited the family, including the artist's wife, Betsy James Wyeth, who sometimes stayed for dinner with the Kuerners.[17]

Karl was able to purchase Ring Farm in 1943.[18] The family raised dairy cattle and pigs; grew hay, grain, and apples; and the pond was even stocked with fish. Yet despite this apparent bounty and the hard work it required to maintain, it was barely enough to feed the family.[19] The profit margins were so thin that the Kuerners relied more often on barter than cash.[20] As Louise recalled, "We were really, really, *really* poor."[21]

Many members of Karl's family were nearby, but only one of Anna's eleven siblings settled the United States. Leaving Philadelphia did not prove to lift her spirits. She spoke little English and was not an active participant in the Chadds Ford community. The "homesick" Anna was hospitalized at least twice at Norristown State Hospital, an inpatient psychiatric facility about thirty miles from Chadds Ford.[22] Louise estimates the first stay began when she was five or six years old.[23] Whether and to what extent Anna may have suffered from mental illness is not clear, and the memories of her difficulties seem painful still for family members living today.

A new association with the Kuerners' German heritage arose during World War II, when a camp for prisoners of war was established in nearby Downingtown.[24] Although Karl was now on the opposite side of the conflict, the naturalized US citizen hired German soldiers who had been given leave to work on local farms, a common practice at the time.[25] These laborers built the Kuerner farmhouse's gateposts, retaining wall, porch support, and chimney. The family estimates that this was done in 1945, with a tragic memory serving as a reminder: the accident at the railroad crossing at the base of Kuerner Hill that killed N. C. Wyeth. Family legend tells that Karl was collecting the workmen that day, so he

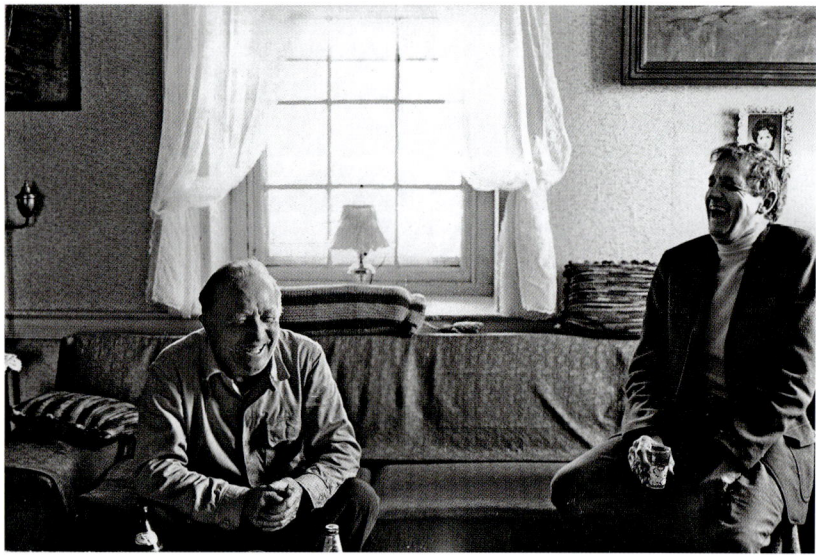

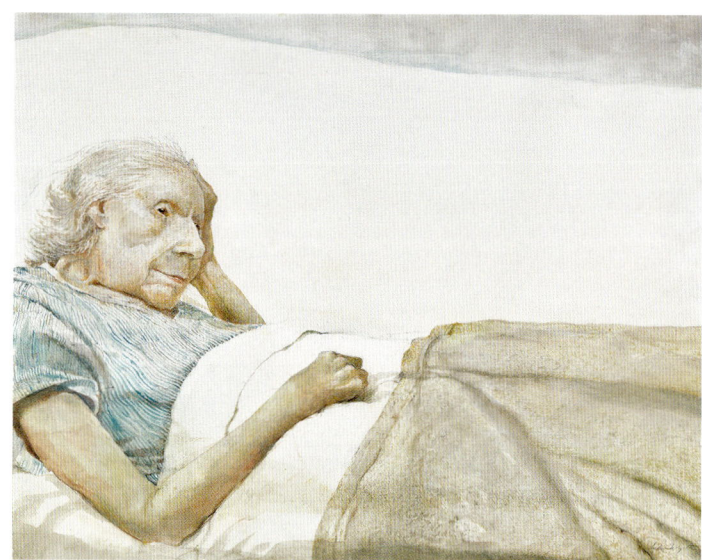

was not on the farm at the time of the accident.[26] With the death of Wyeth's father, the farm took on a still deeper meaning for the artist. It was the site of a terrible loss, but he found perhaps a lingering paternal presence in Karl, eighteen years his senior.

In 1959, Wyeth completed the landmark tempera *Groundhog Day* (p. 80), a view of the Kuerner kitchen. Much has been written about the subtle threat of violence implicit in this work.[27] In contrast, when Louise saw the painting years after its completion, she vividly recalled no such thing, rather the cozy smell of her mother's pancakes. To the Kuerner children, this kitchen was home.[28] While Wyeth's paintings often emphasize the difficulties of farm life and allude to Karl's military history, the children no doubt saw other dimensions to their father. While he necessarily performed the sometimes brutal duties of soldier and farmer, there is little evidence that he was prone to violence in his domestic life. During the time that his wife was hospitalized, Karl refused that his children be placed in foster care and instead hired a housekeeper, despite his meager income. In regard to the sense of menace that was sometimes assigned to him in Wyeth's art, in particular through the artist's 1948 portrait of him (p. 67), Karl demurred: "The Wyeths say that Andy was really painting his father more than me."[29]

One also gets a sense of Karl's lighter side from a photo of him and Wyeth laughing (fig. 4). The publication of the image, shot by Hans Namuth, in the national magazine *Show* in 1964 is also evidence that the farm and its inhabitants were becoming well known, much as Christina and Alvaro Olson of Cushing, Maine, had become public figures after the popularity of *Christina's World* (1948), perhaps the artist's best-known painting. In the late 1960s, journalist Gene Logsdon contacted Karl for a full interview, which would appear in his book *Wyeth People* (1969).[30] The success of Wyeth's artwork had brought farm and family into the spotlight.

As the children grew, they left the farm for new lives, with the exception of Karl Jr., who married in 1956 but stayed on the farm to work. He and his wife, Margaret, had a son named Karl J. Kuerner the following year. Having never known his home without Wyeth's presence, Karl J. began art lessons with Wyeth's sister Carolyn, further knitting the two families together.

In 1970, the eldest Karl was diagnosed with leukemia.[31] A neighbor arrived to help tend the garden: Helga Testorf, a Prussian immigrant in her late thirties who lived across the road with her husband and four children. With her distinct accent and recent memories of a shared homeland, she was a natural fit for the family, and gradually she took on more household chores and nursing duties.[32] Testorf also captured the attention of Wyeth, who had long been enamored with Germanic culture. One of the artist's first paintings of her poses her in a traditional dirndl in the Kuerner kitchen (p. 104). Soon, Testorf posed nude in the privacy of the same third-floor room where Wyeth's striking 1948 portrait of Karl had been set. The series that was to become "The Helga Pictures" began in earnest, but the family asked the artist and model to continue it elsewhere. They complied, and as Karl J. Kuerner notes, most of the artist's depictions of Testorf during the following years were not interior scenes, but outside views of the house and farm.[33]

While the eldest Karl had agreed to sit for Wyeth on numerous occasions, Anna proved a more elusive subject. Perhaps the changes within the household, including the specter of her husband's mortality, led her to reconsider. When she finally agreed to sit in January 1971, she posed for just three weeks.[34] A small panel would be the only tempera portrait of Anna (p. 101). Through the 1970s, Wyeth completed a few watercolor portraits, but most other depictions are of her in motion: climbing stairs, doing yard work, or cooking. She was usually seen as a figure within the context of the farm, still wary of neglecting her never ending cycle of chores to interact with the artist, who had by then become a long-established fixture of the household.

By 1978 Karl was in the end stages of his illness, and Wyeth was preparing a final tempera of him. *Spring* (p. 122) depicts the patriarch lying within a snow drift at the base of his now famous hill. Though the painter intended to depict Karl becoming a part of the land he loved, the family may have expected an updated view of the powerful man seen in his portrait thirty years before.[35] The Surrealist quality of the scene offended the family, who considered it to be disrespectful.[36]

Wyeth continued to take inspiration from Kuerner Farm and its family, including the next generation of Kuerners, among them Karl J., who had become a professional painter. After Anna died, in 1997, her son stayed on to continue the farm work, even after the property was gifted to the Brandywine Conservancy two years later, under an arrangement that ensured the family retained use of the barn to continue to care for their animals.[37]

Wyeth's final Kuerner works include a portrait of Margaret Kuerner, Karl J.'s mother, in 2006 (fig. 5). She posed only after much convincing; *Spring* was still on her mind. In the end, she and the family were pleased with her more conventional depiction.[38] She passed away shortly afterward, and Wyeth died in 2009. Karl Jr. passed away in 2018, leaving his son to maintain the barn while continuing his artistic career from his home overlooking the property. The farm and family that the young Karl and Anna worked to create had survived the lean years. The home that they had established when they were young immigrants had seen two new generations thrive, and for better or worse, Andrew Wyeth had ushered them into the limelight. The property's protection under the auspices of the Brandywine Conservancy, its status as a National Historic Landmark, and the artwork that the farm and its inhabitants inspired will ensure that the Kuerner story will be told for decades to come.

Notes

1. Betsy James Wyeth, *Wyeth at Kuerners* (Boston: Houghton Mifflin, 1976), 3.

2. Marta McCave, "Karl Kuerner, Wyeth's Friend, Dies at 80," *The News Journal* [Wilmington, DE], January 8, 1979, 25.

3. "A Brief Look at the Battle of Verdun," Mémorial de Verdun Champ de Bataille, accessed March 4, 2024, https://memorial-verdun.fr/en/learning-resource-centre/the-battle-of-verdun-historic-events.

4. Karl J. Kuerner, in conversation with the author, November 30, 2023.

5. "Louise Kuerner Edwards and Karl W. Kuerner, Jr., April 17, 2013," video interview by Mary Cronin and Christine Podmaniczky. Walter and Leonore Annenberg Research Center, Brandywine Museum of Art, Chadds Ford, PA.

6. "Karl J. Kuerner, Wyeth," interview by Glenn Holsten, March 23, 2017, American Masters Digital Archive (WNET), accessed March 4, 2024, https://www.pbs.org/wnet/americanmasters/archive/interview/karl-kuerner.

7. Betsy James Wyeth, "Tempera Books," object page for *Anna Kuerner*, n.d. Andrew & Betsy Wyeth Study Center, Brandywine Museum of Art, Chadds Ford, PA. Although this source reports that the Kuerners were married in 1921, Karl is listed as unmarried on the passenger manifest for his crossing to the United States in 1923, while the 1925 passenger manifest for Anna, which uses her maiden name, lists Karl as her "intended husband." See "New York, U.S., Arriving Passenger and Crew Lists (including Castle Garden and Ellis Island), 1820–1957" (accessed via Ancestry.com, May 4, 2024). It is possible that they were married at Ellis Island before Anna and Louise were granted entrance to the United States (see Vincent J. Cannato, "Moral Turpitude," chap. 13 in *American Passage: The History of Ellis Island* [New York: Harper, 2009]). The US Census in 1930 lists their ages when married as twenty-eight for Karl and twenty-six for Anna. See "US Census Bureau, Fifteenth Census of the United States: 1930 Population Schedule" (accessed via Ancestry.com, December 5, 2023). It may be that the 1921 date was invented to conform to societal norms, but the reason for the discrepancy ultimately remains unknown. In regard to the death of the Kuerners' infant son, see Richard Meryman, *Andrew Wyeth: A Secret Life* (New York: HarperCollins, 1996), 199.

8. Louise Kuerner Edwards, interview by Cronin and Podmaniczky.

9. Ibid.

10. Ibid.

11. Ibid., and Meryman, *Secret Life*, 199.

12. Walter Licht et al., "The Original People and Their Land: The Lenape, Pre-History to the 18th Century," West Philadelphia Collaborative History, accessed March 4, 2024, https://collaborativehistory.gse.upenn.edu/stories/original-people-and-their-land-lenape-pre-history-18th-century.

13. Karl J. Kuerner, conversation, November 2023; Lydia N. Kessler, in conversation with the author, March 4, 2023. Kessler, whose uncle knew Karl before the families emigrated, recalled her memories of visiting Kuerner Farm gatherings with her family. Her account is echoed by Helga Testorf, in conversation with the author, March 6, 2024, and throughout Meryman, *Secret Life*. The consistency of this characterization spreads over many years.

14. Meryman, *Secret Life*, 199.

15. Louise Kuerner Edwards, interview by Cronin and Podmaniczky.

16. "Farm Where Andrew Wyeth Painted Landscapes Opens," *Lewiston* [ME] *Sun Journal*, June 13, 2004, accessed March 4, 2024, https://www.sunjournal.com/2004/06/13/farm-andrew-wyeth-painted-landscapes-opens.

17. Meryman, *Secret Life*, 203.

18. Robert Wise Consulting, *The Kuerner Farm: Historic Structures Report* (Chadds Ford, PA: Brandywine Conservancy, 2000), 18.

19. Gene Logsdon, *Wyeth People* (Dallas: Taylor Publishing, 1969), 33.

20. Louise Kuerner Edwards, interview by Cronin and Podmaniczky.

21. Louise Kuerner Edwards, quoted in Meryman, *Secret Life*, 288.

22. Karl J. Kuerner, in conversation with the author, August 1, 2022.

23. Louise Kuerner Edwards, interview by Cronin and Podmaniczky.

24. J. R. Ertell, "German POWs at VFGH," *The Historical Society of the Phoenixville Area Newsletter* 35, no. 4 (September 2012), 2–5, accessed December 28, 2023, https://hspa-pa.org/Newsletter/2012%20Sept%20Newsletter.pdf.

25. "Prisoner of War Camps at Gettysburg During World War II," National Park Service, accessed December 28, 2023, https://www.nps.gov/articles/gettysburgww2.htm.

26. Karl J. Kuerner, in conversation with the author, January 5, 2024.

27. This is especially well detailed in Anne Classen Knutson et al., *Andrew Wyeth: Memory & Magic* (New York: Rizzoli, 2005).

28. Louise Kuerner Edwards, interview by Cronin and Podmaniczky.

29. Karl Kuerner, quoted in Logsdon, *Wyeth People*, 35.

30. Logsdon, *Wyeth People*, 29.

31. Karl J. Kuerner, conversation, January 2024.

32. Helga Testorf, conversation, March 2024.

33. Karl J. Kuerner, conversation, August 2022.

34. Betsy James Wyeth, "Tempera Books," object page for *Anna Kuerner*, n.d. The fact that Wyeth typically spent much longer on his tempera portraits is evident in the "Tempera Books" as well. For comparison, the object page

for *My Young Friend*, a portrait of another local Chadds Ford model, records that this tempera took the artist four months to complete, from November 1969 through February 1970.

35. Betsy James Wyeth, "Black Books," object page for *Spring*, 2003. Andrew & Betsy Wyeth Study Center, Brandywine Museum of Art, Chadds Ford, PA.
36. Karl J. Kuerner, conversation, November 2023.
37. One of these animals, a Percheron horse named Dentzel, is depicted in *Fenced In* (p. 148) and *Karlanna* (p. 149).
38. Karl J. Kuerner, conversation, November 2023.

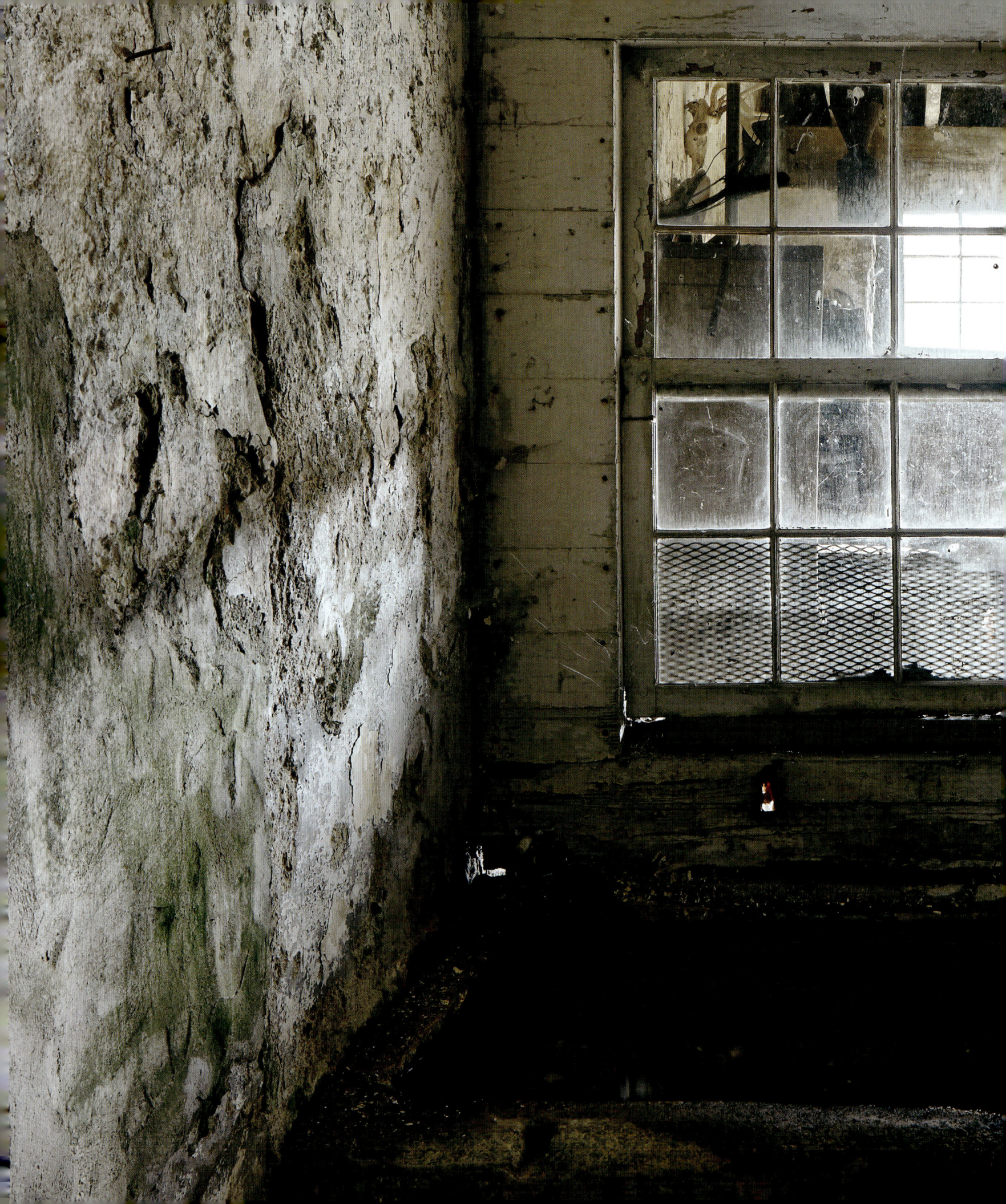

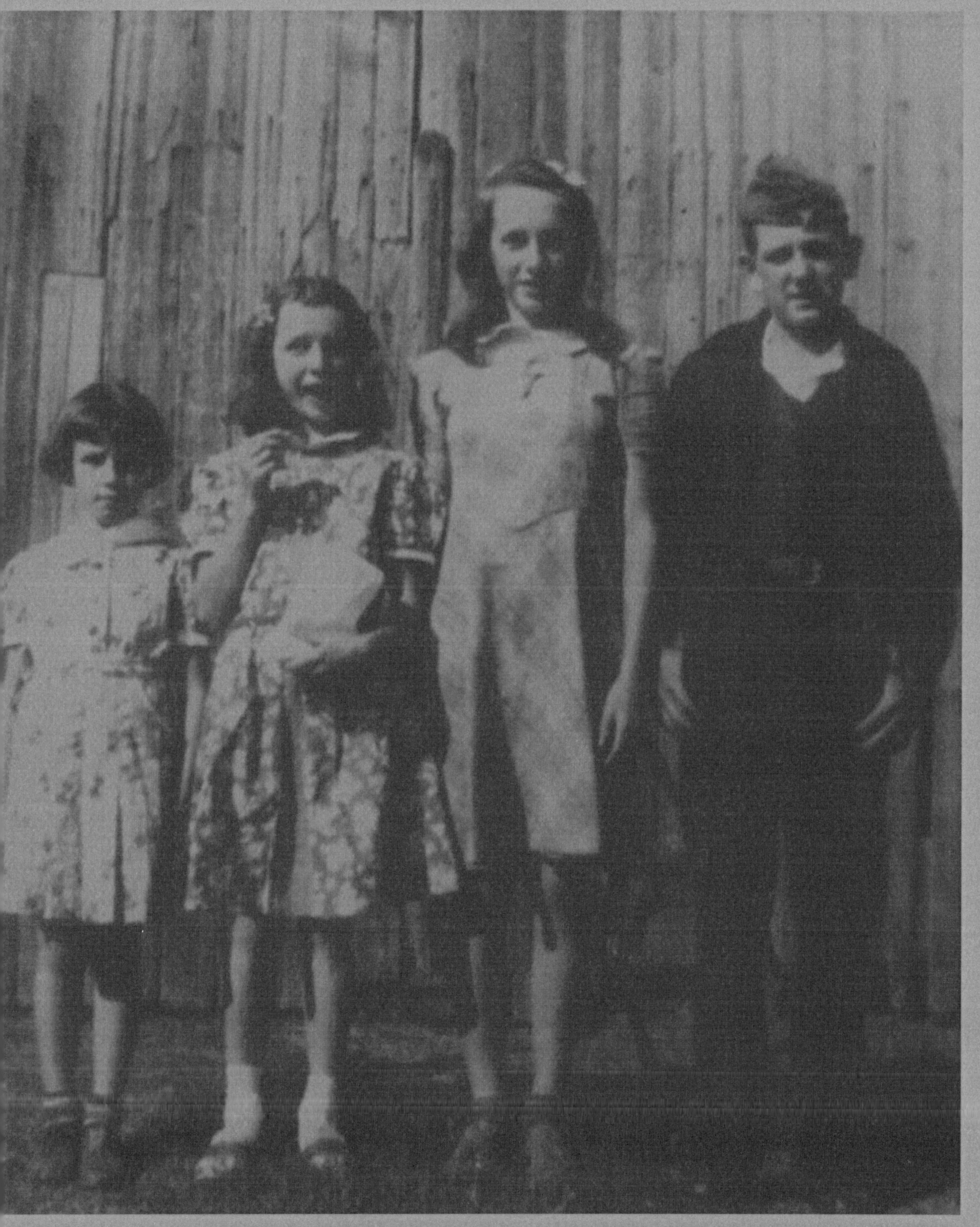

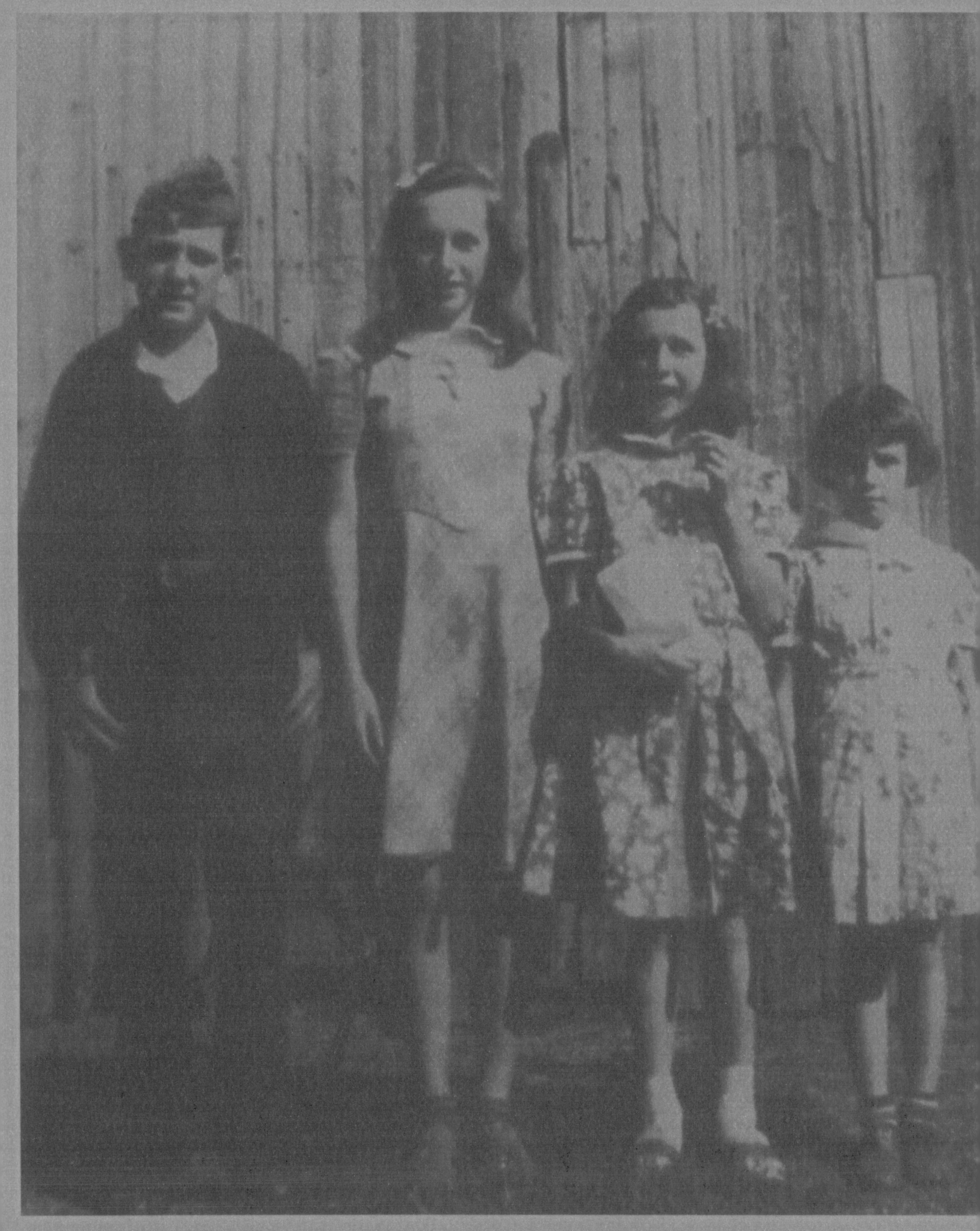

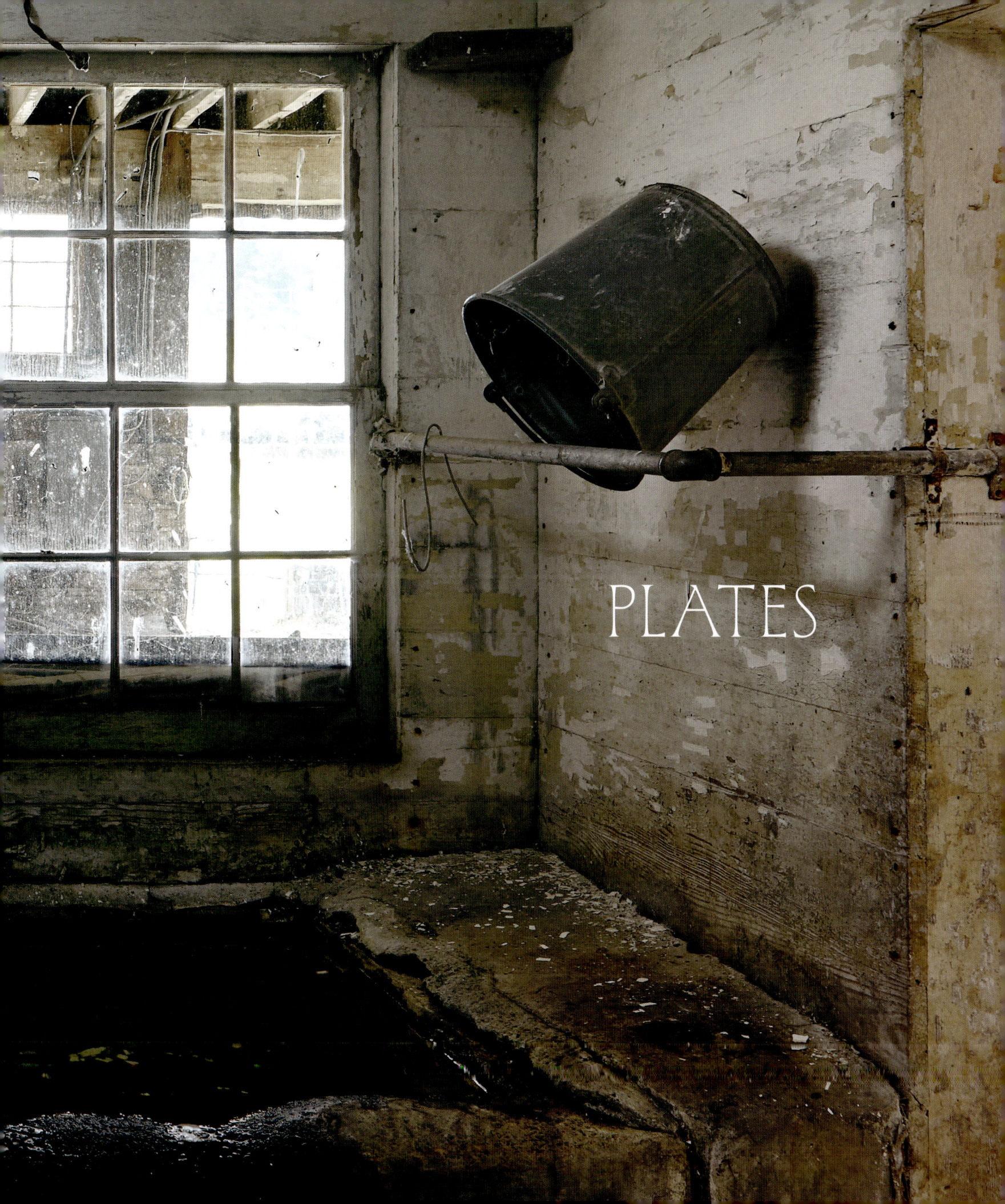

PLATES

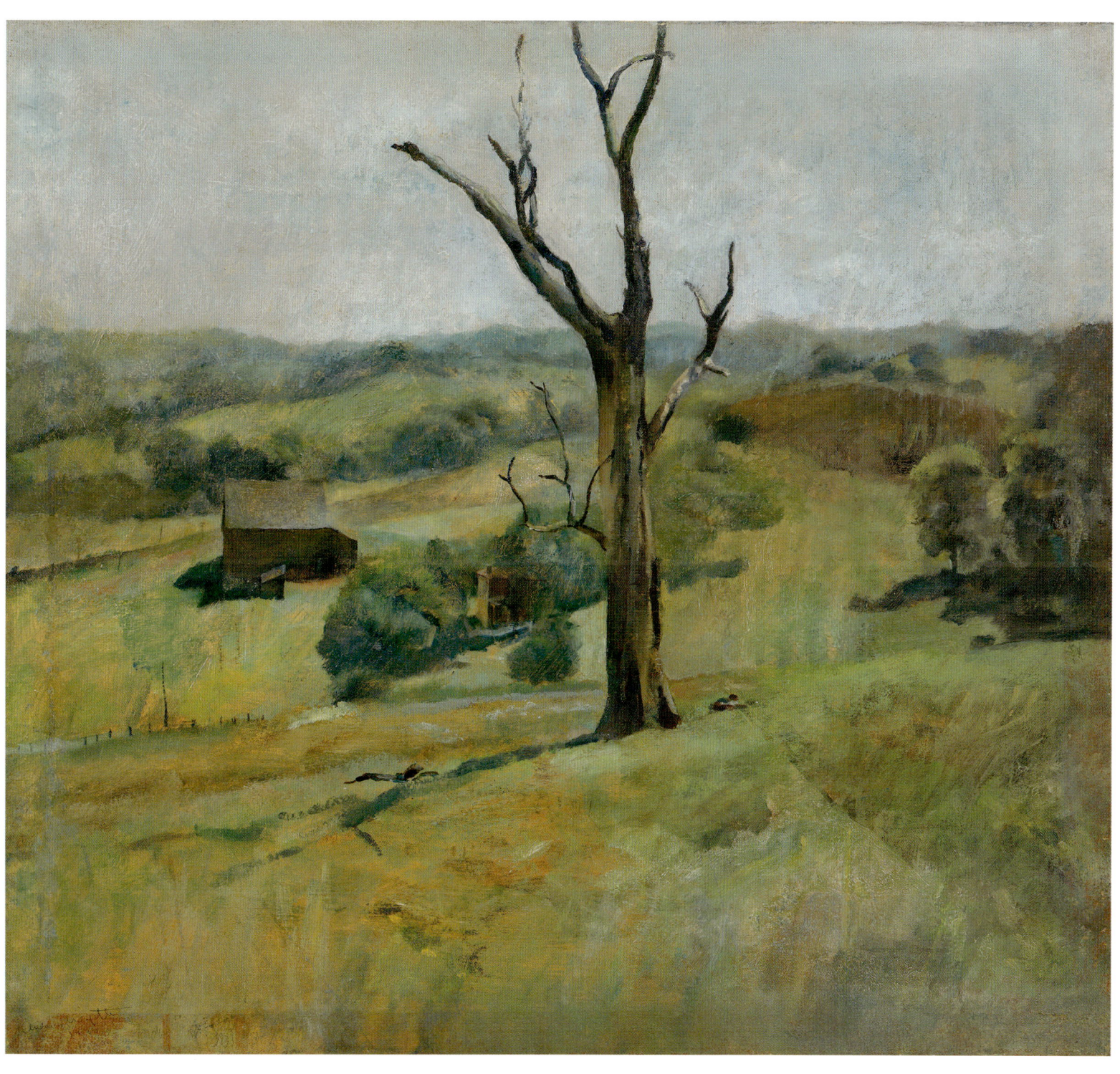

Chestnut Tree, 1933. Oil on canvas, 30 × 33 inches

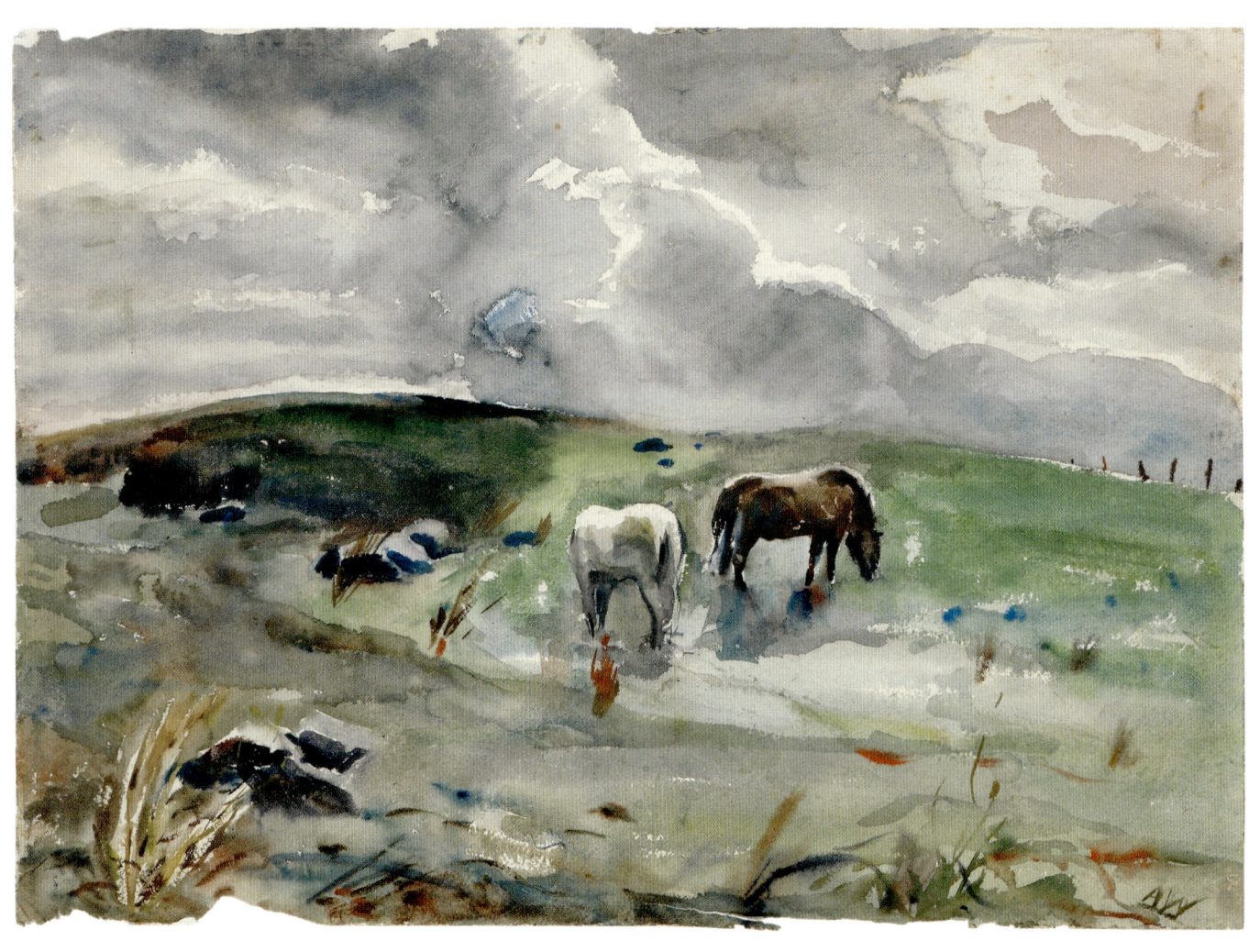

Green Hill, 1934. Watercolor on paper, 15 × 21 inches

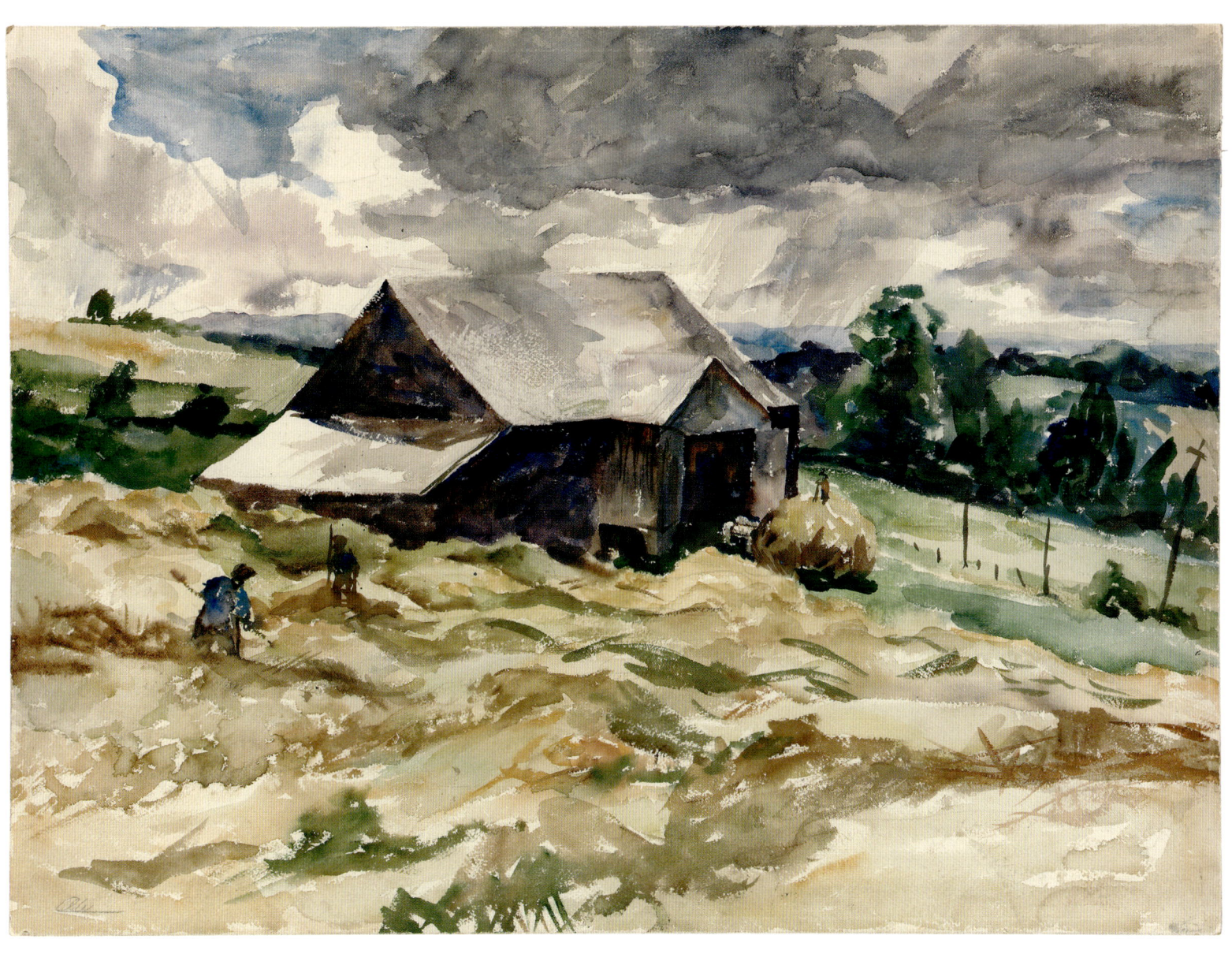

Haying at Kuerners, 1934. Watercolor on paper, 22 × 30 inches

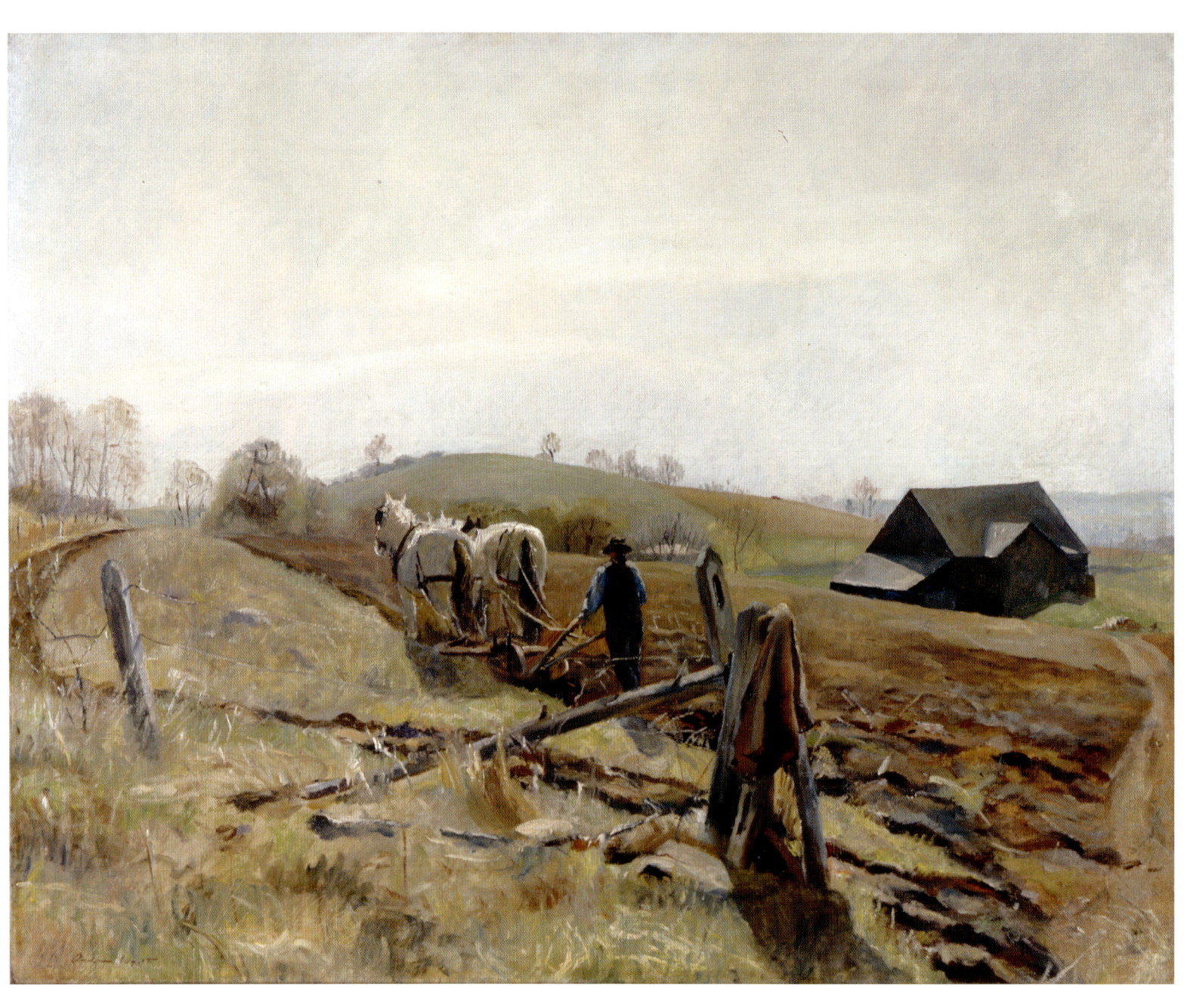

Spring Landscape at Kuerners, 1935. Oil on canvas, 32 × 40 inches

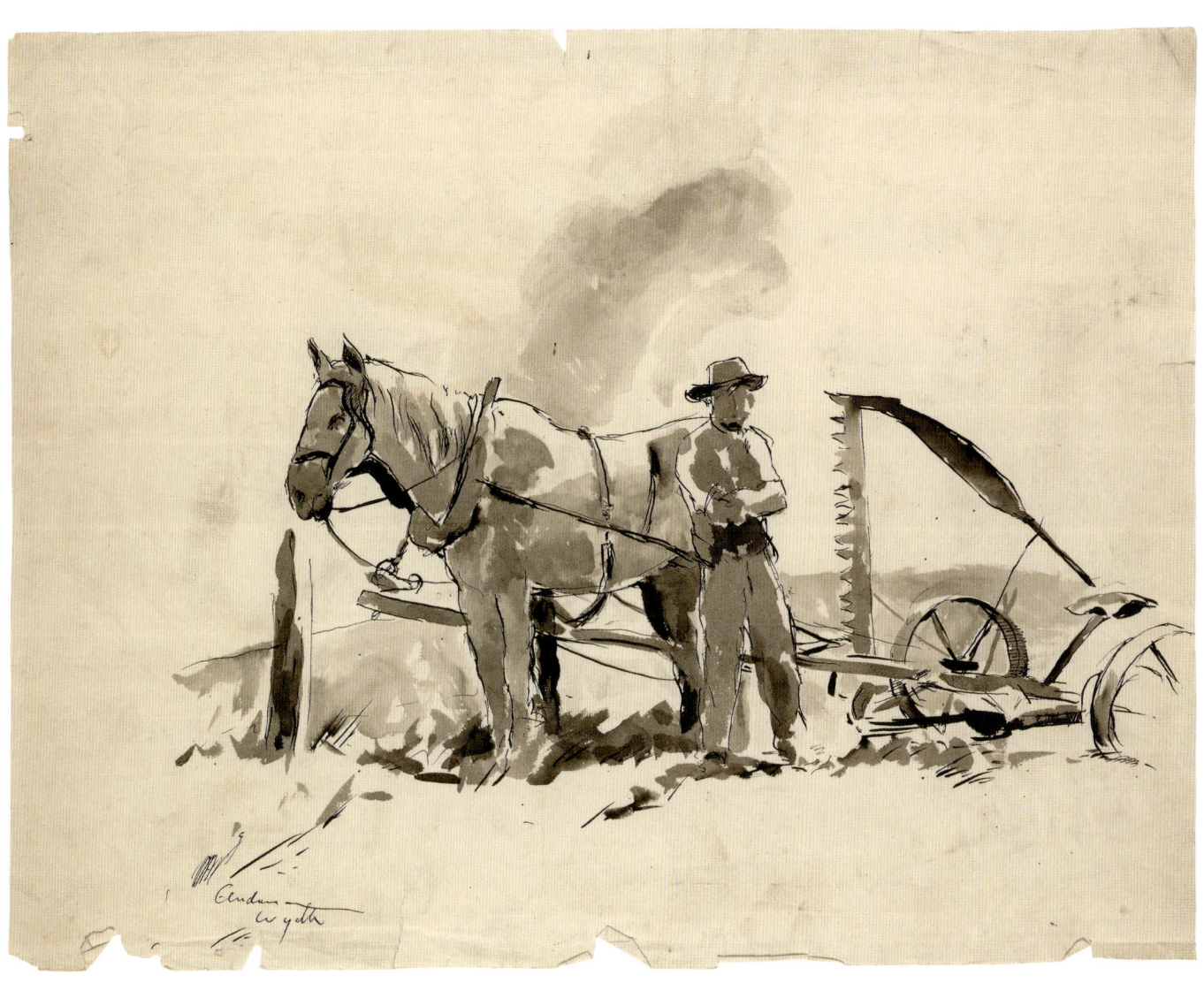

Untitled, 1935. Ink wash on paper, 15 ¾ × 20 ½ inches

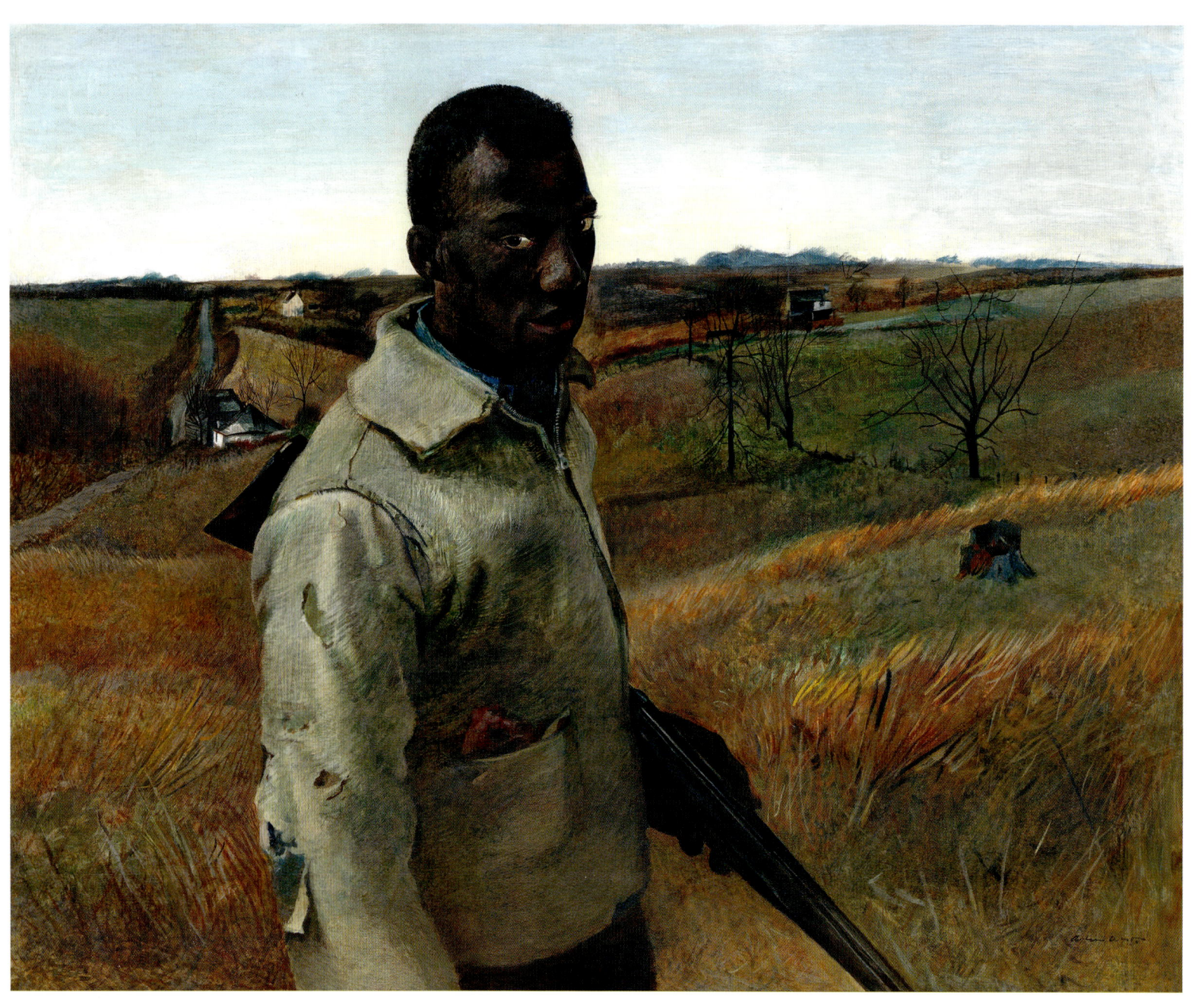

Black Hunter, 1938. Egg tempera on panel, 32 × 40 inches

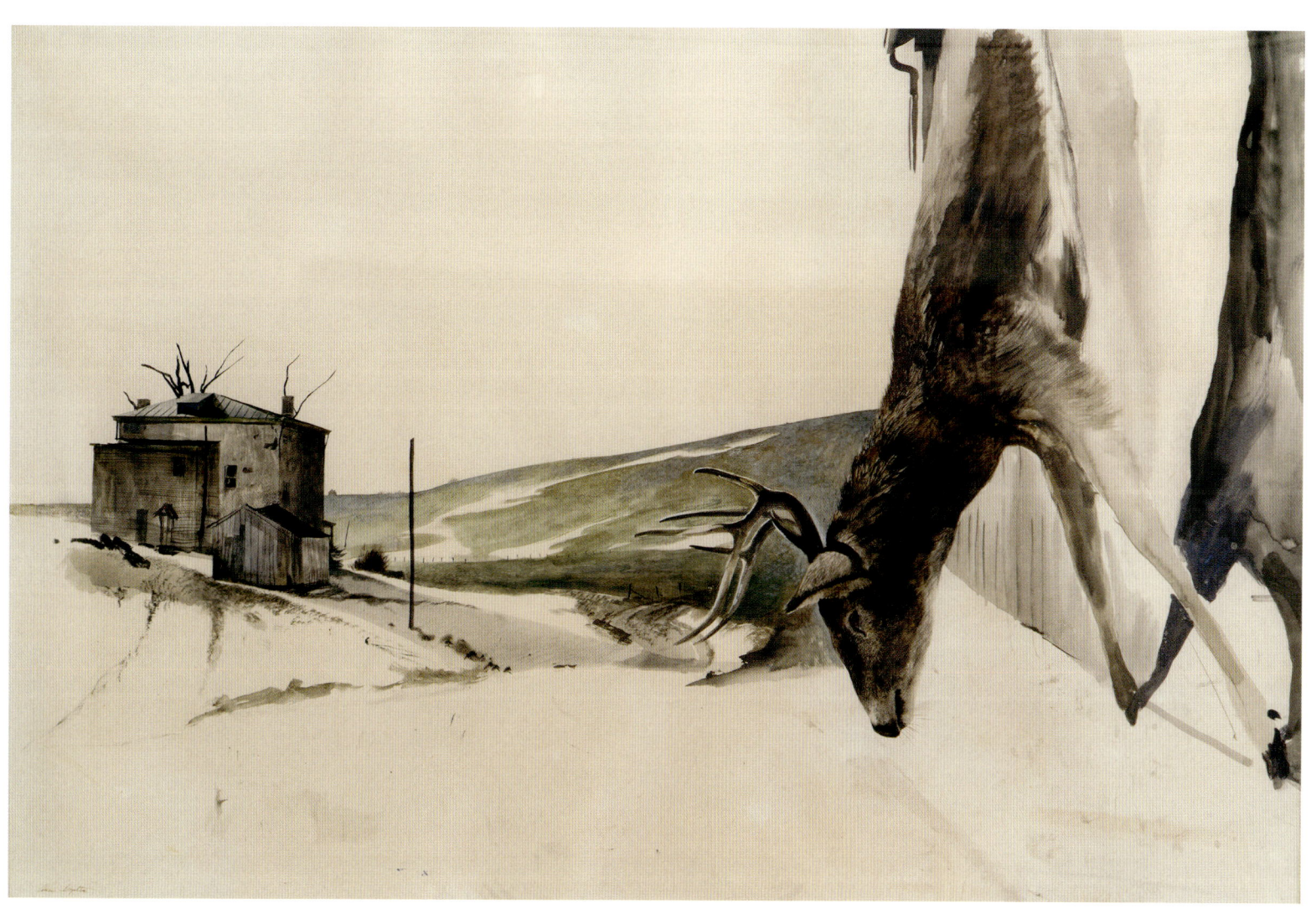

Winter Morning, 1944. Drybrush watercolor on paper, 25 ½ × 38 ⅜ inches

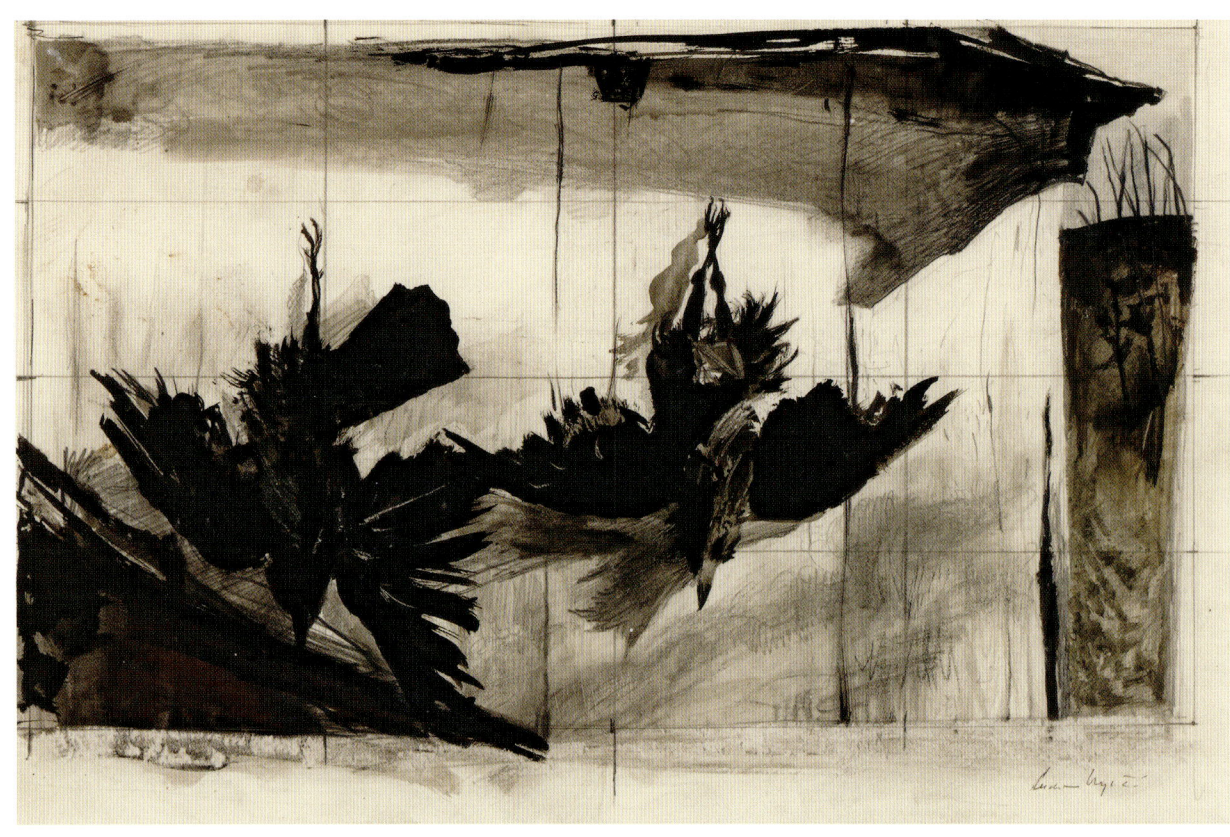

Woodshed Study, 1944. Ink wash, watercolor, and pencil on paper, 16 × 20 ¾ inches

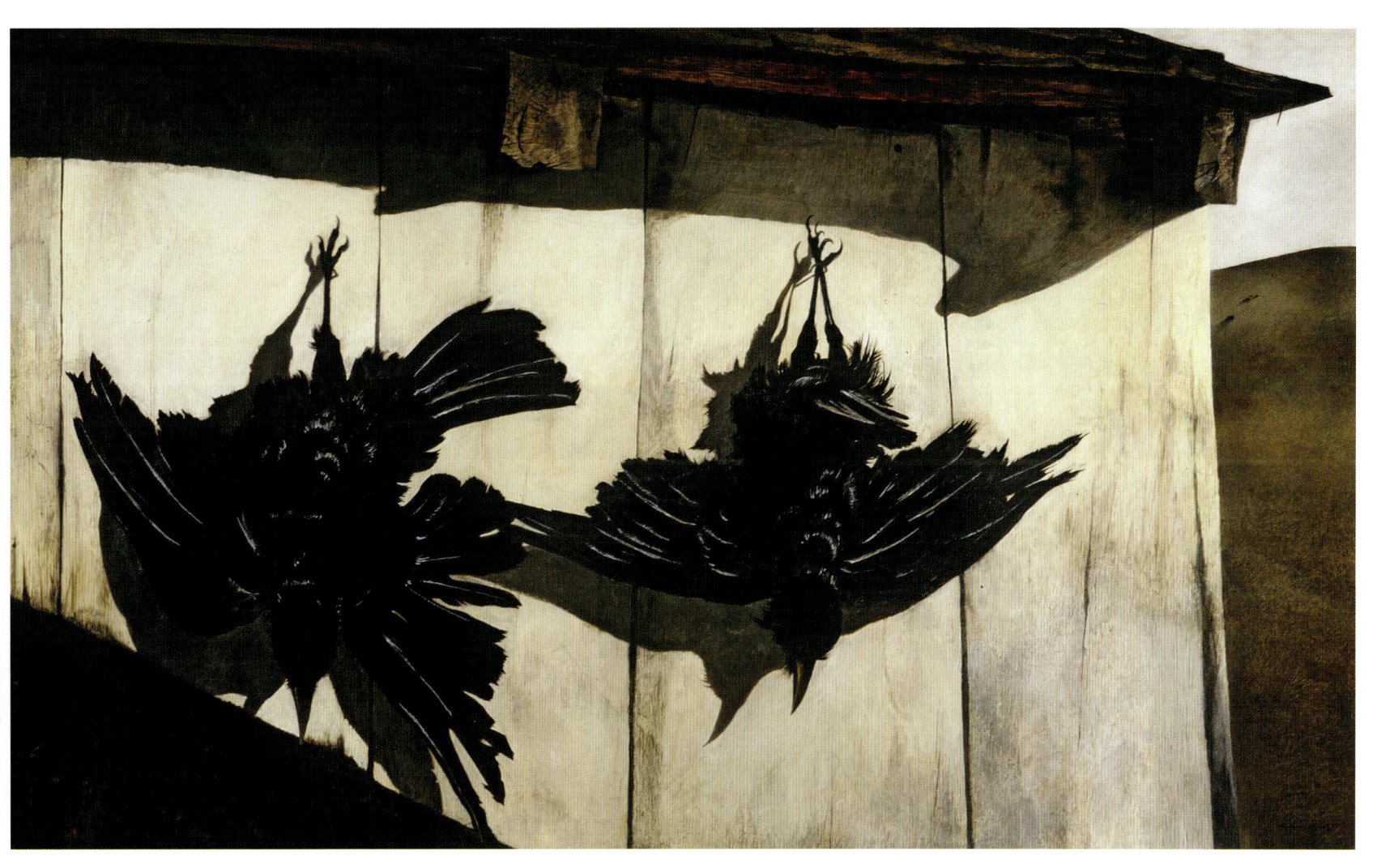

Woodshed, 1944. Egg tempera on panel, 31 ½ × 56 ¾ inches

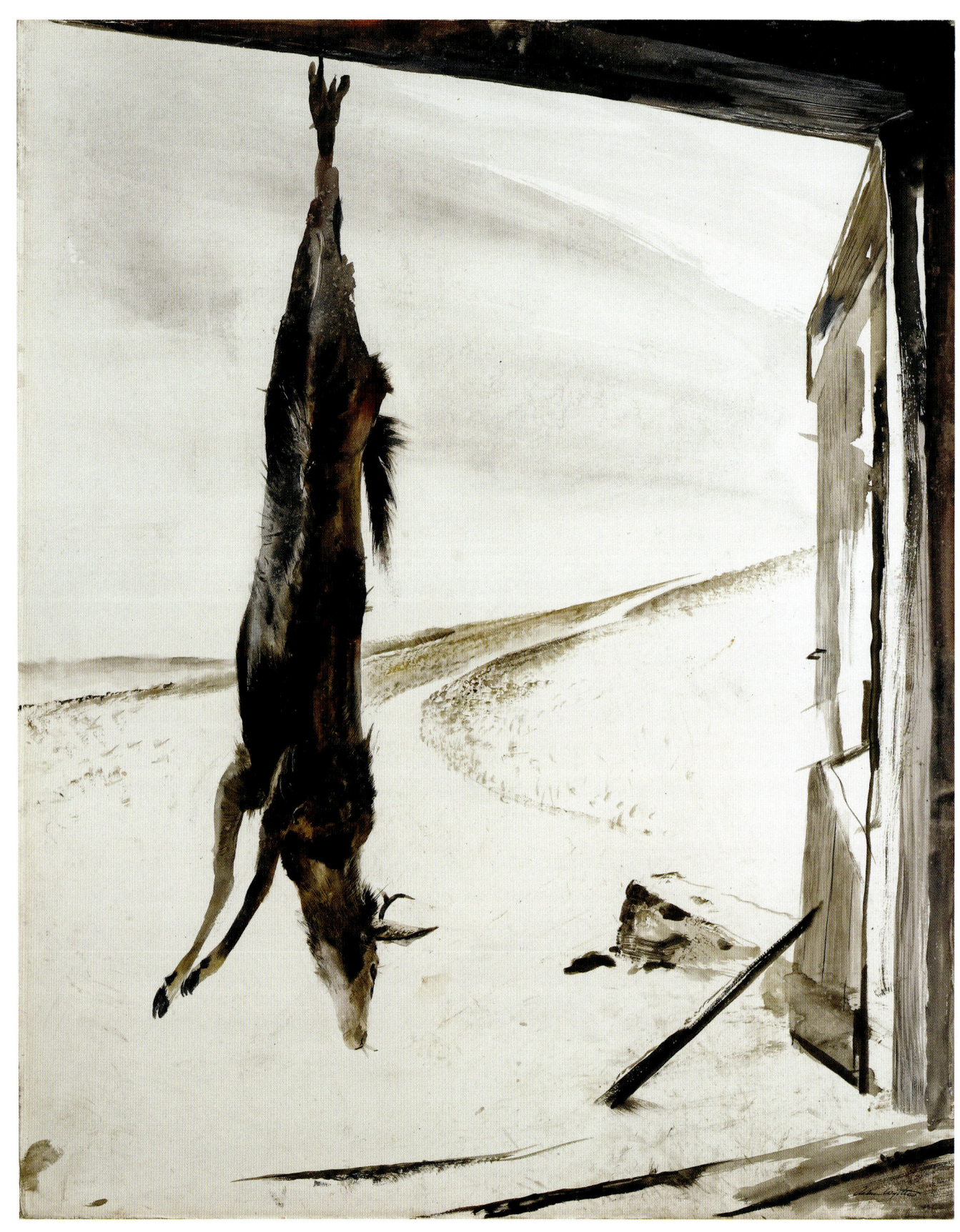

Young Buck, 1944. Watercolor on paper, 29 × 22 ¾ inches

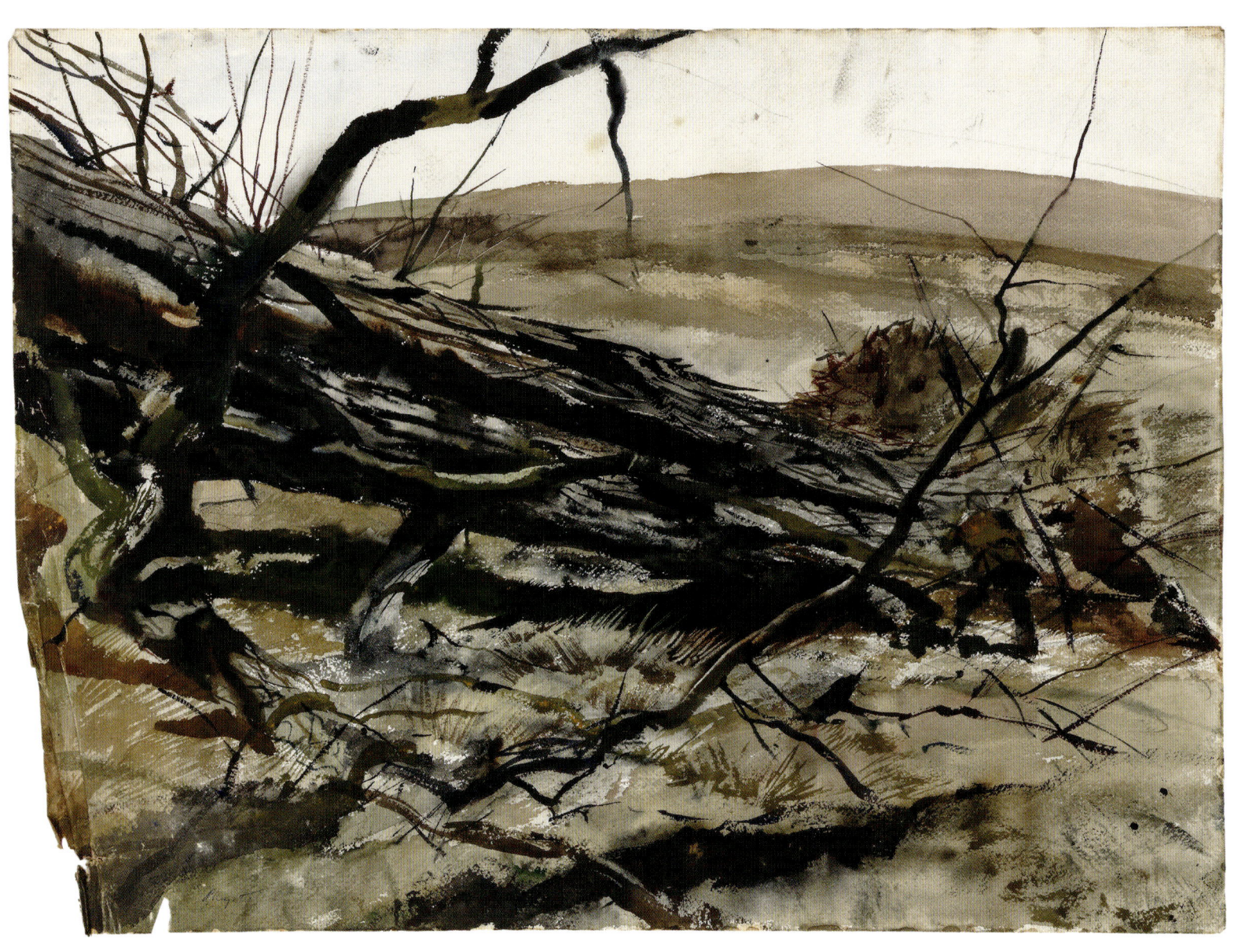

Untitled, 1946. Watercolor on paper, 21 ½ × 29 ½ inches

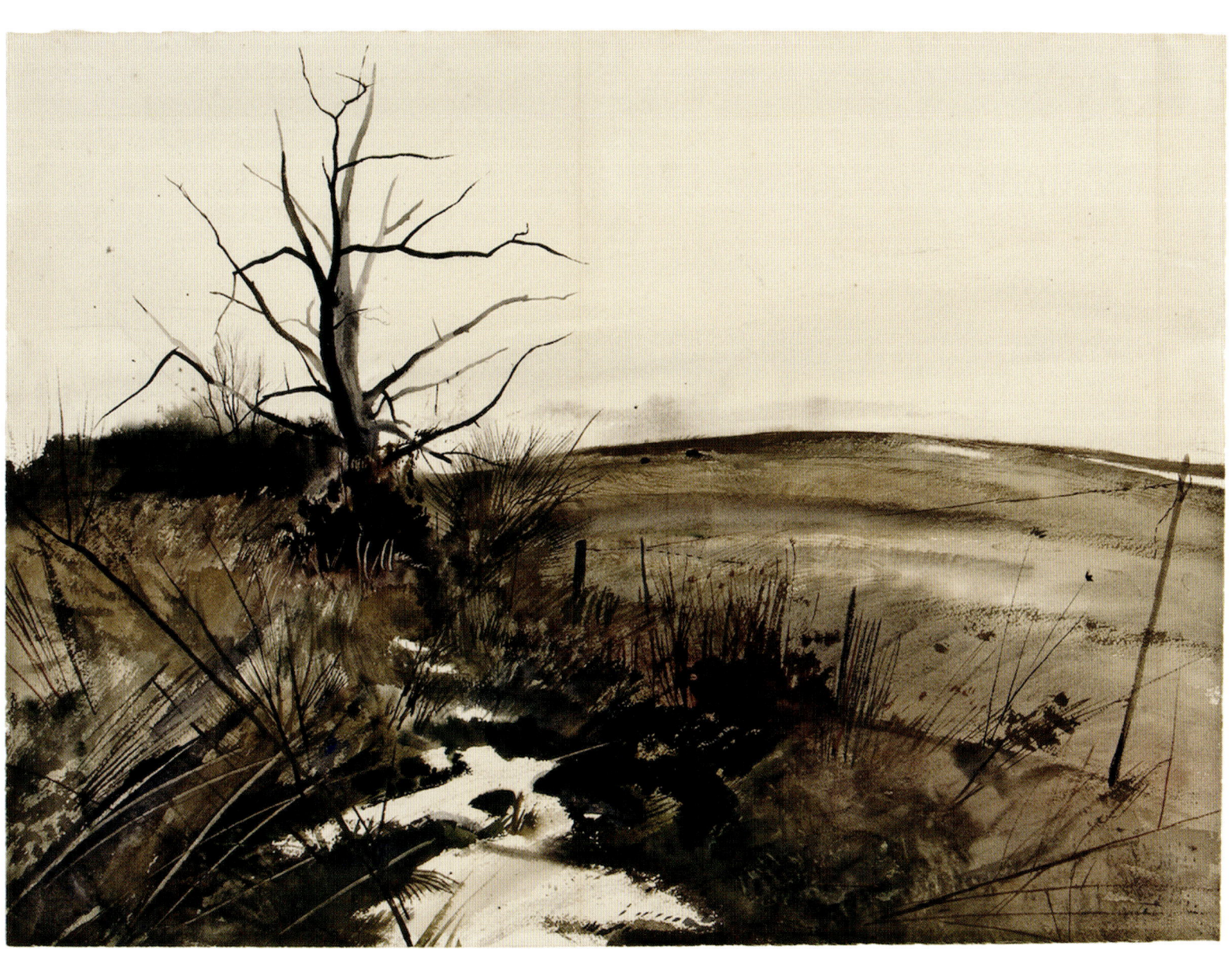

End of Winter, Study for Winter, 1946, 1946. Watercolor on paper, 20 ¾ × 28 ¾ inches

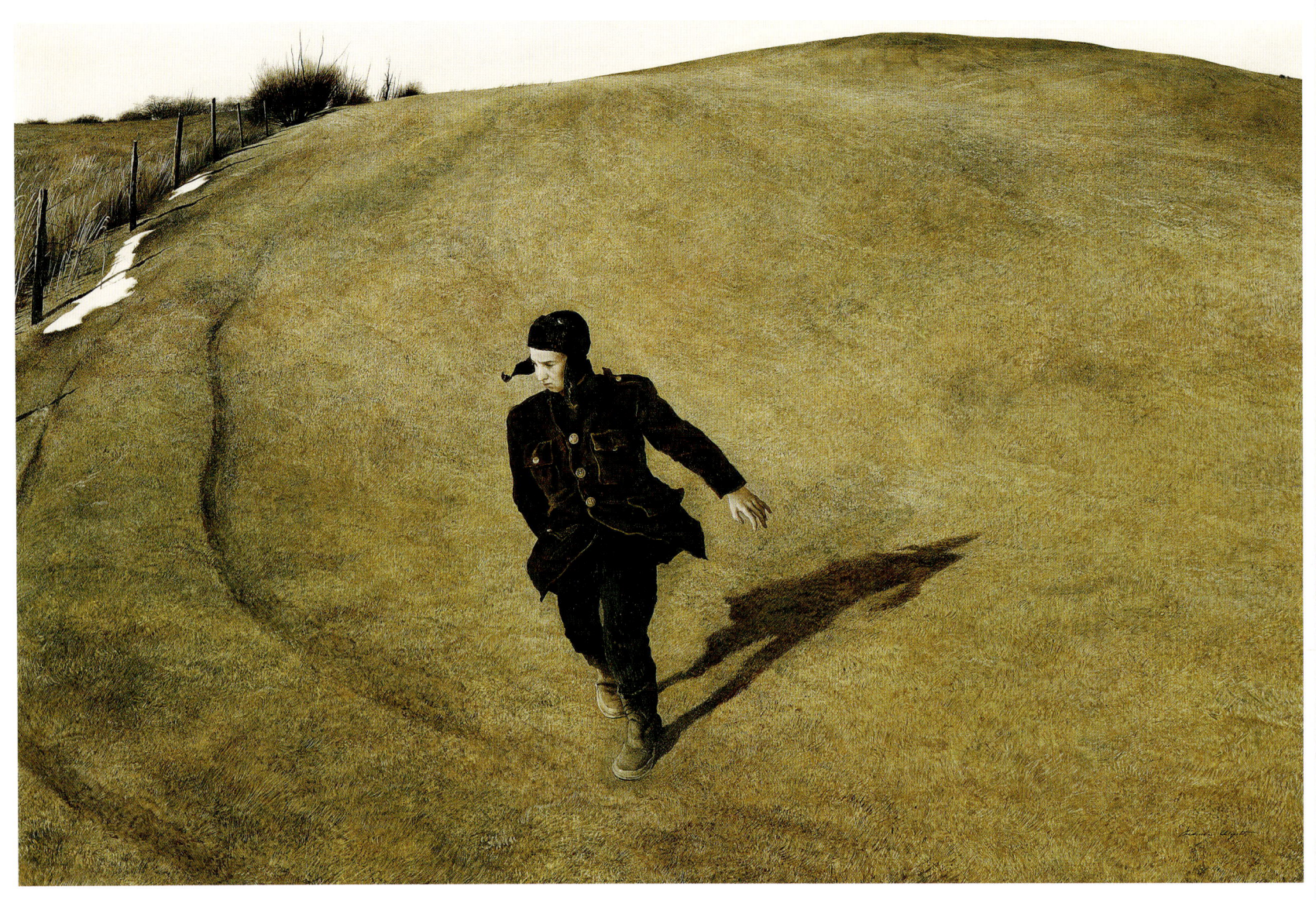

Winter, 1946, 1946. Egg tempera on panel, 31 ⅜ × 48 inches

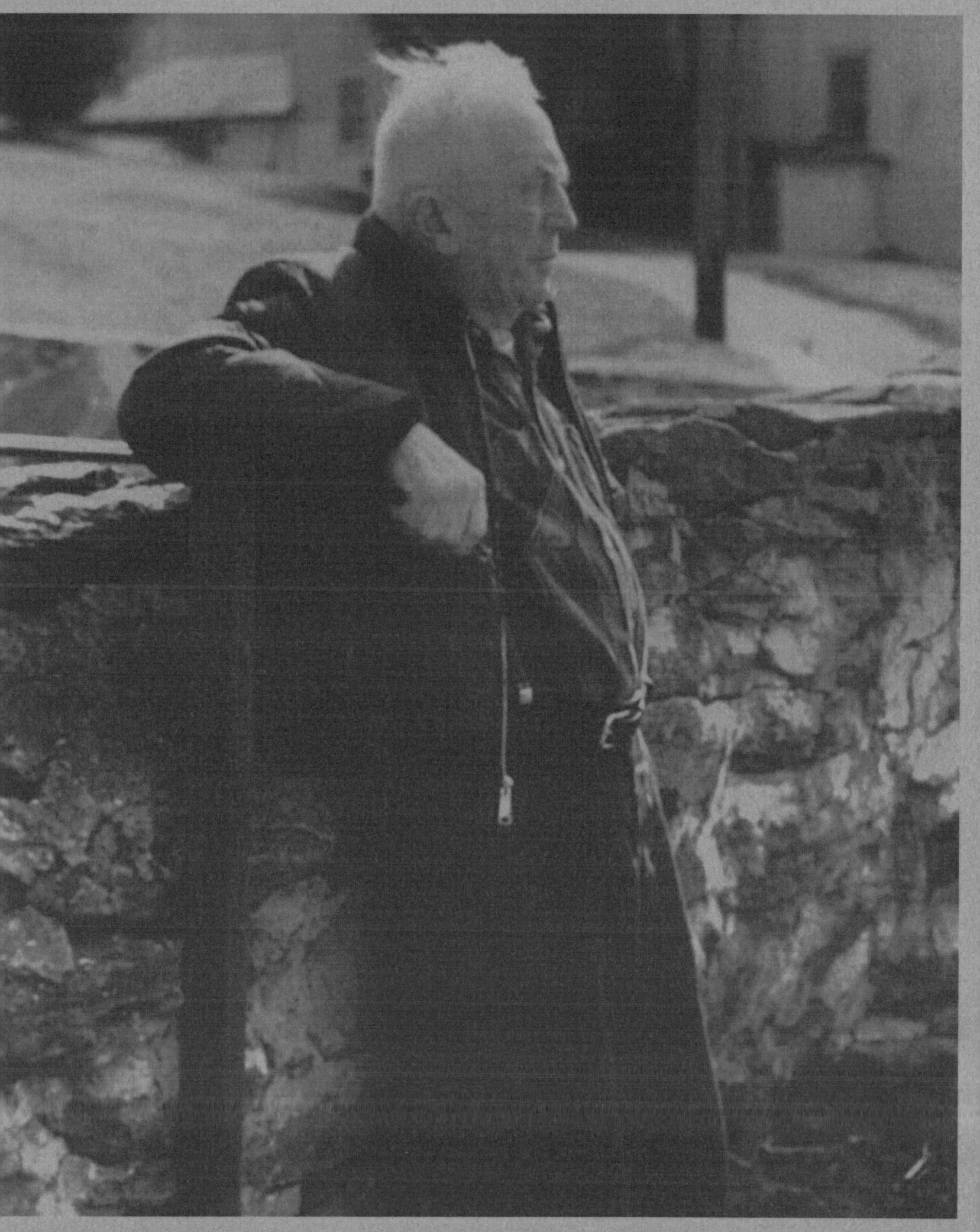

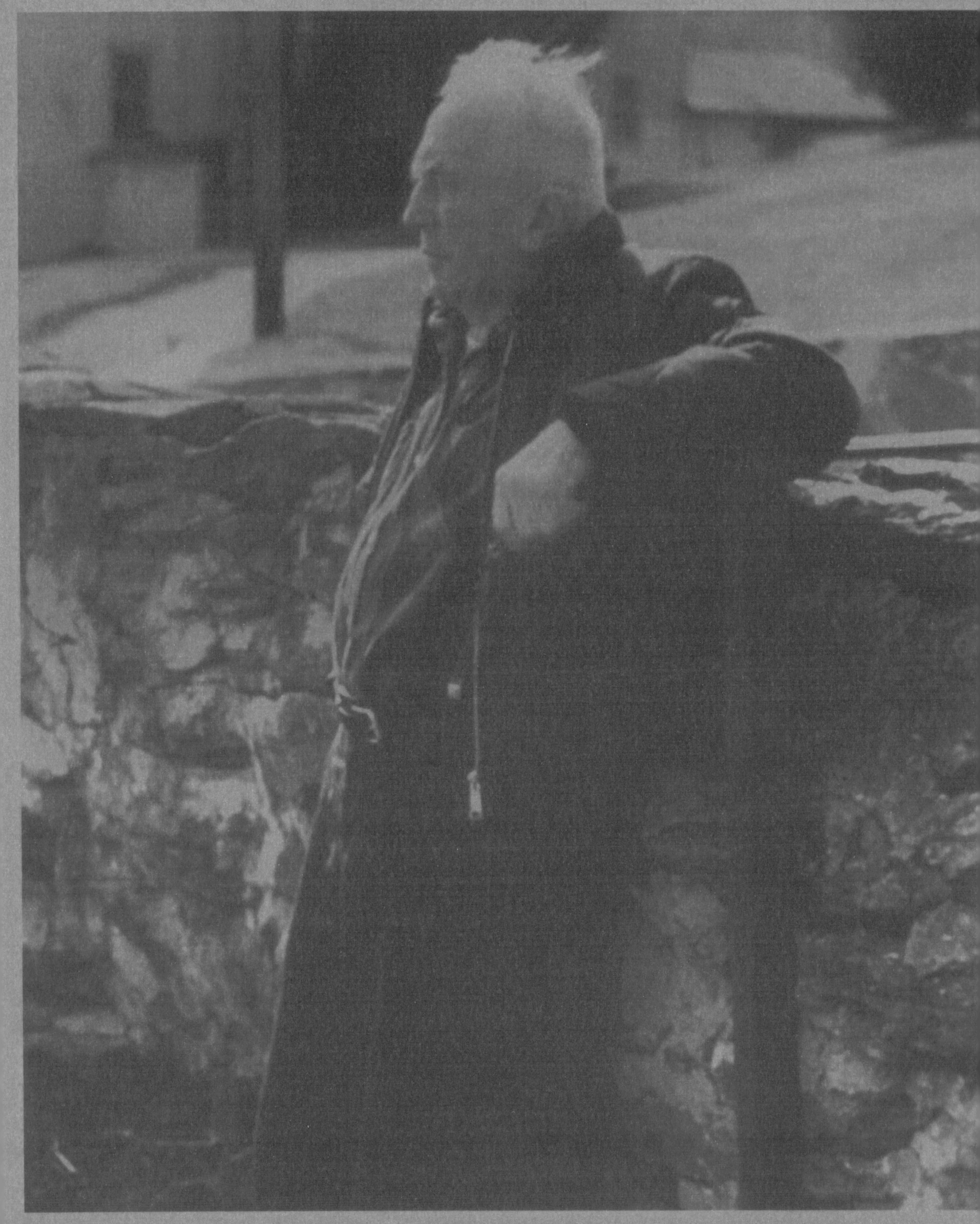

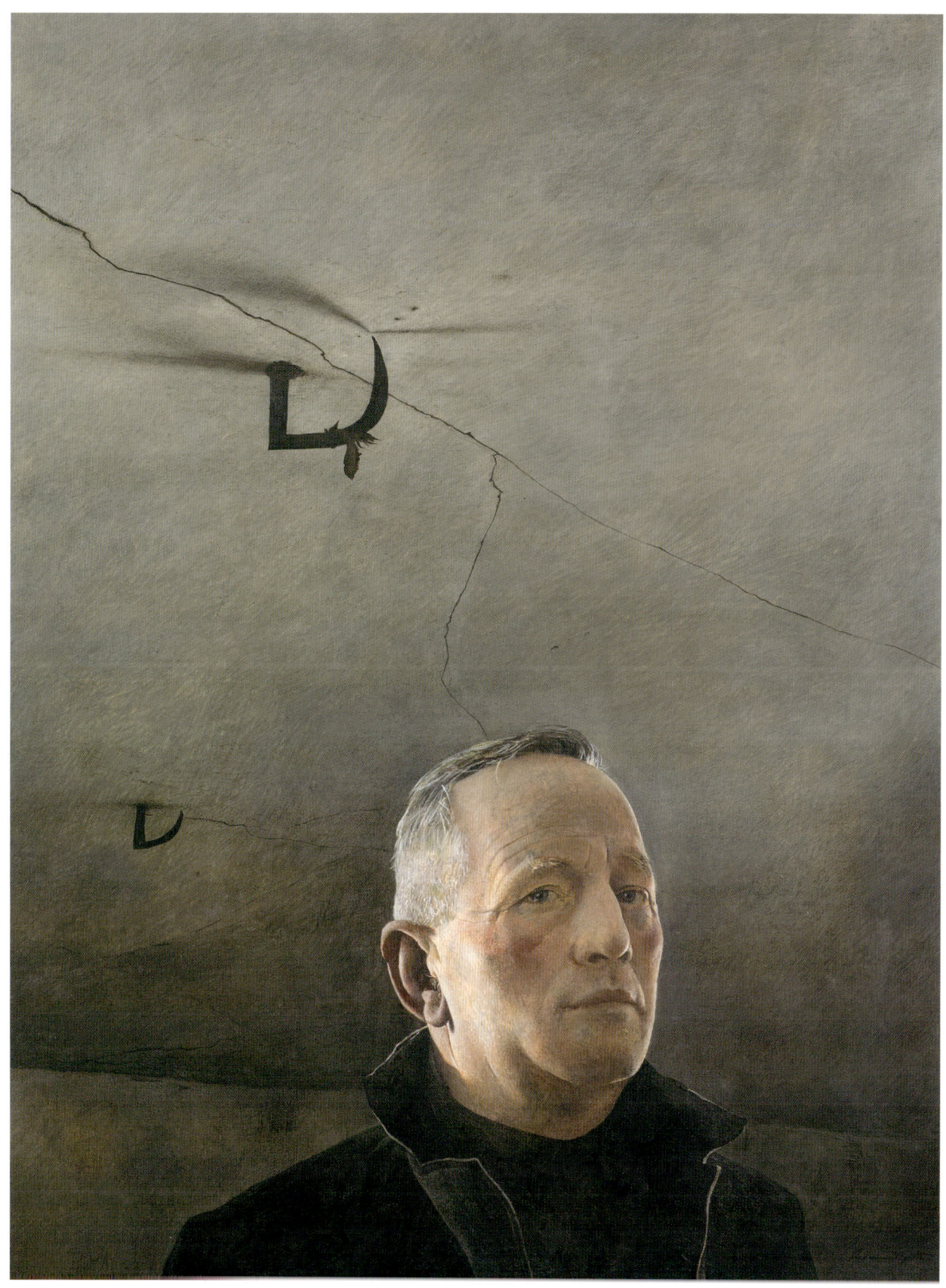

Karl, 1948. Egg tempera on panel, 30 ½ × 23 ½ inches

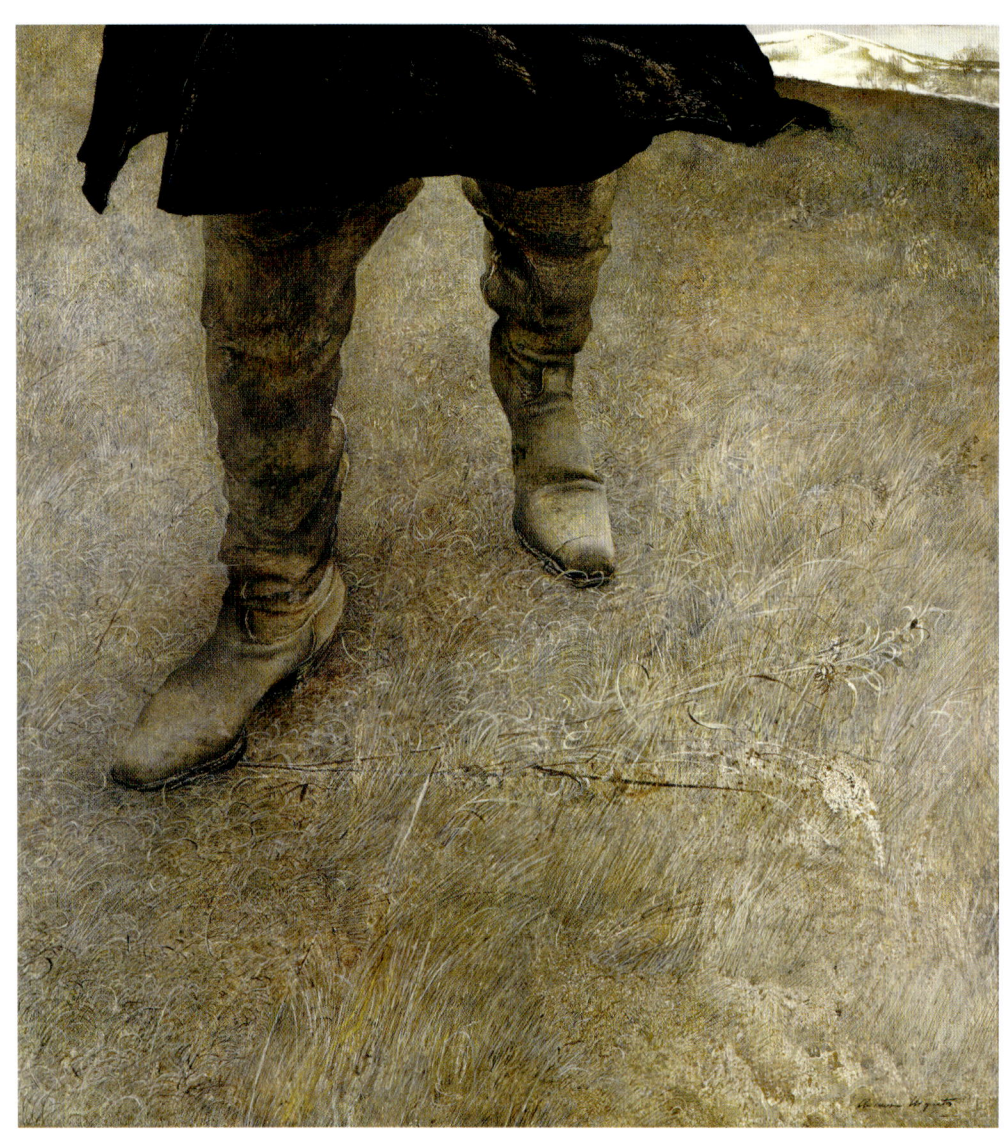

Trodden Weed, 1951. Egg tempera on panel, 20 × 18 ¼ inches

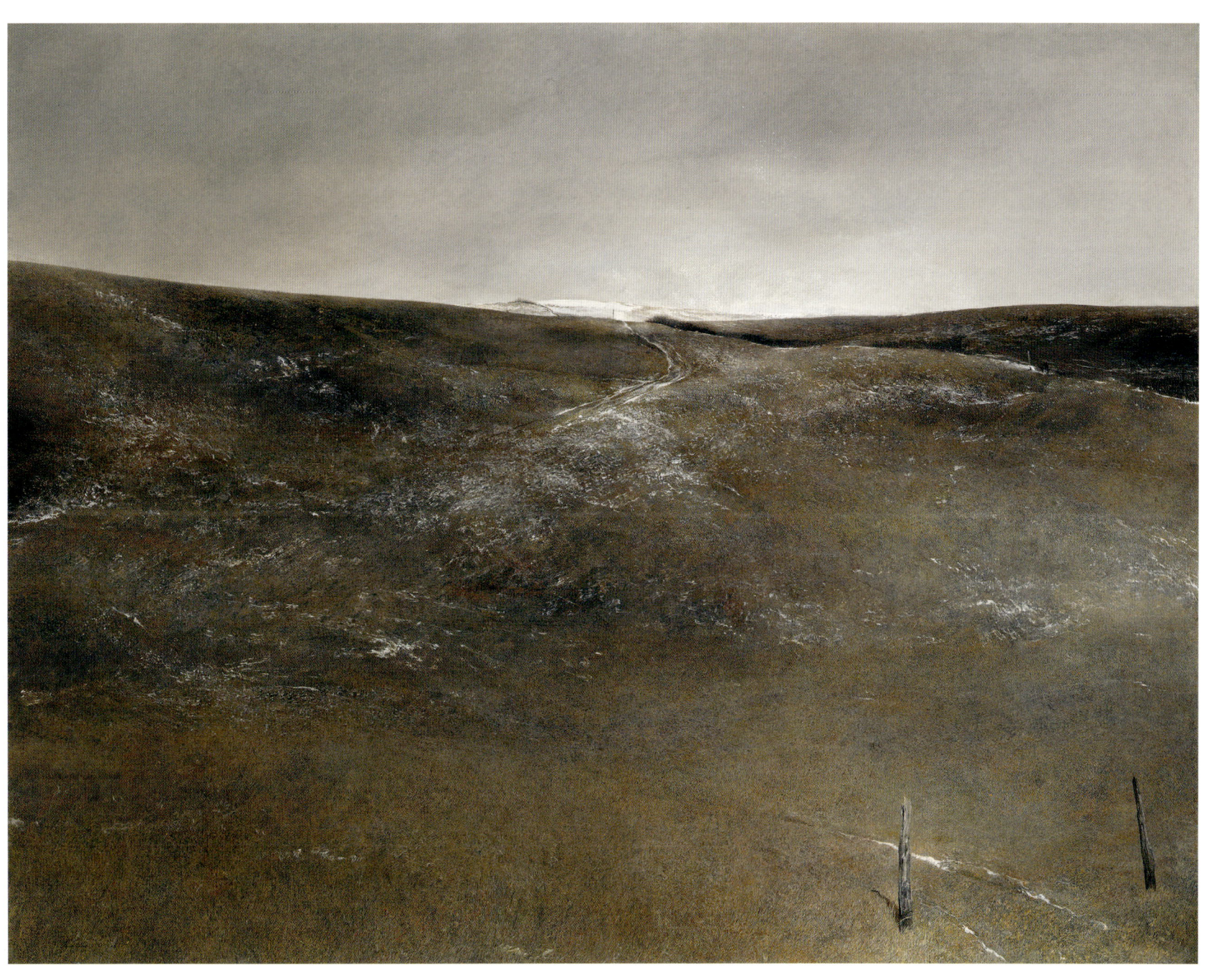

Snow Flurries, 1953. Egg tempera on panel, 37 ½ × 48 inches

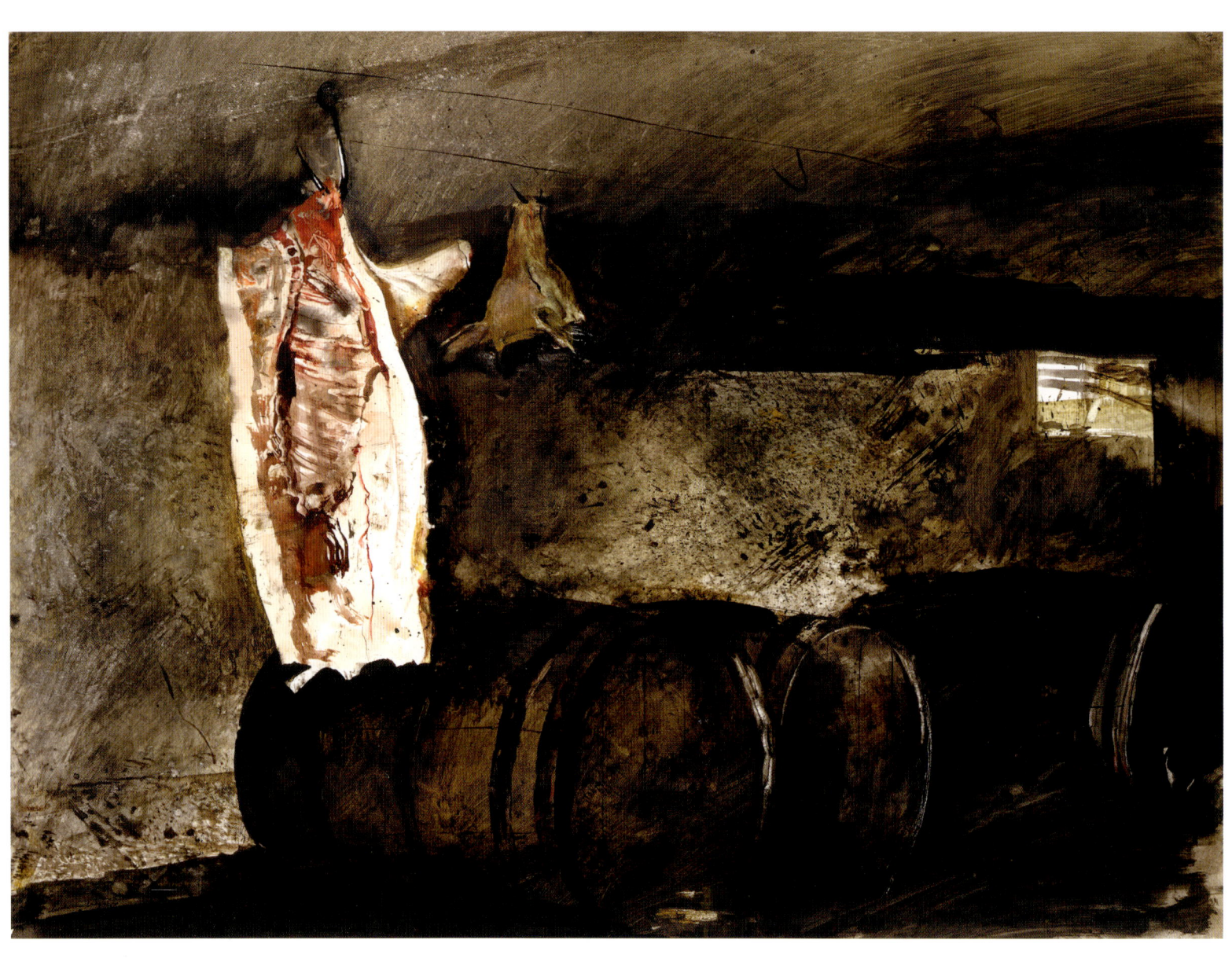

Cider and Pork, 1956. Watercolor on paper, 21 ¾ × 29 ¼ inches

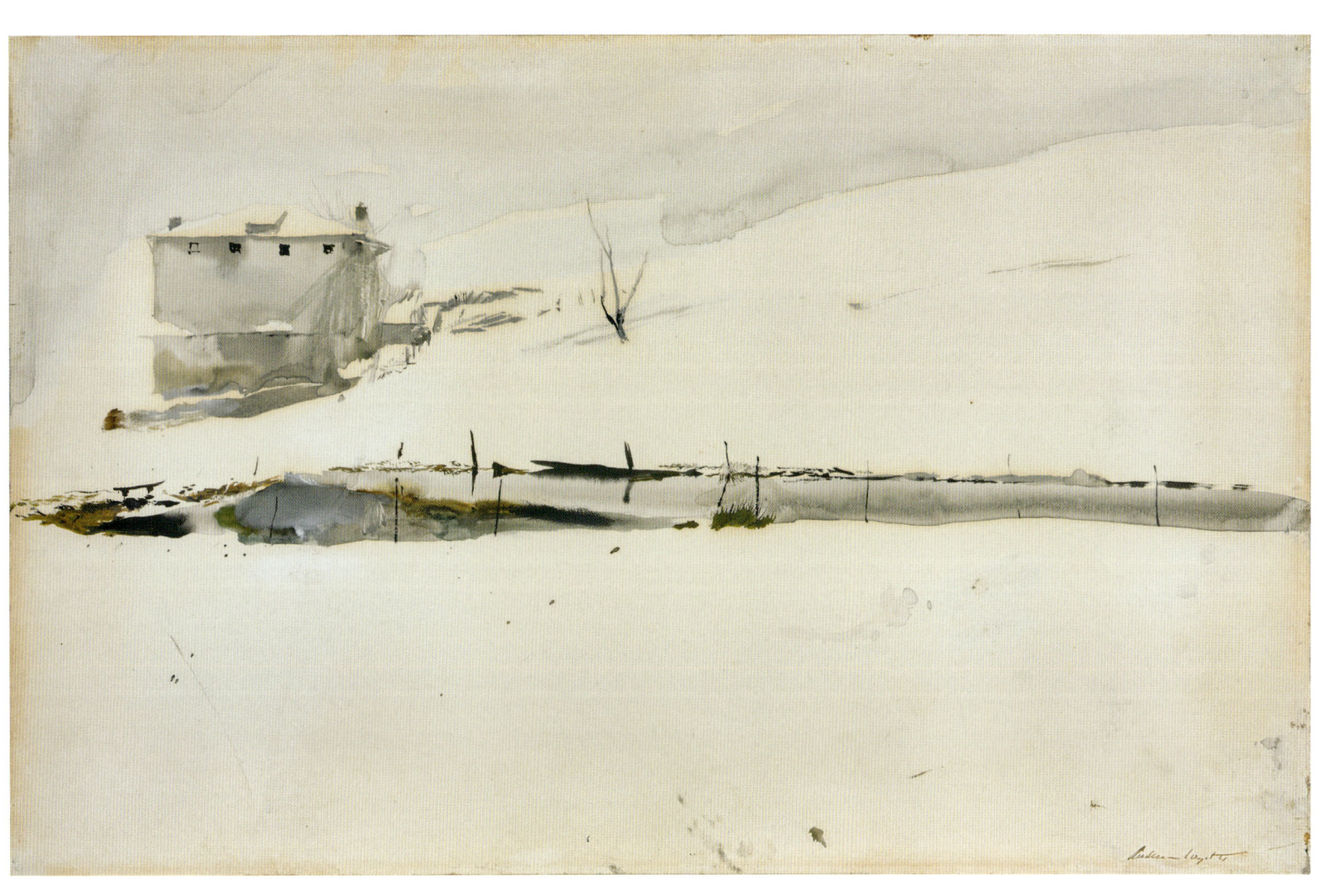

Farm Pond, Study for Brown Swiss, 1957. Watercolor on paper, 13 ¼ × 21 ⅞ inches

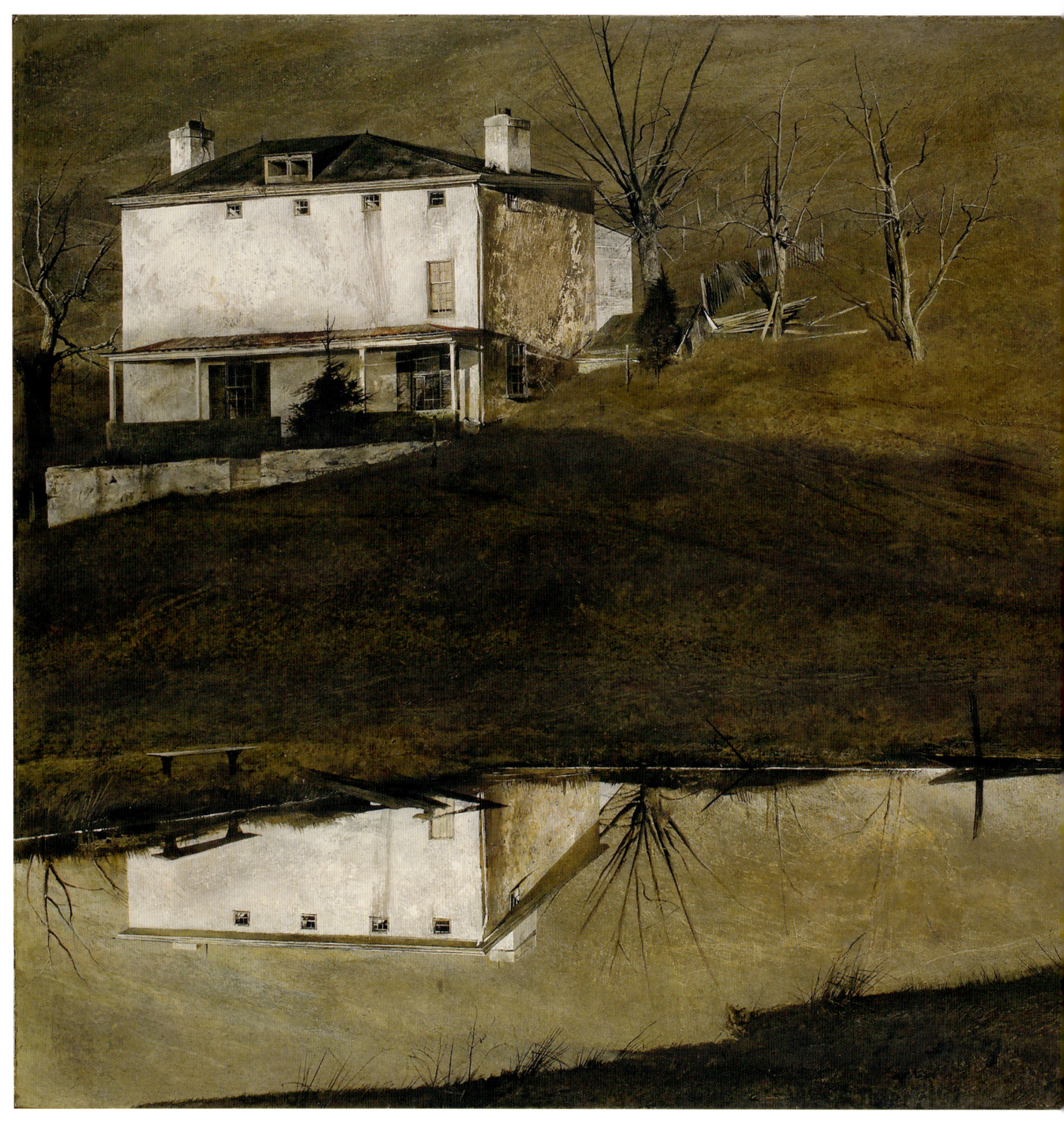

Brown Swiss, 1957. Egg tempera on panel, 30 × 60 ⅛ inches

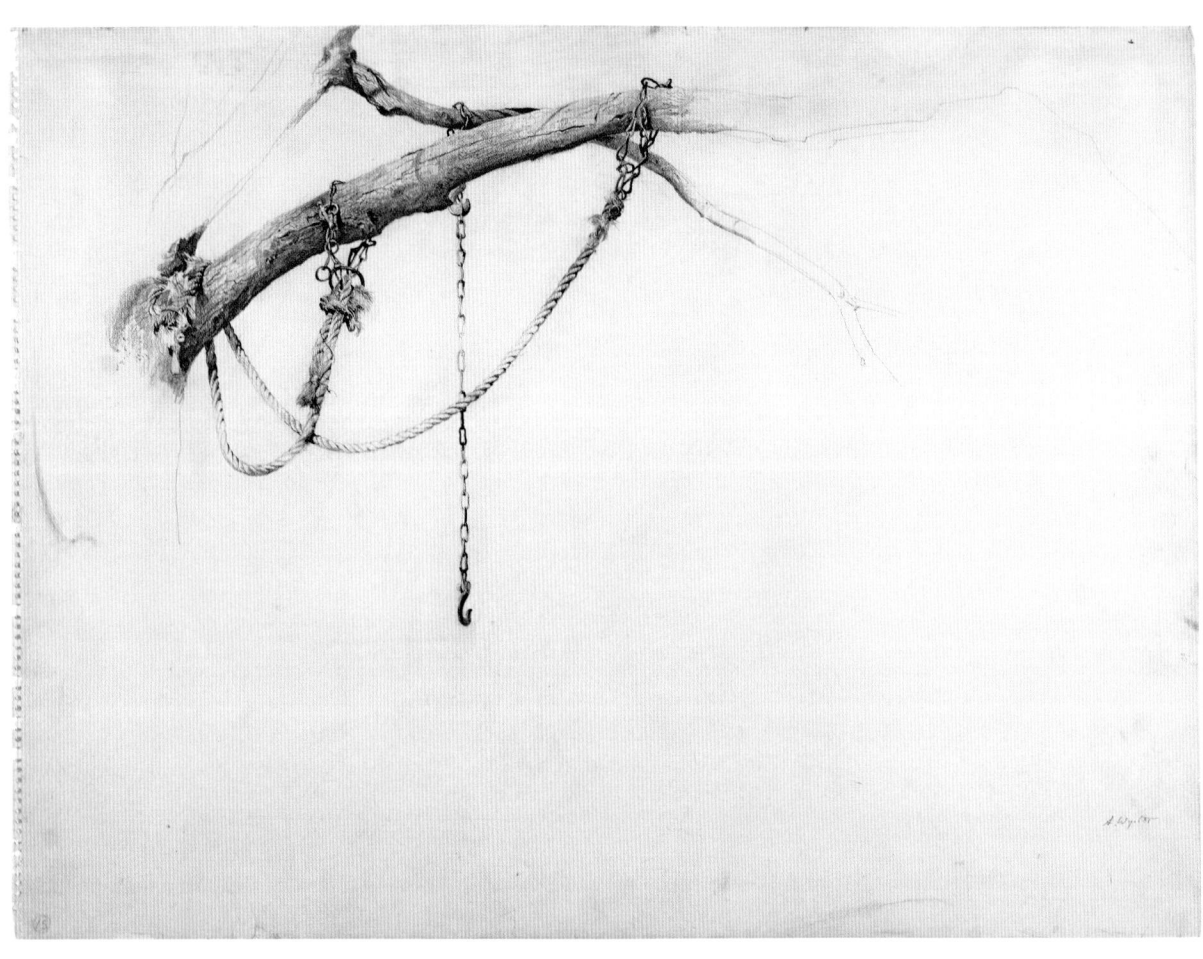

Rope and Chains, Study for Brown Swiss, 1957. Pencil on paper, 17 ¾ × 23 ½ inches

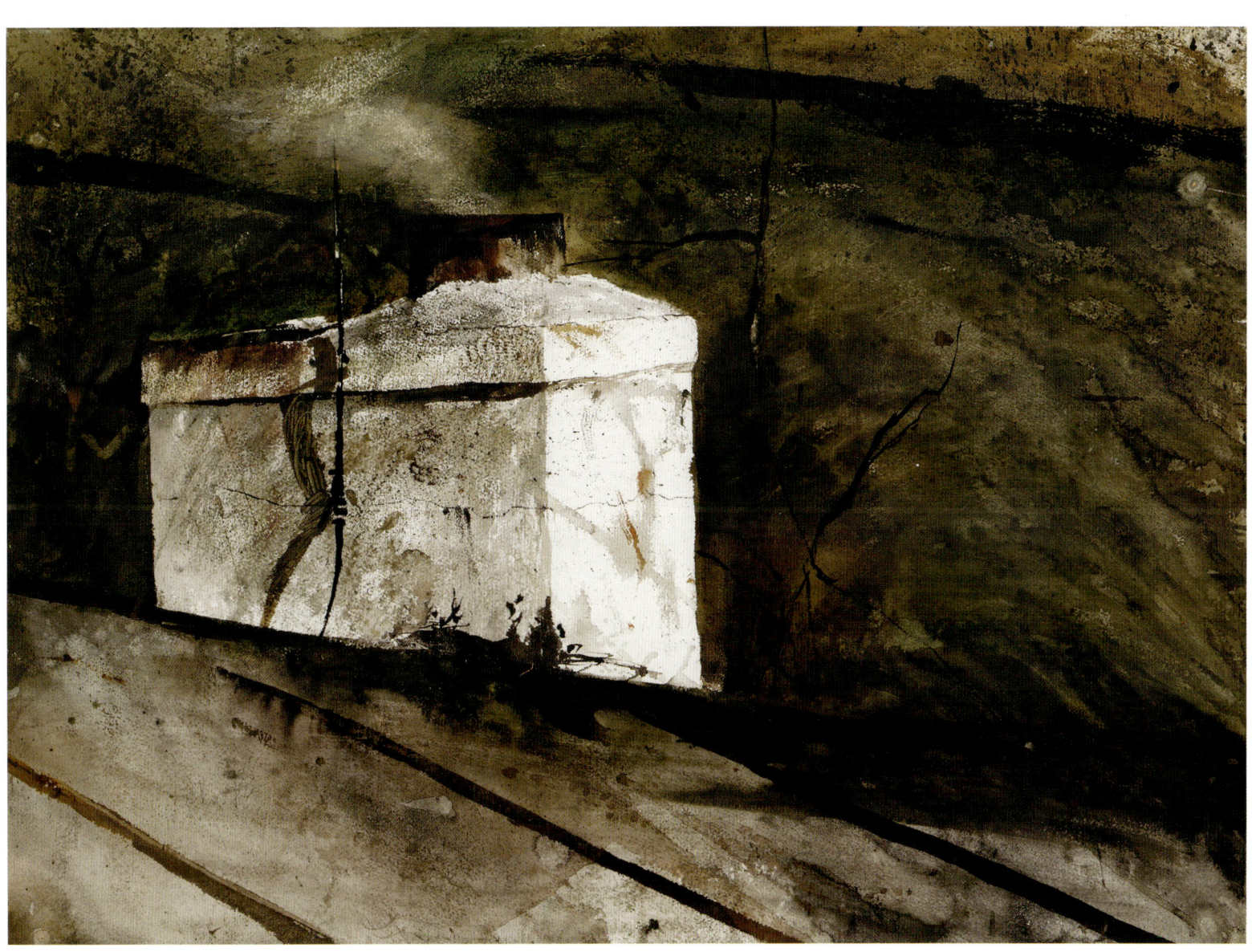

Chimney Smoke, 1957. Watercolor on paper, 21 ⅜ × 29 ¾ inches

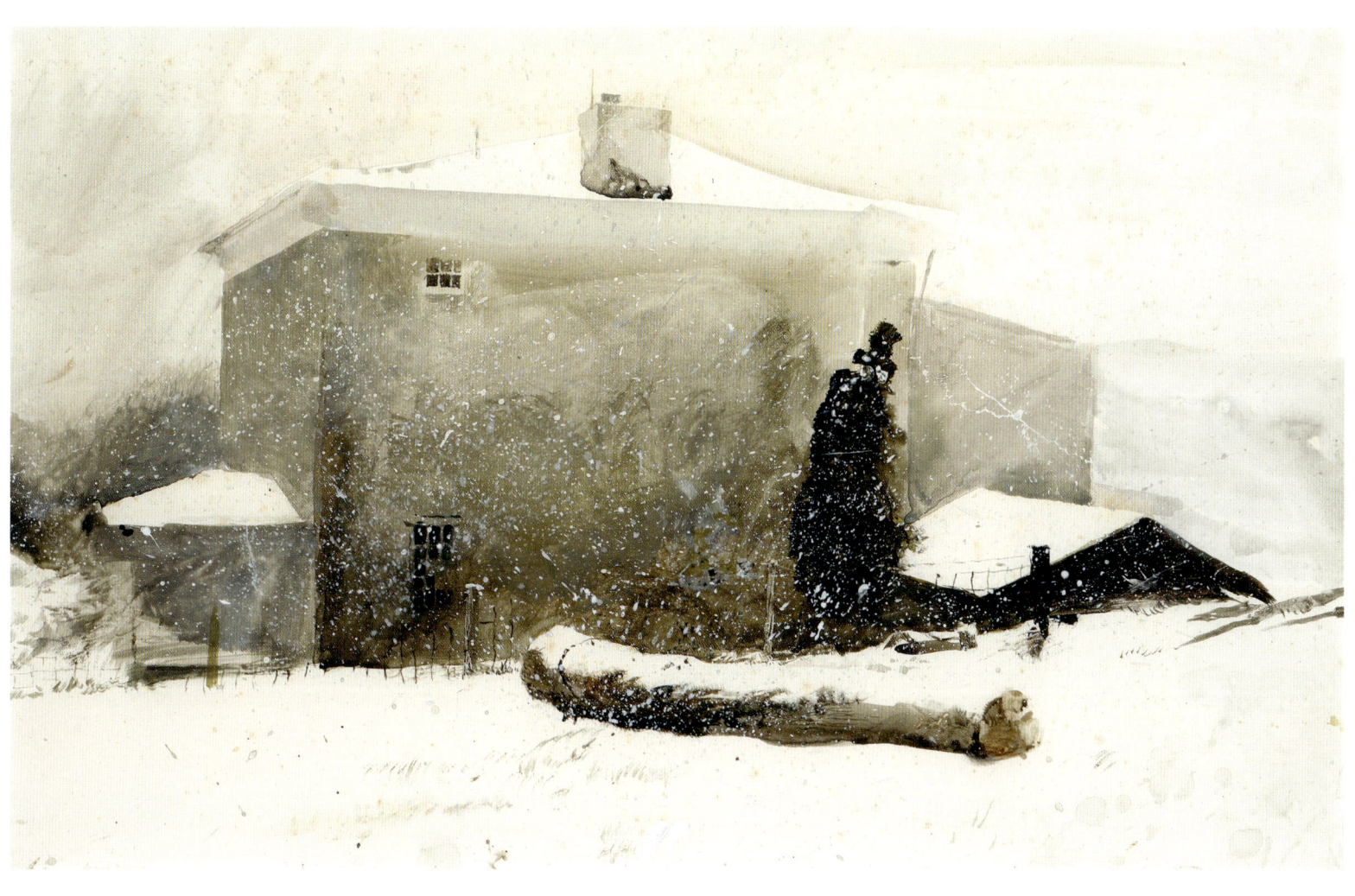

First Snow, Study for Groundhog Day, 1959. Drybrush watercolor on paper, 13 ⅜ × 21 ⅛ inches

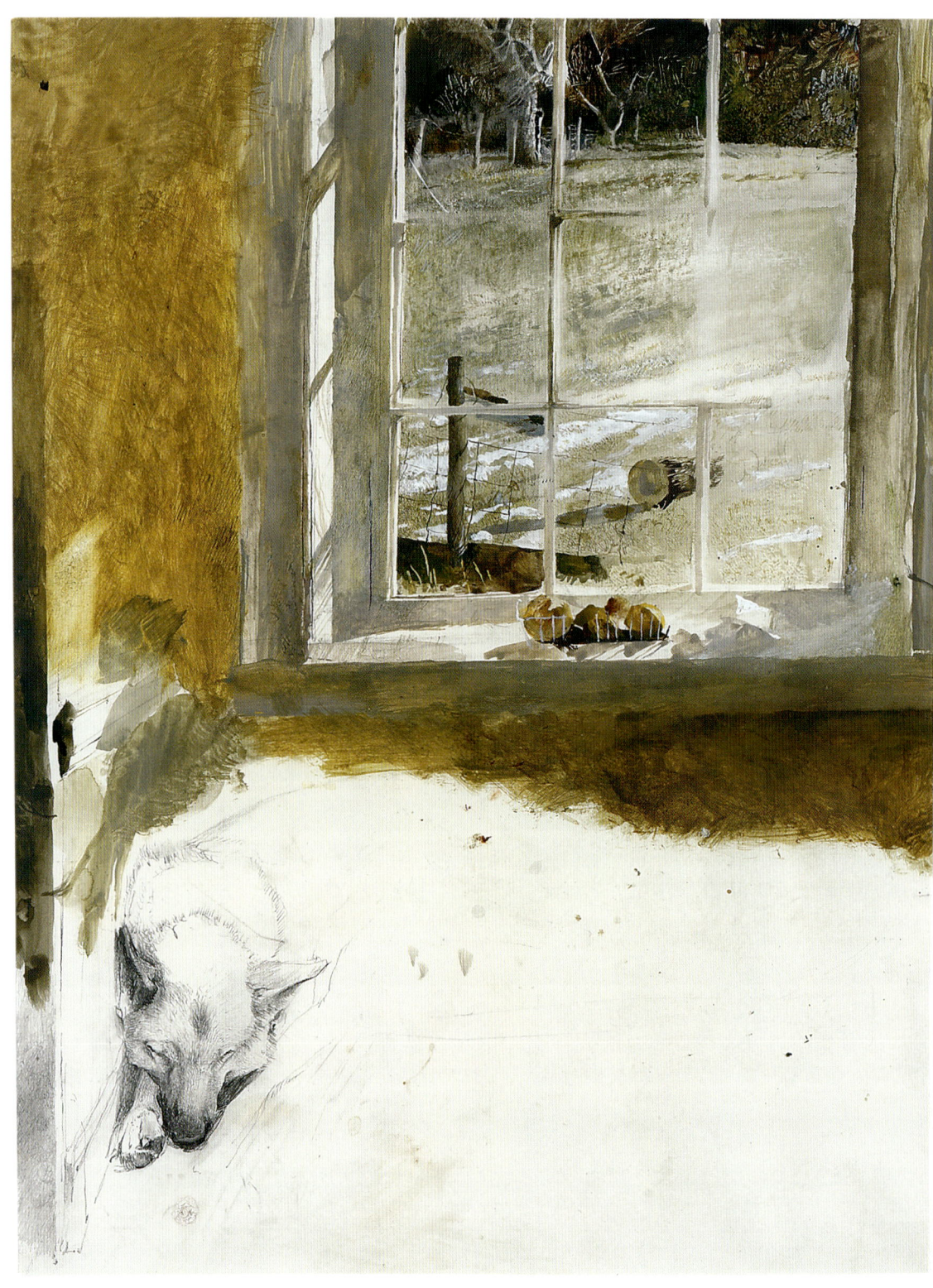

Groundhog Day Study, 1959. Watercolor and pencil on paper, 23 × 17 ⅞ inches

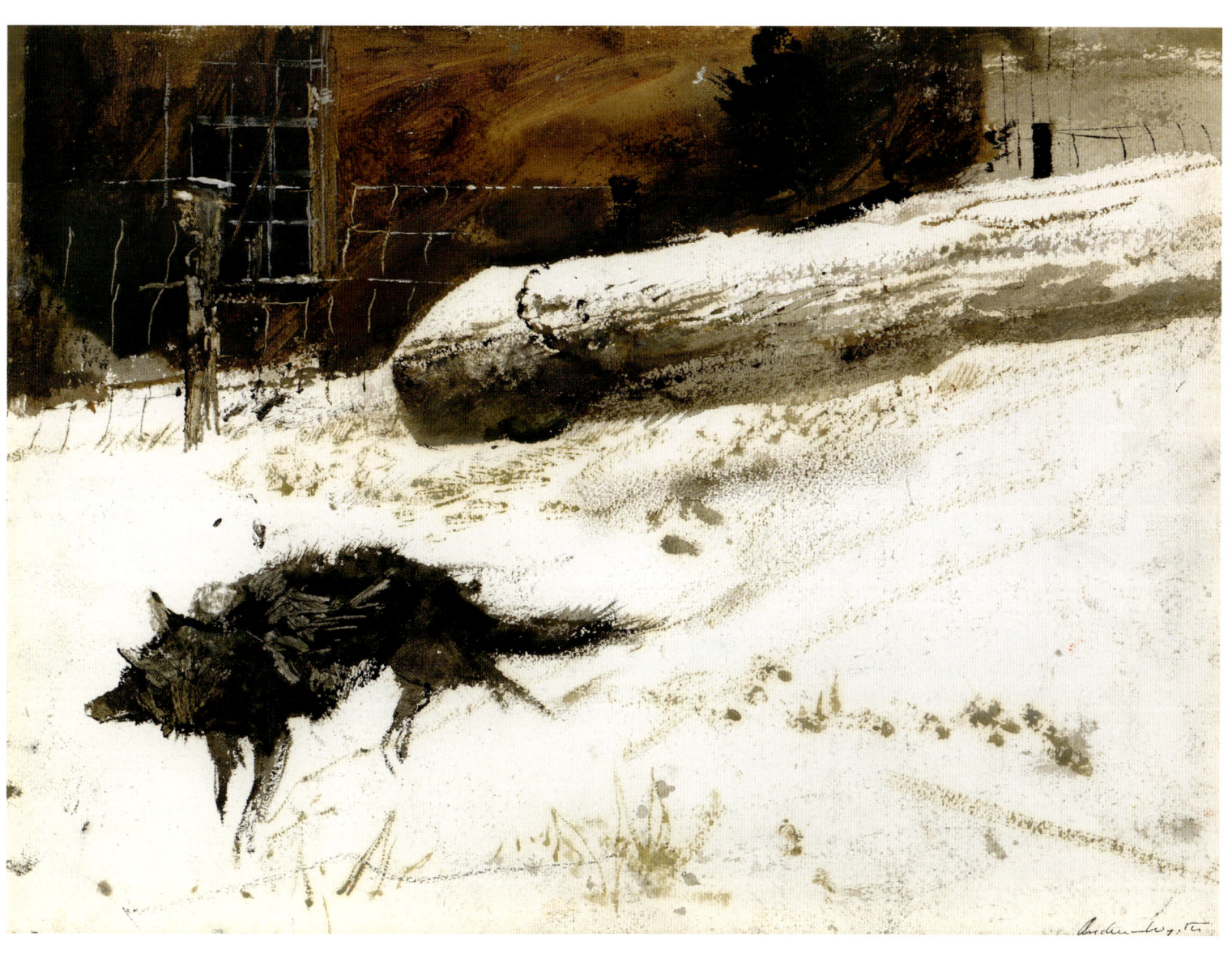

Wild Dog, Study for Groundhog Day, 1959. Watercolor on paper, 13 ½ × 19 inches

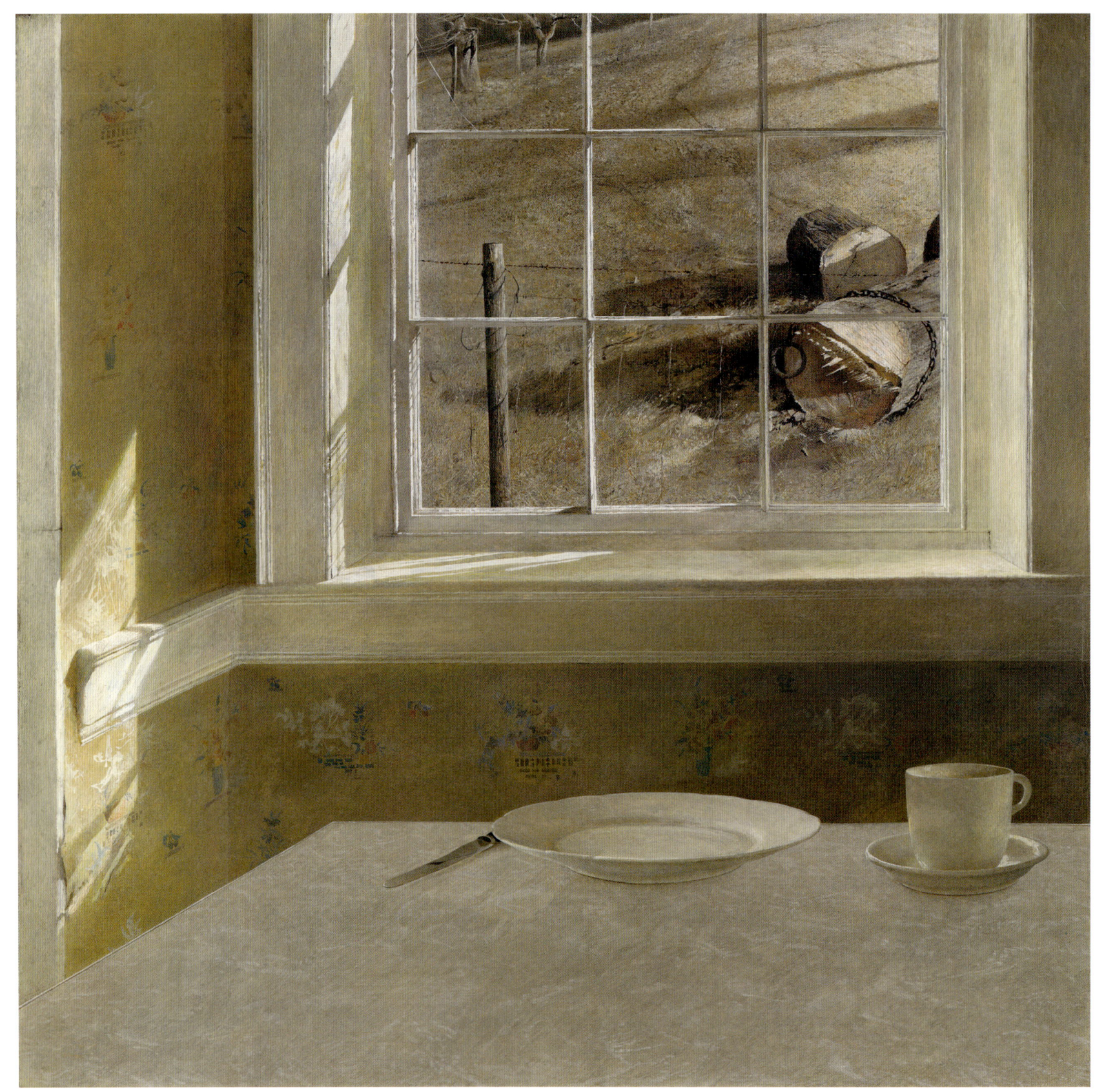

Groundhog Day, 1959. Egg tempera on panel, 31 × 31 ¾ inches

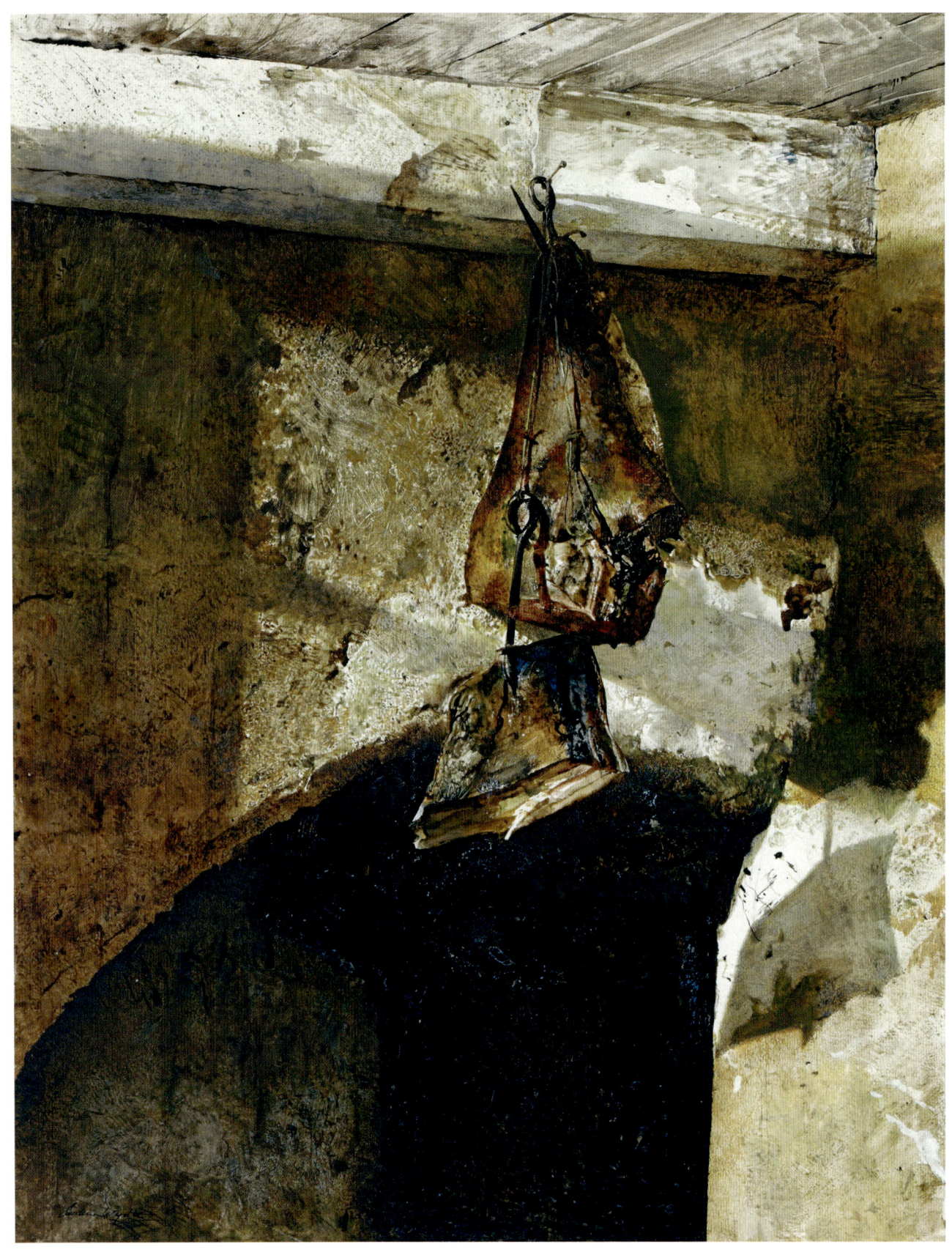

Below the Kitchen, 1960. Drybrush watercolor on paper, 23 × 17 ¾ inches

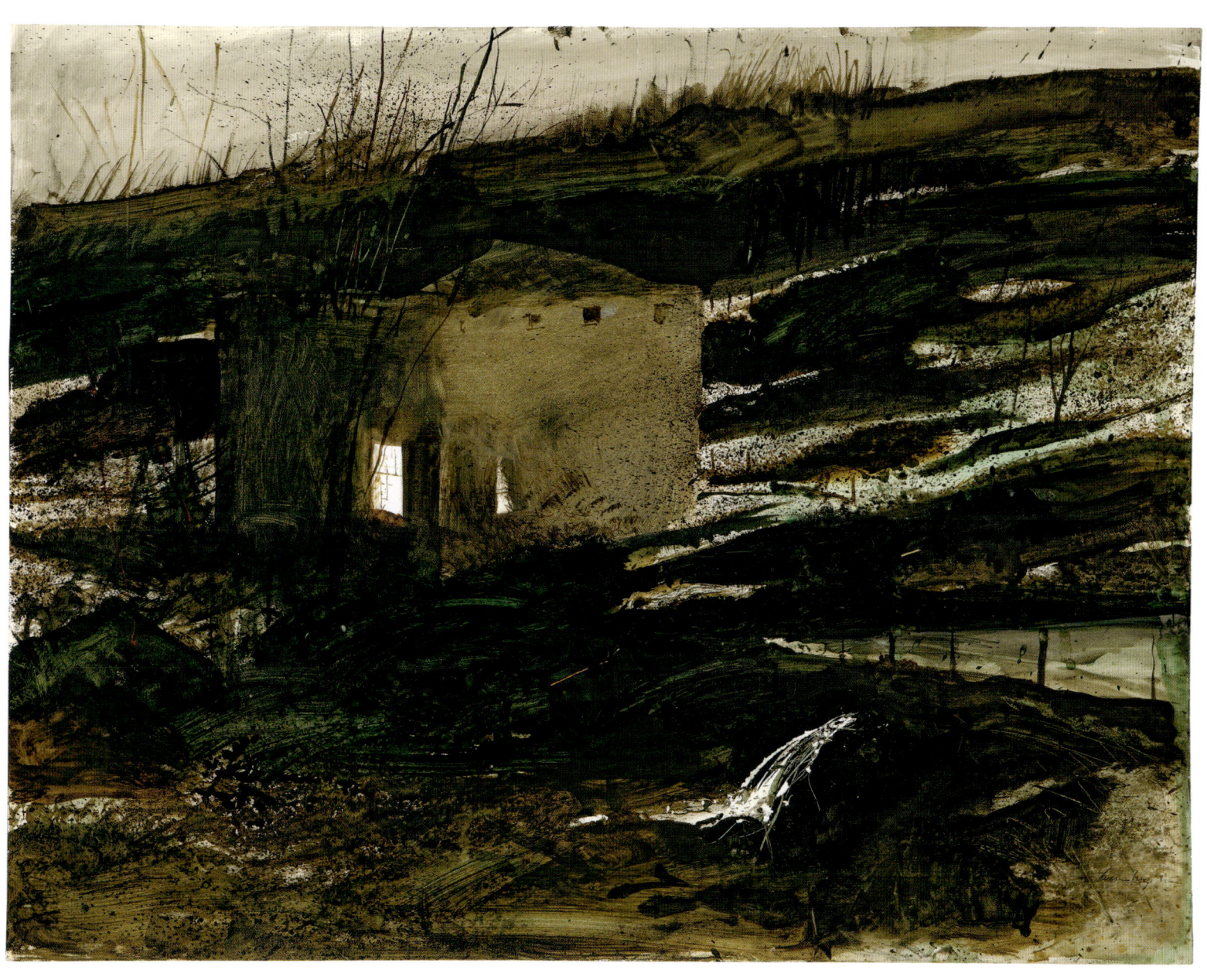

Night Light at Kuerners, 1960. Watercolor on paper, 22 ⅛ × 28 ½ inches

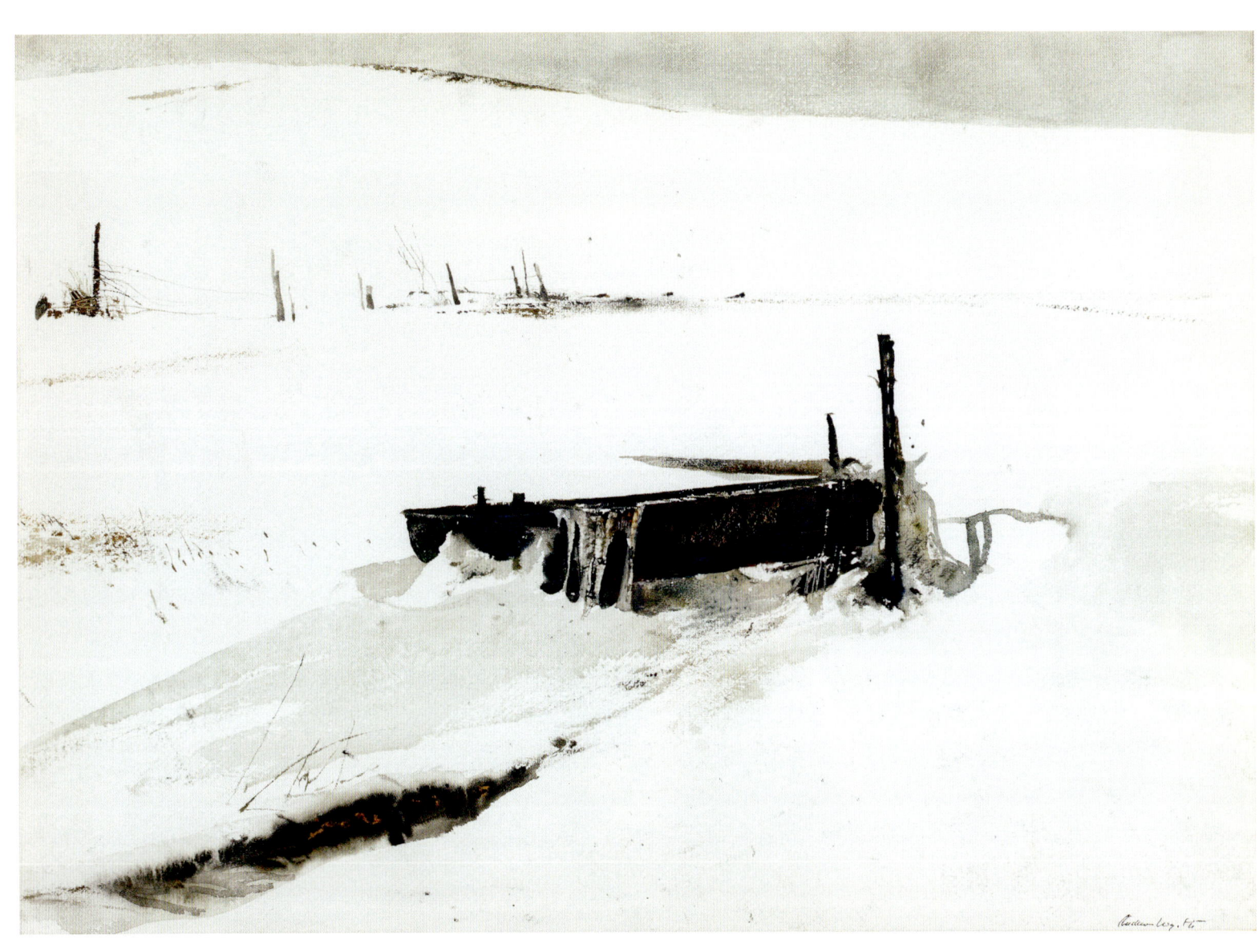

Watering Trough, 1960. Watercolor on paper, 21 ½ × 29 inches

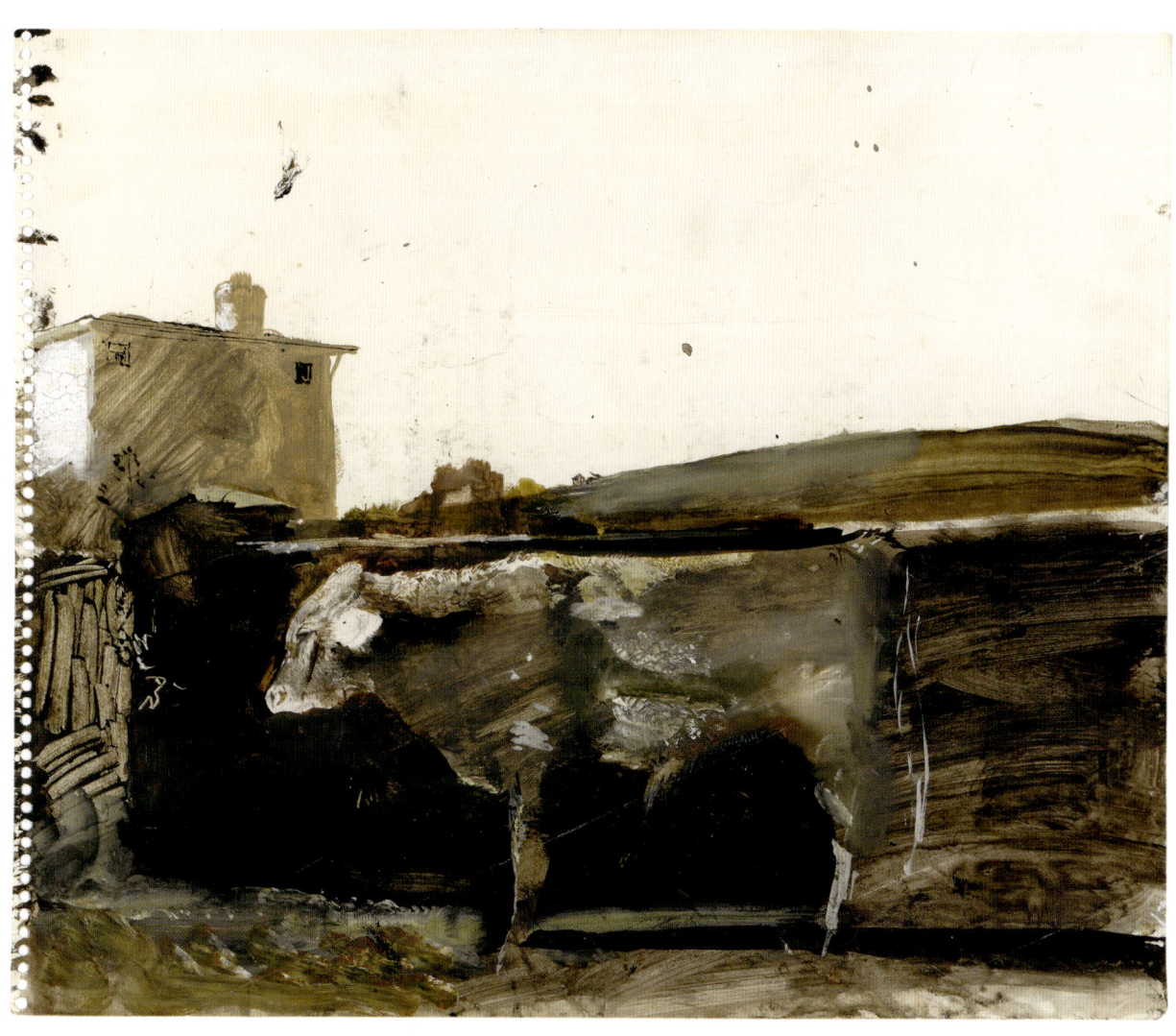

Young Bull Study, 1960. Watercolor on paper, 14 × 16 ½ inches

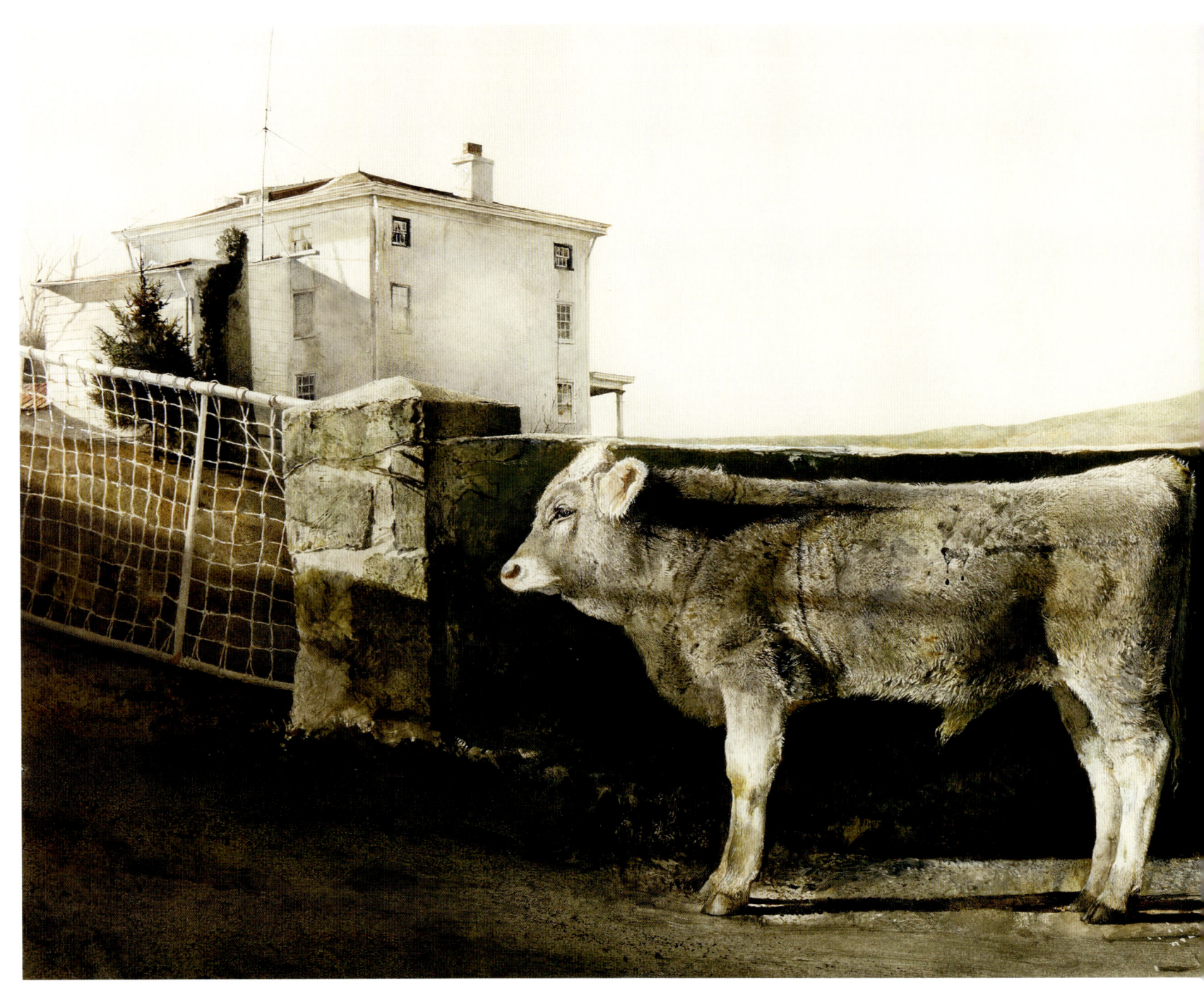

Young Bull, 1960. Drybrush watercolor on paper, 19 ¾ × 41 ¼ inches

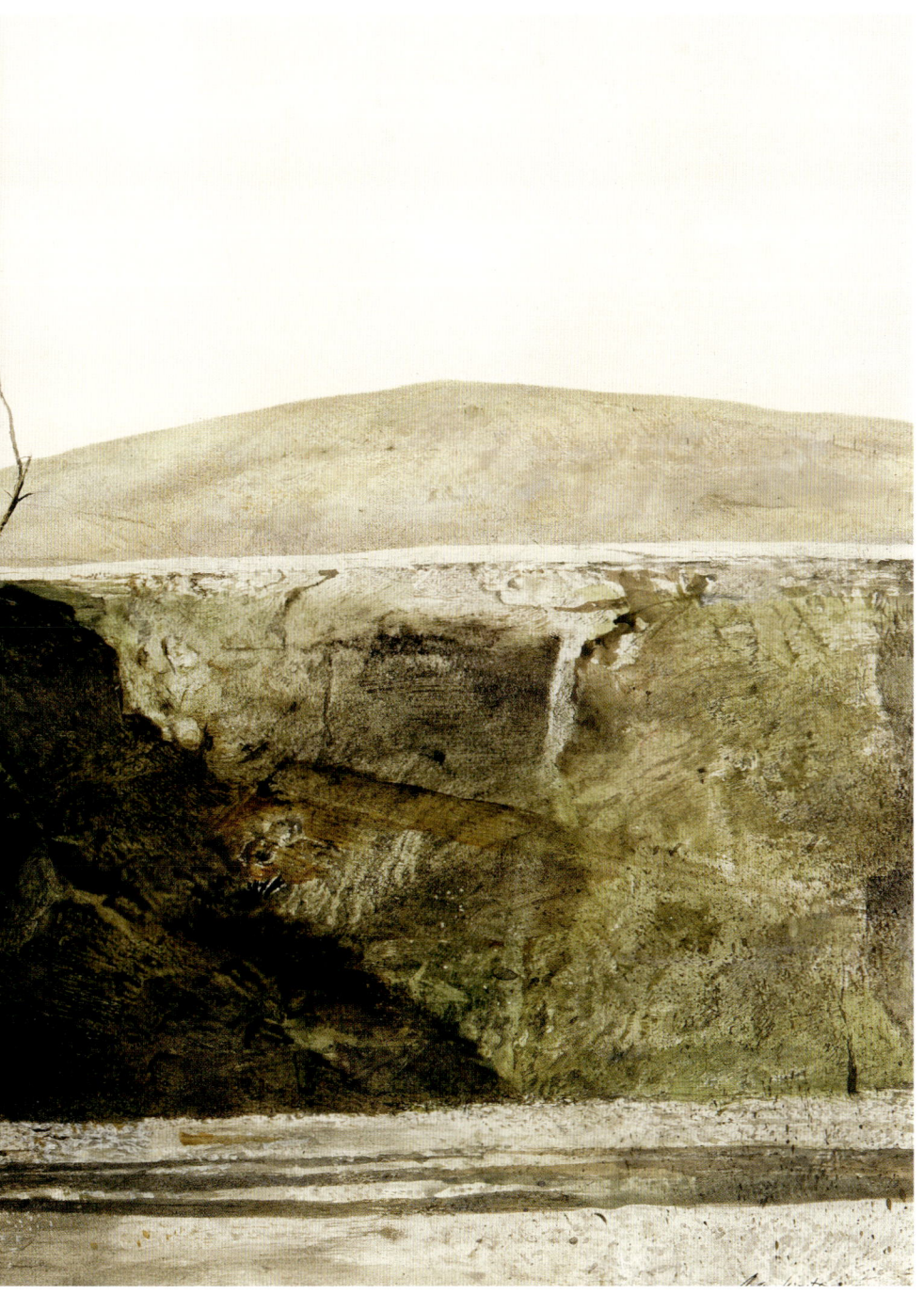

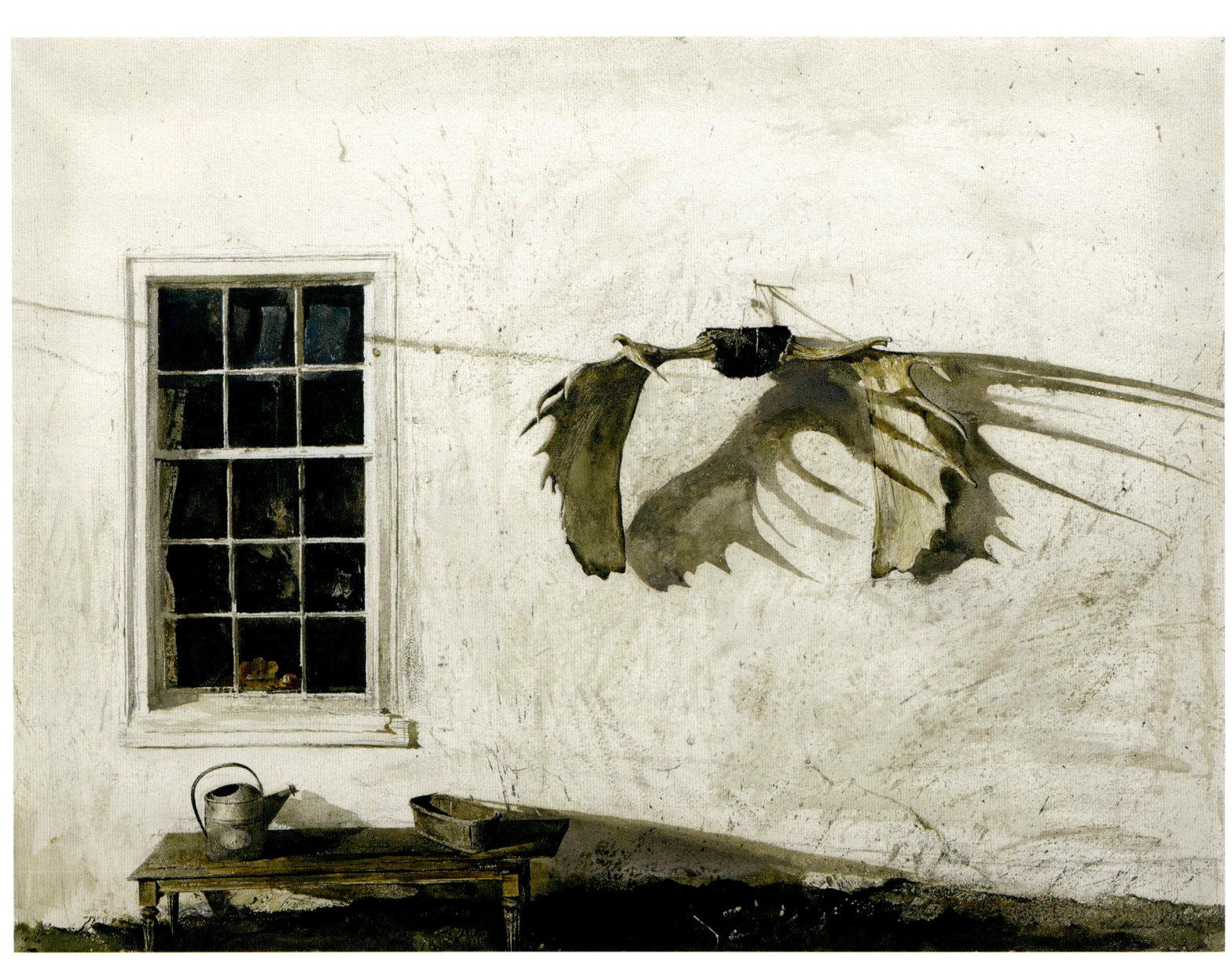

The Trophy, 1963. Watercolor on paper, 22 ⅜ × 30 ½ inches

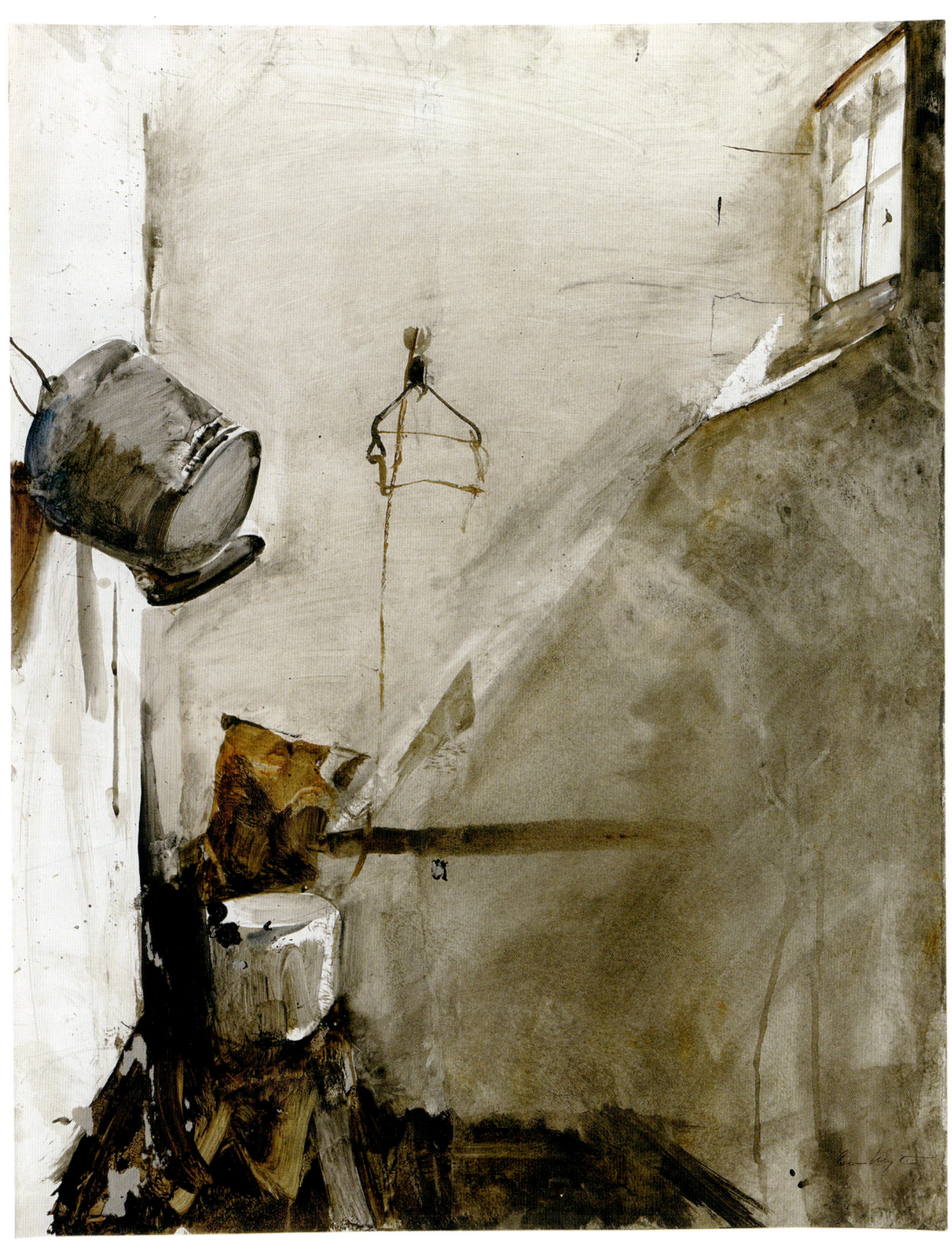

Milk Room Study, 1964. Watercolor on paper, 28 ¾ × 23 ¾ inches

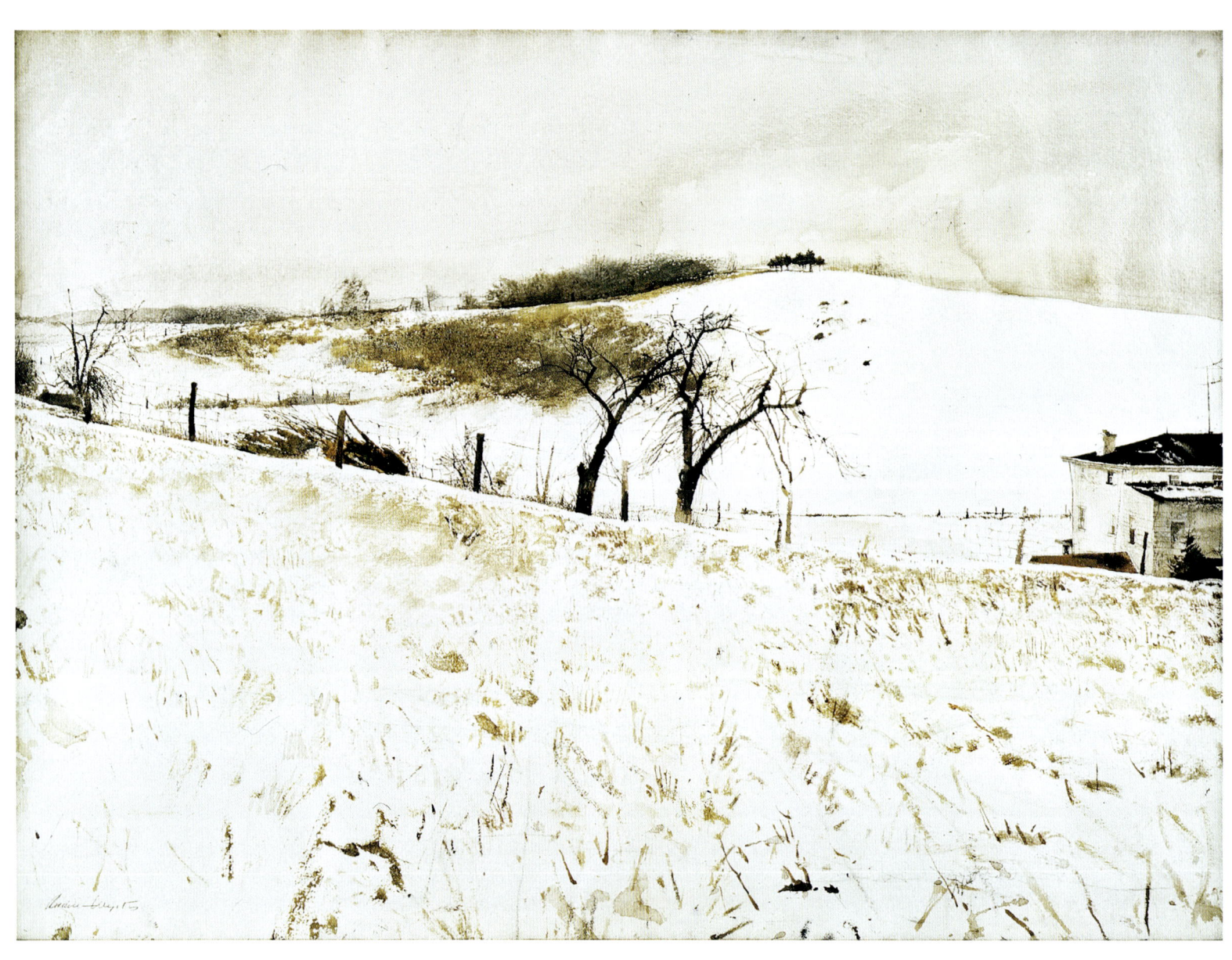

Fence Line, 1967. Watercolor on paper, 21 × 30 inches

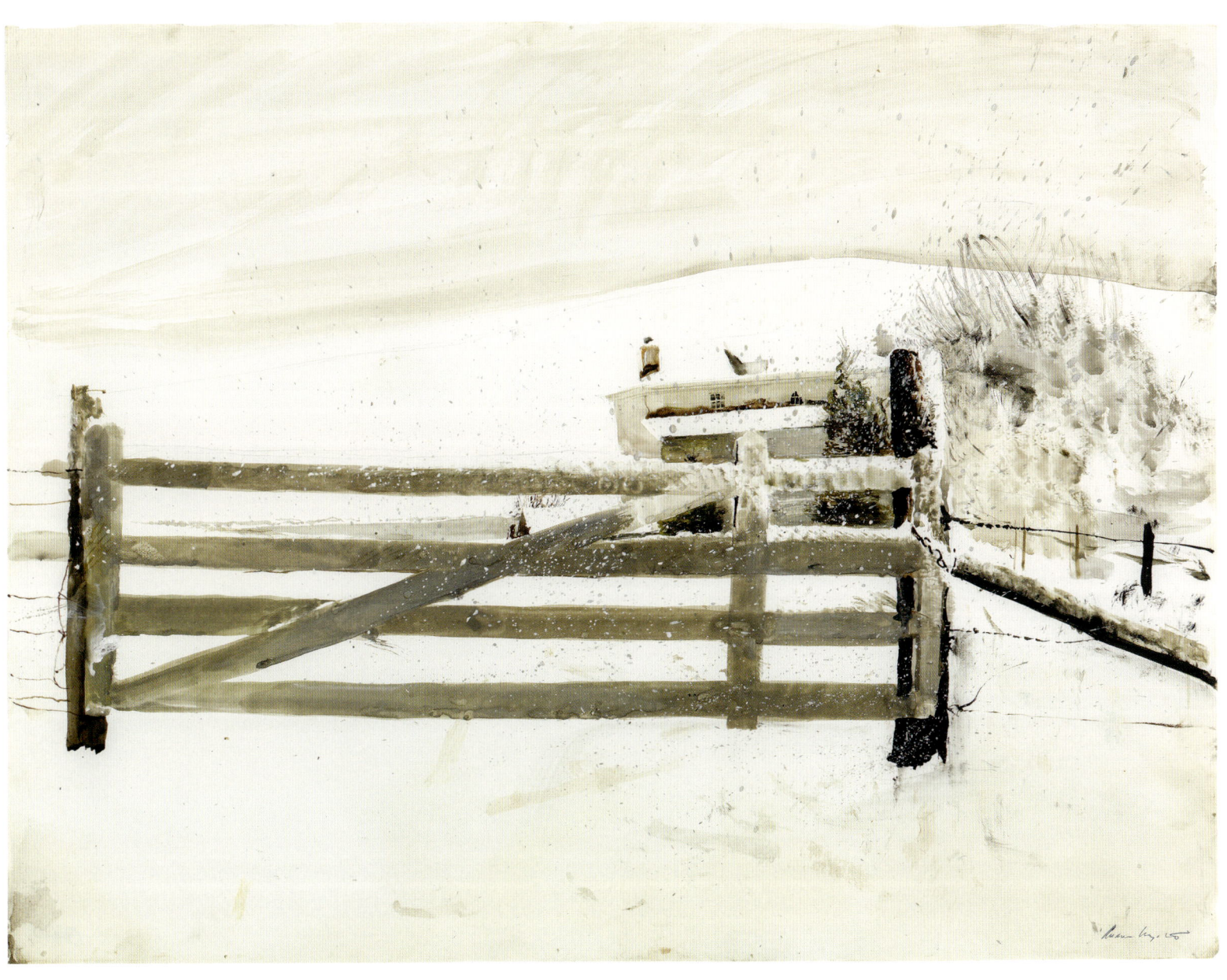

Gate Chain – 1st version, 1967. Watercolor on paper, 22 × 29 inches

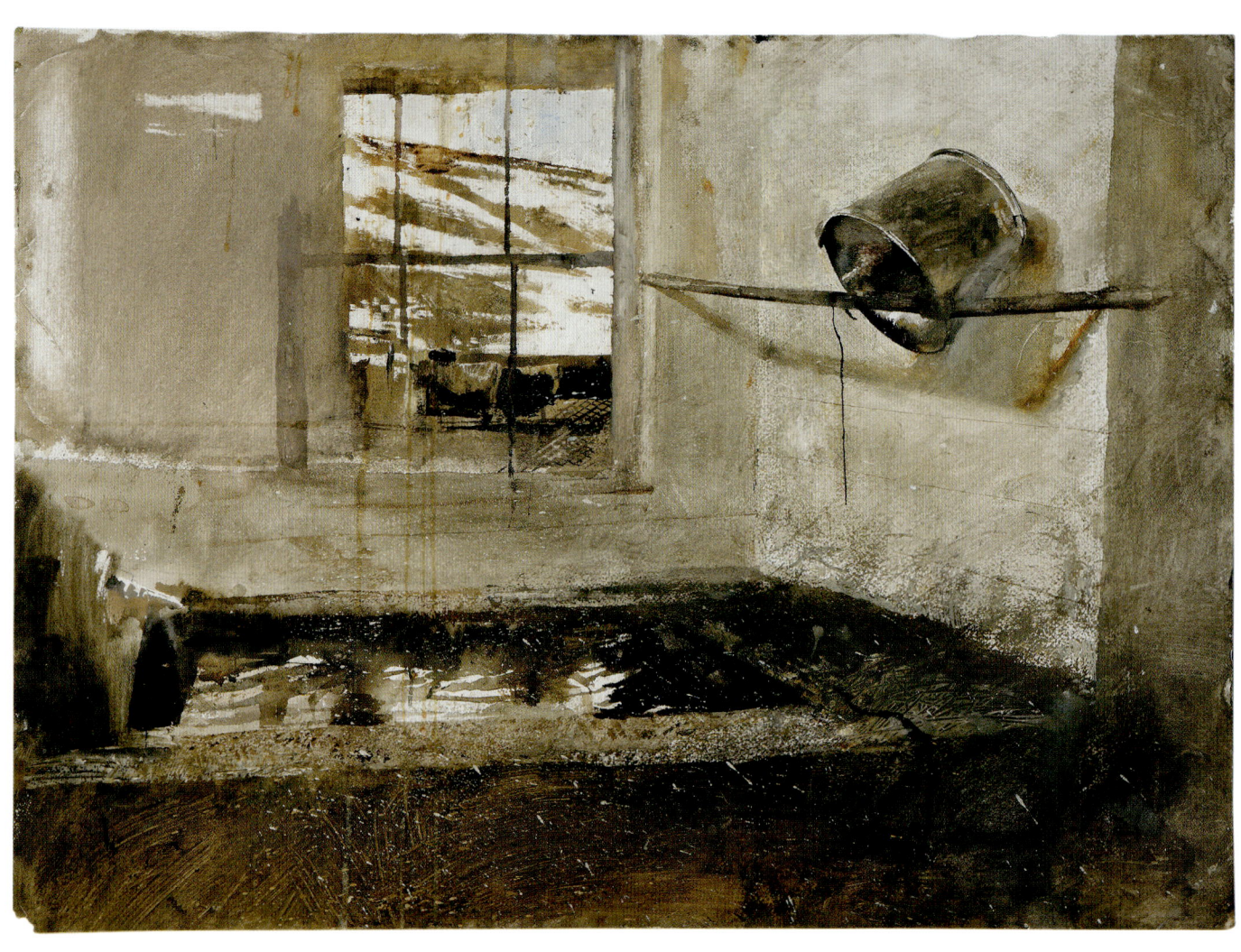

Spring Fed Study, 1967. Watercolor on paper, 21 ¾ × 29 ⅞ inches

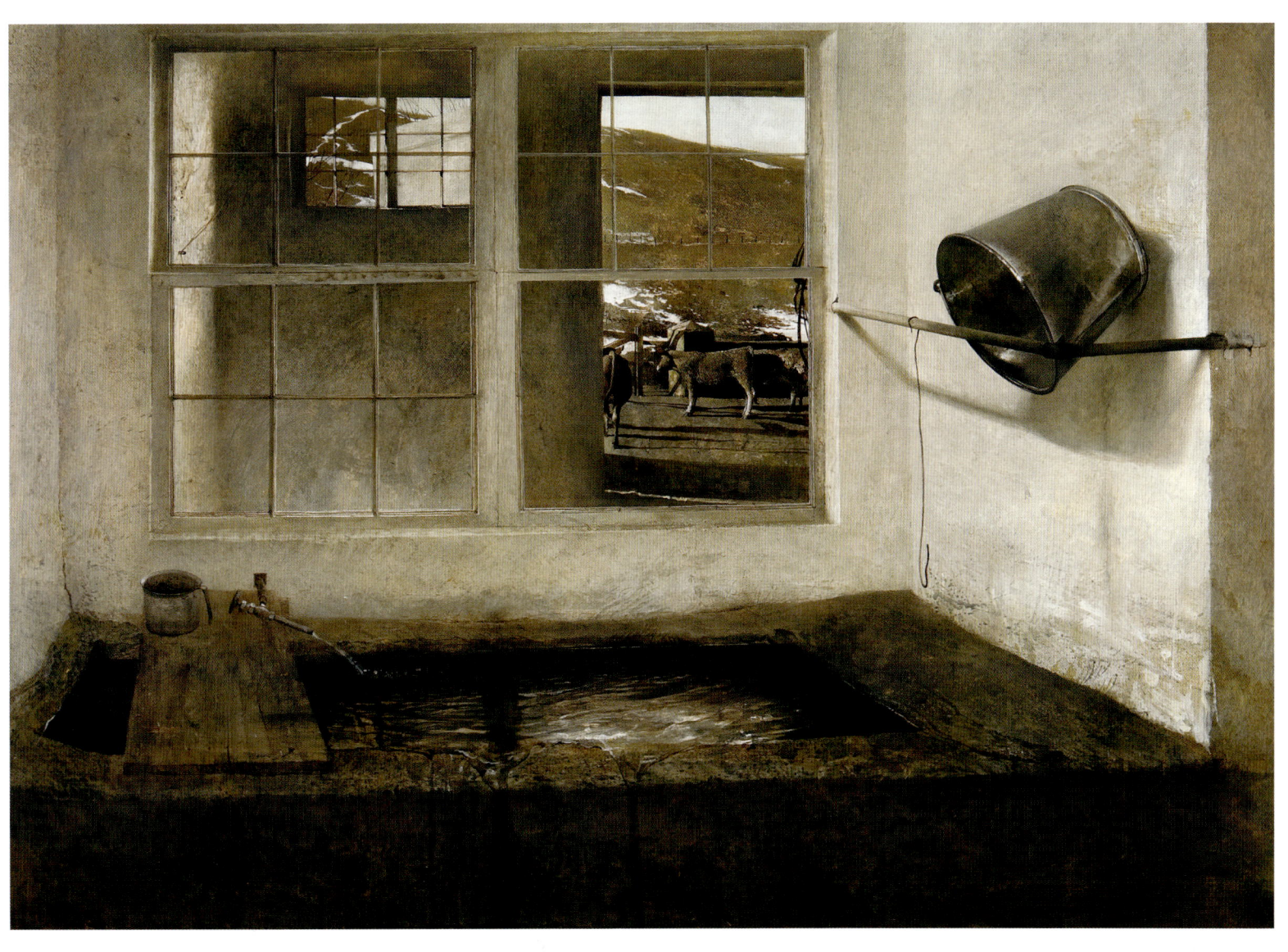

Spring Fed, 1967. Egg tempera on panel, 27 ½ × 39 ½ inches

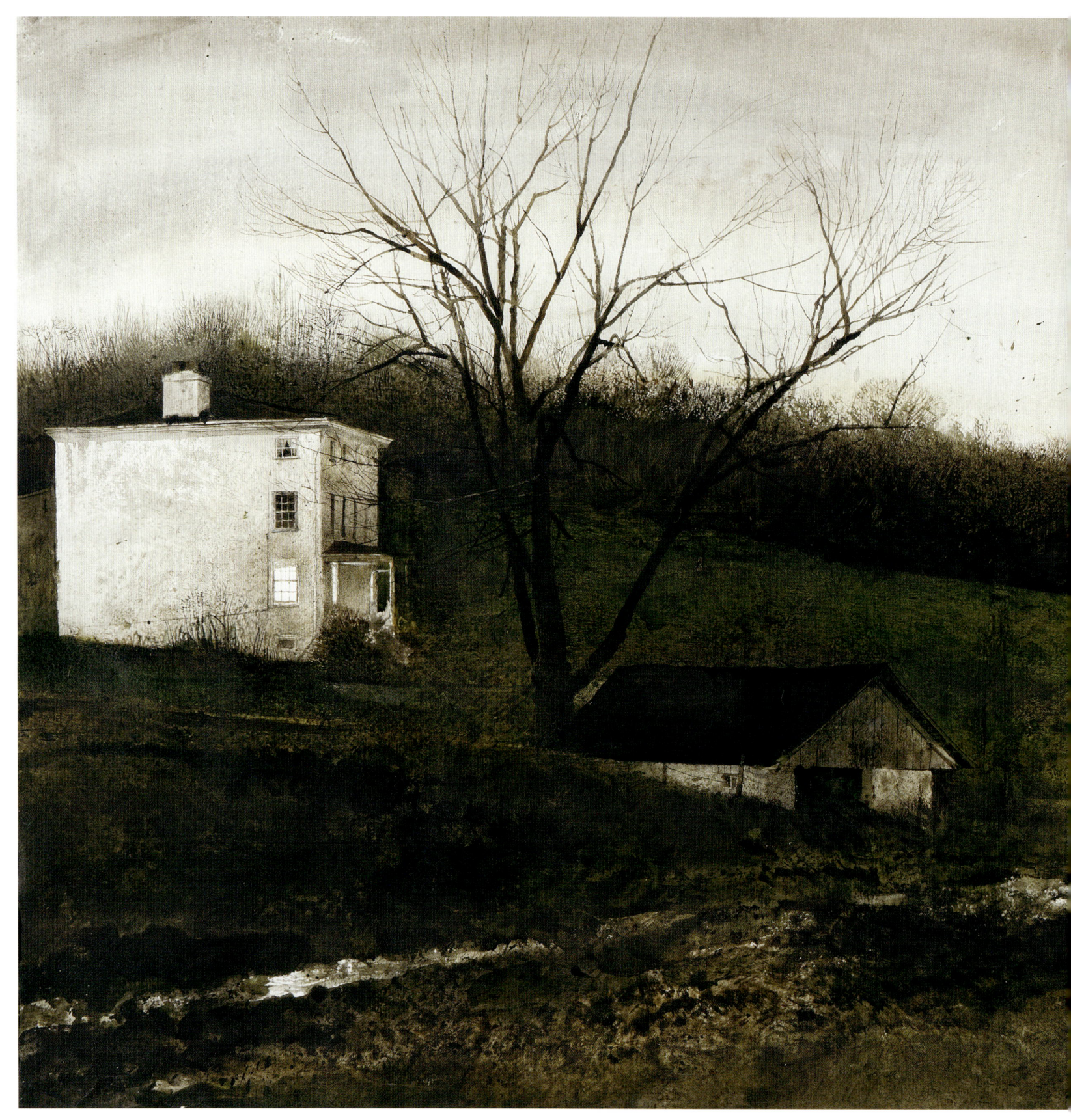

Evening at Kuerners, 1970. Drybrush watercolor on paper, 25 ½ × 39 ¾ inches

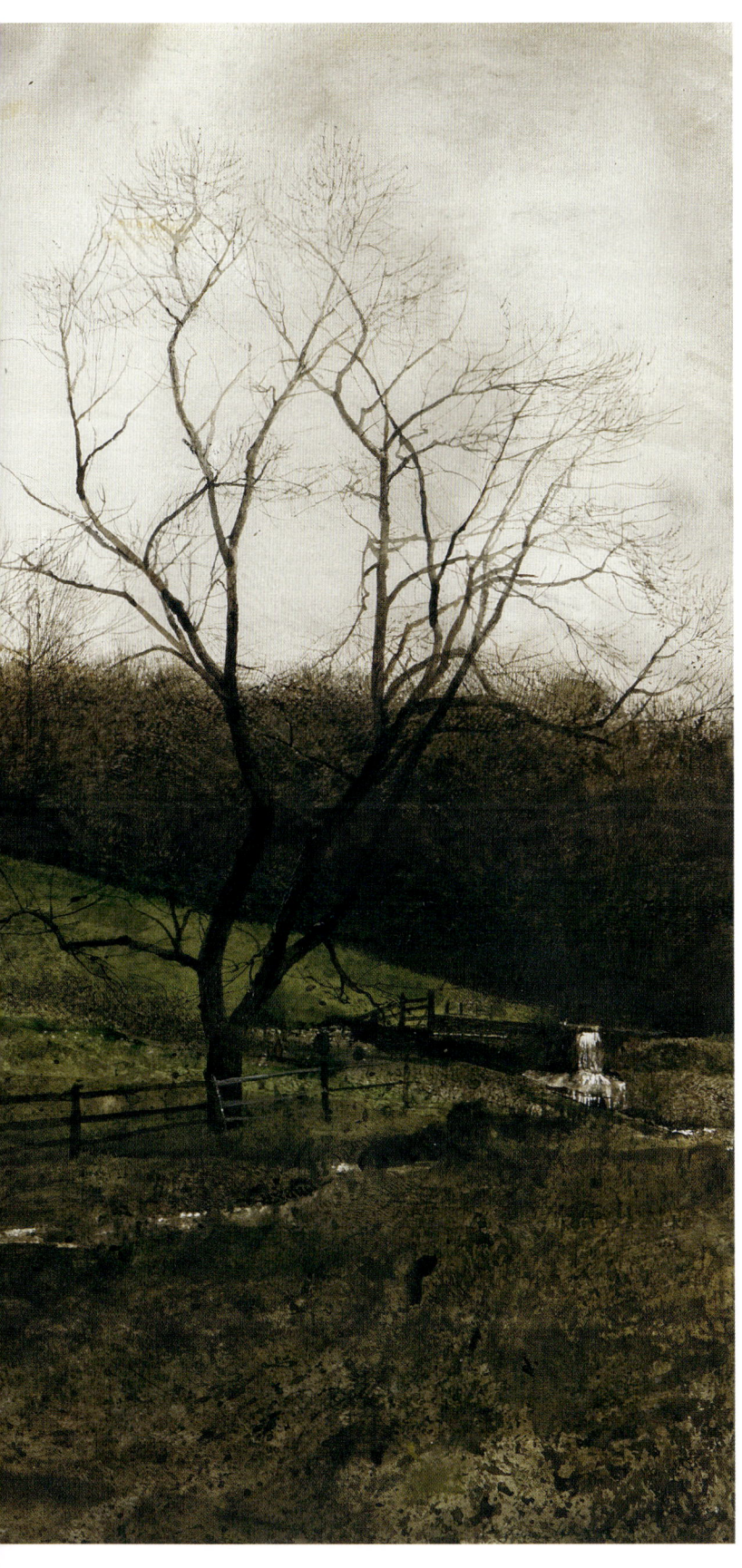

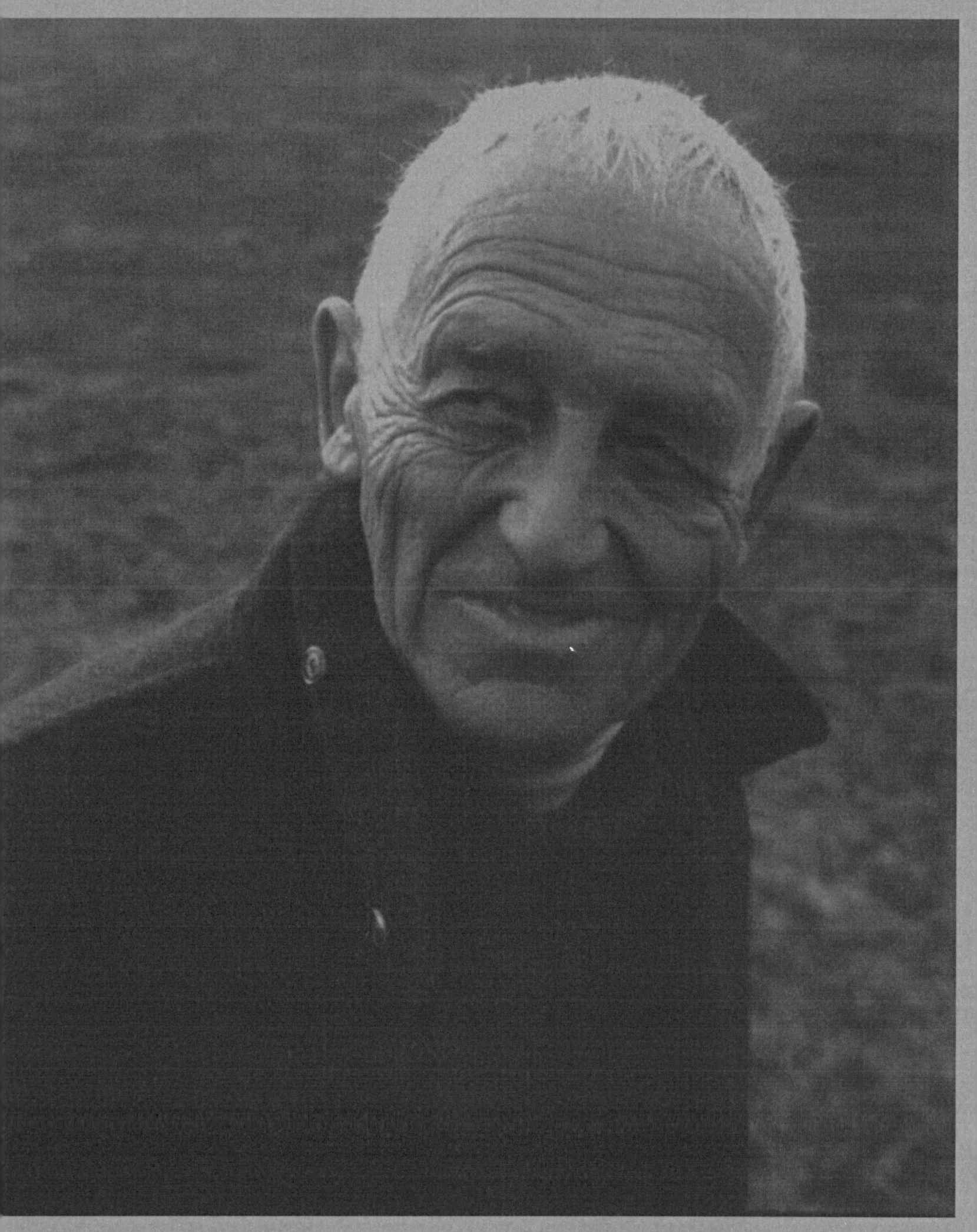

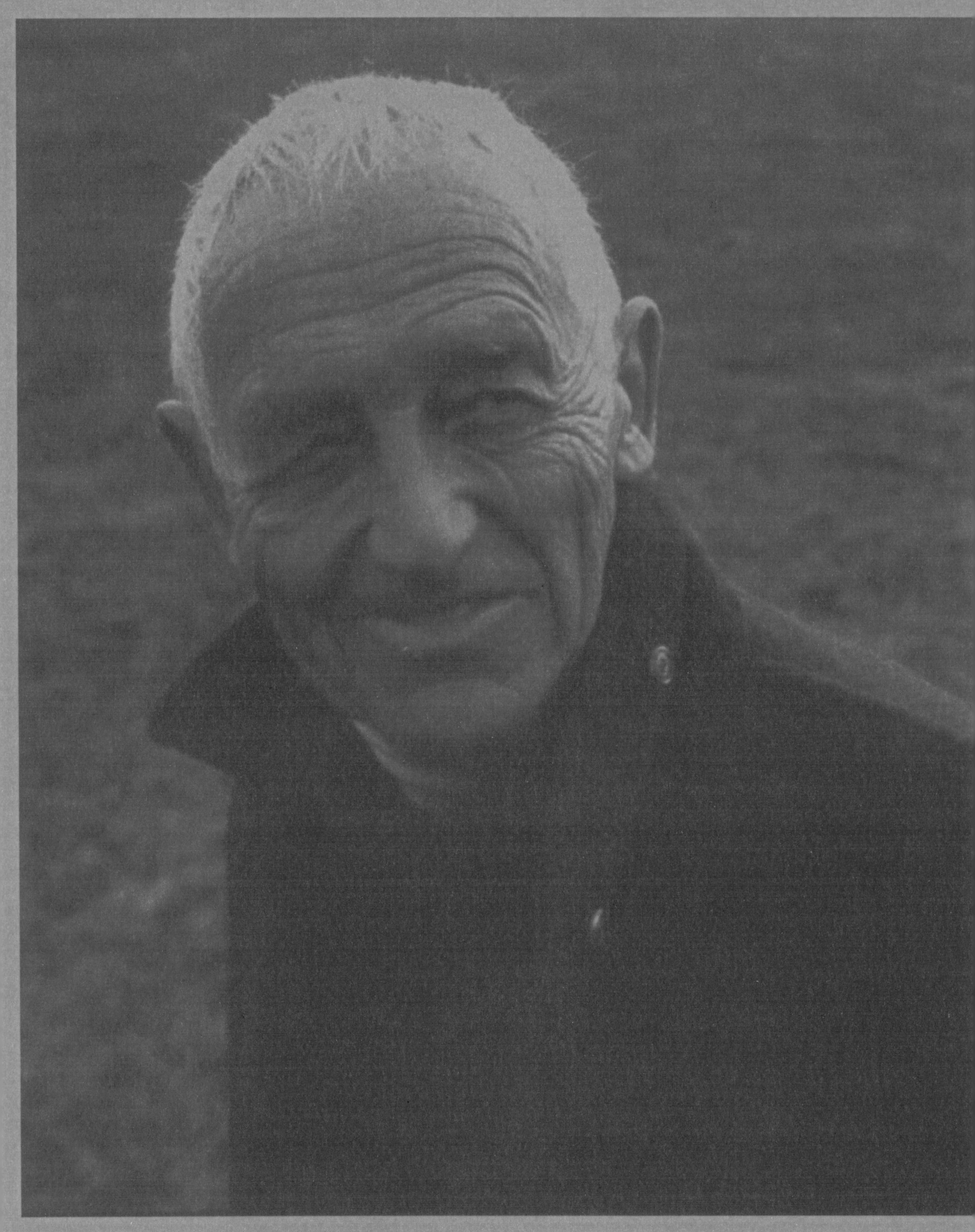

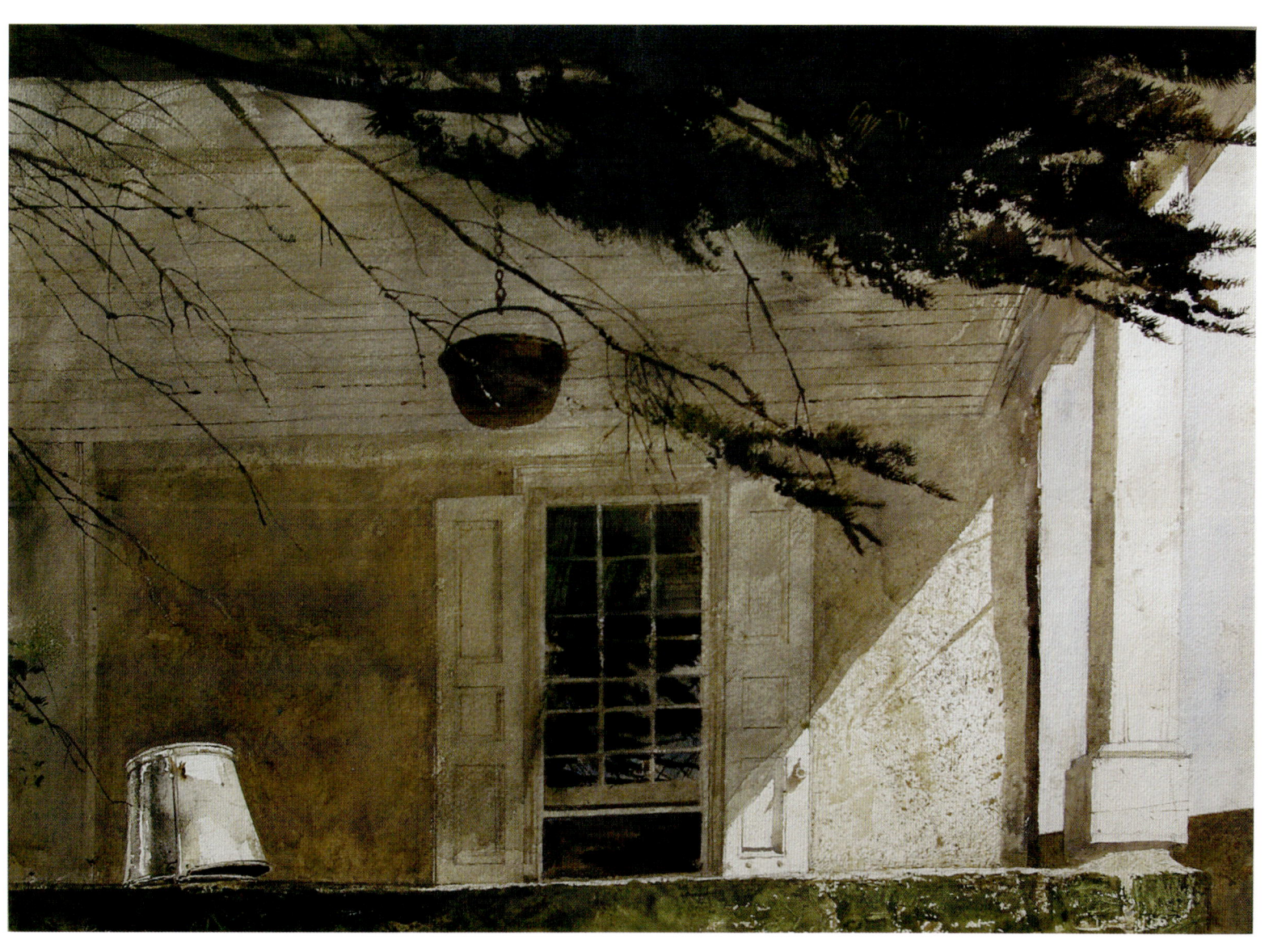

The Porch, 1970. Watercolor on paper, 21 ½ × 29 ¾ inches

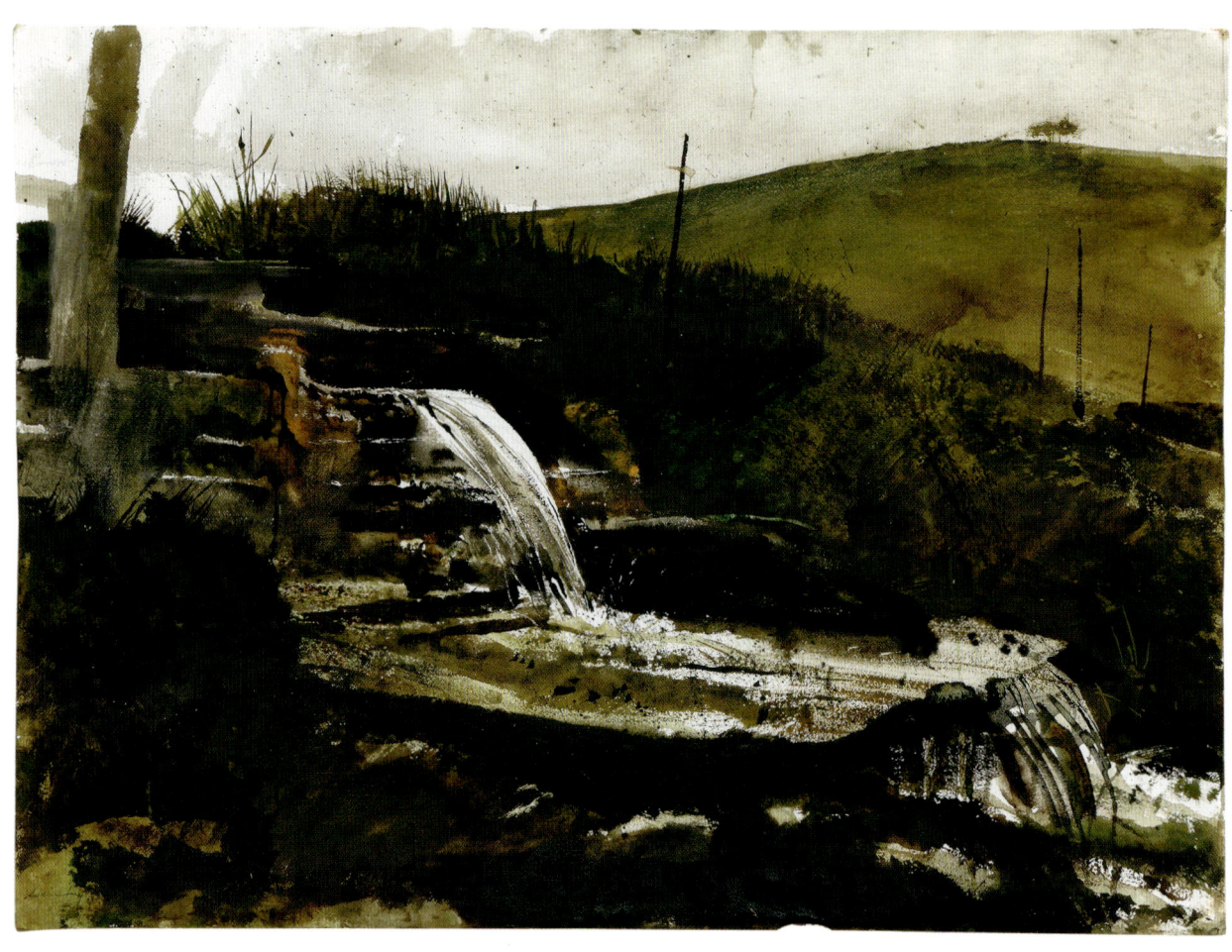

Spillway – 1st version, 1970. Watercolor on paper, 21 ¾ × 30 inches

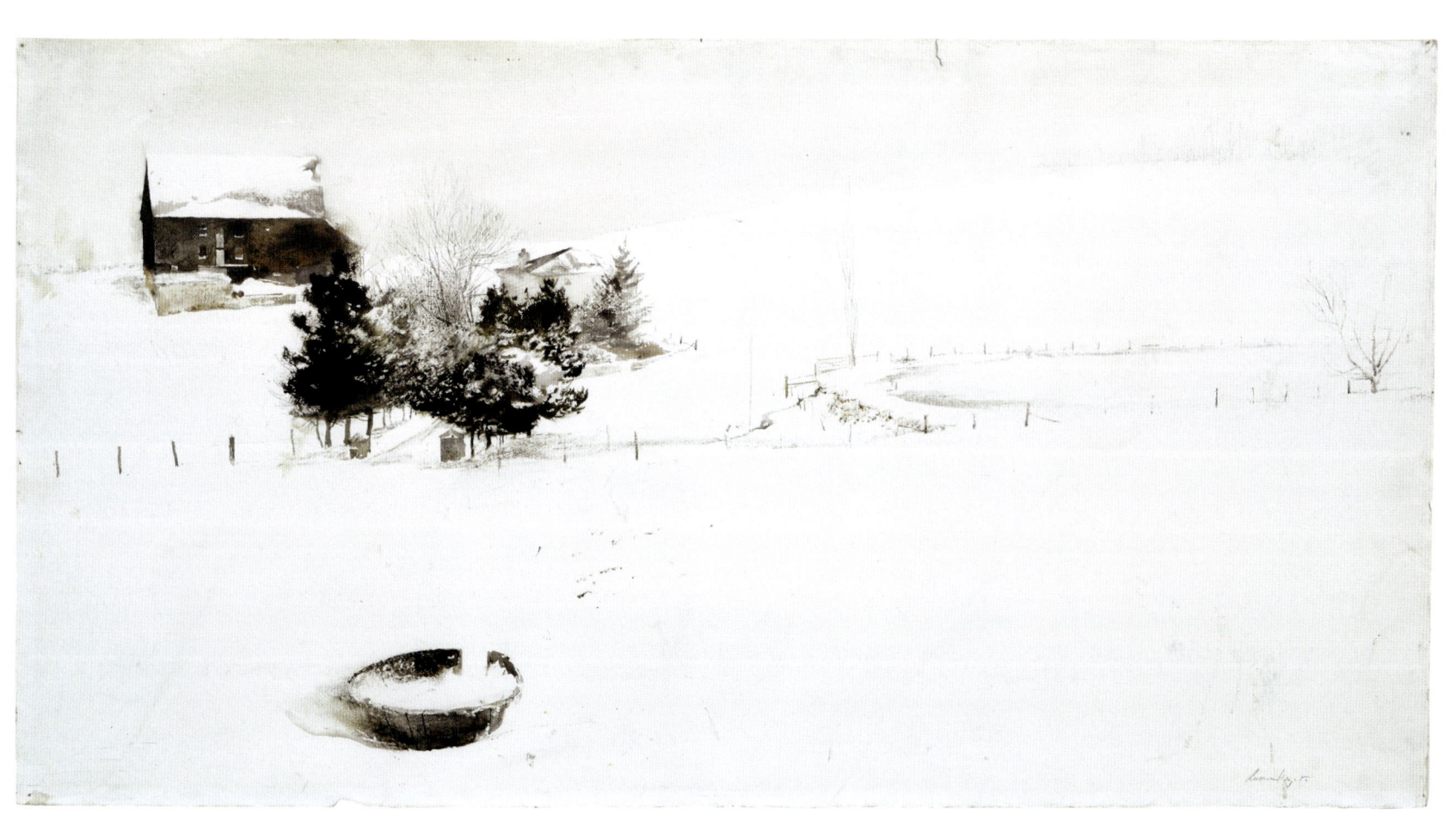

After Christmas, 1971. Watercolor on paper, 21 ½ × 40 inches

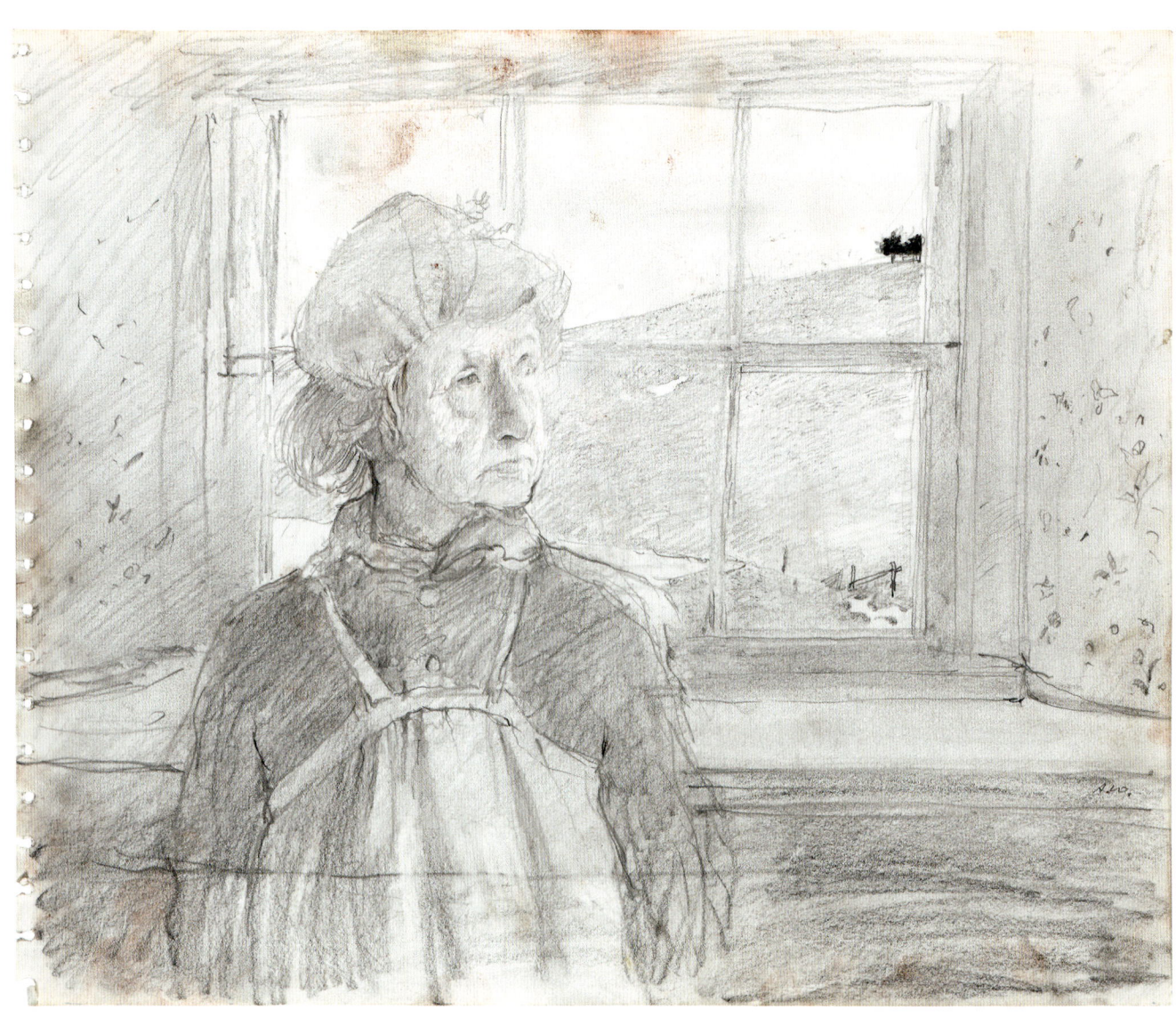

Anna Kuerner Study, 1971. Pencil on paper, 14 × 16 ¾ inches

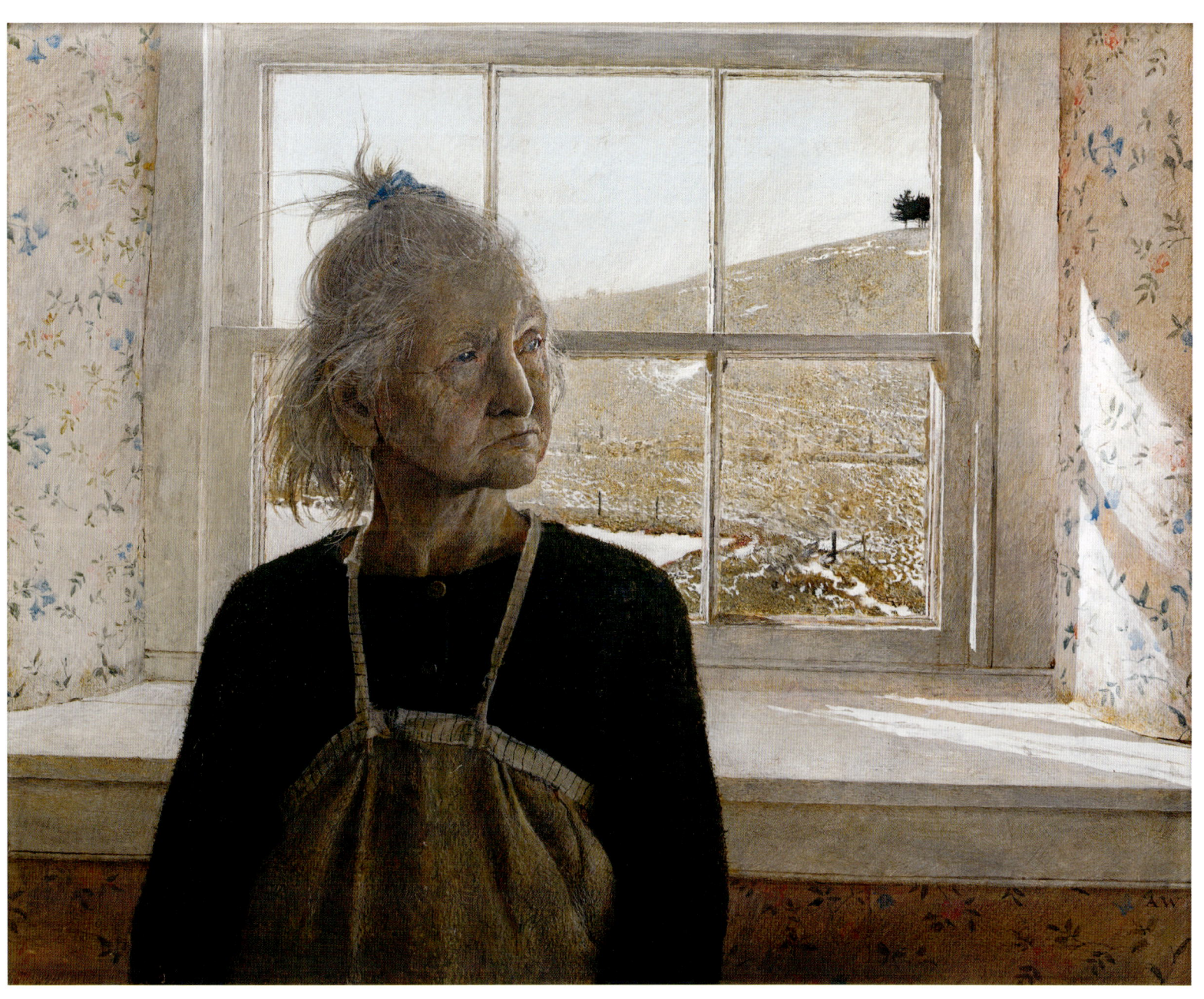

Anna Kuerner, 1971. Egg tempera on panel, 13½ × 17 inches

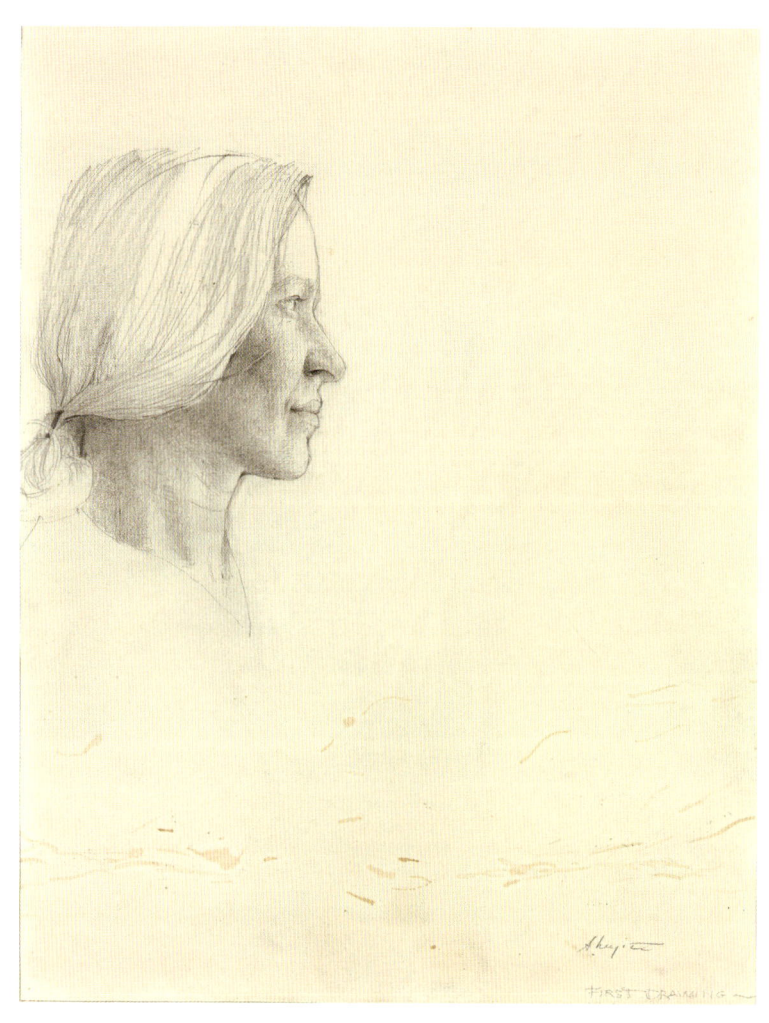

First drawing, 1971. Pencil on paper, 14 × 11 inches

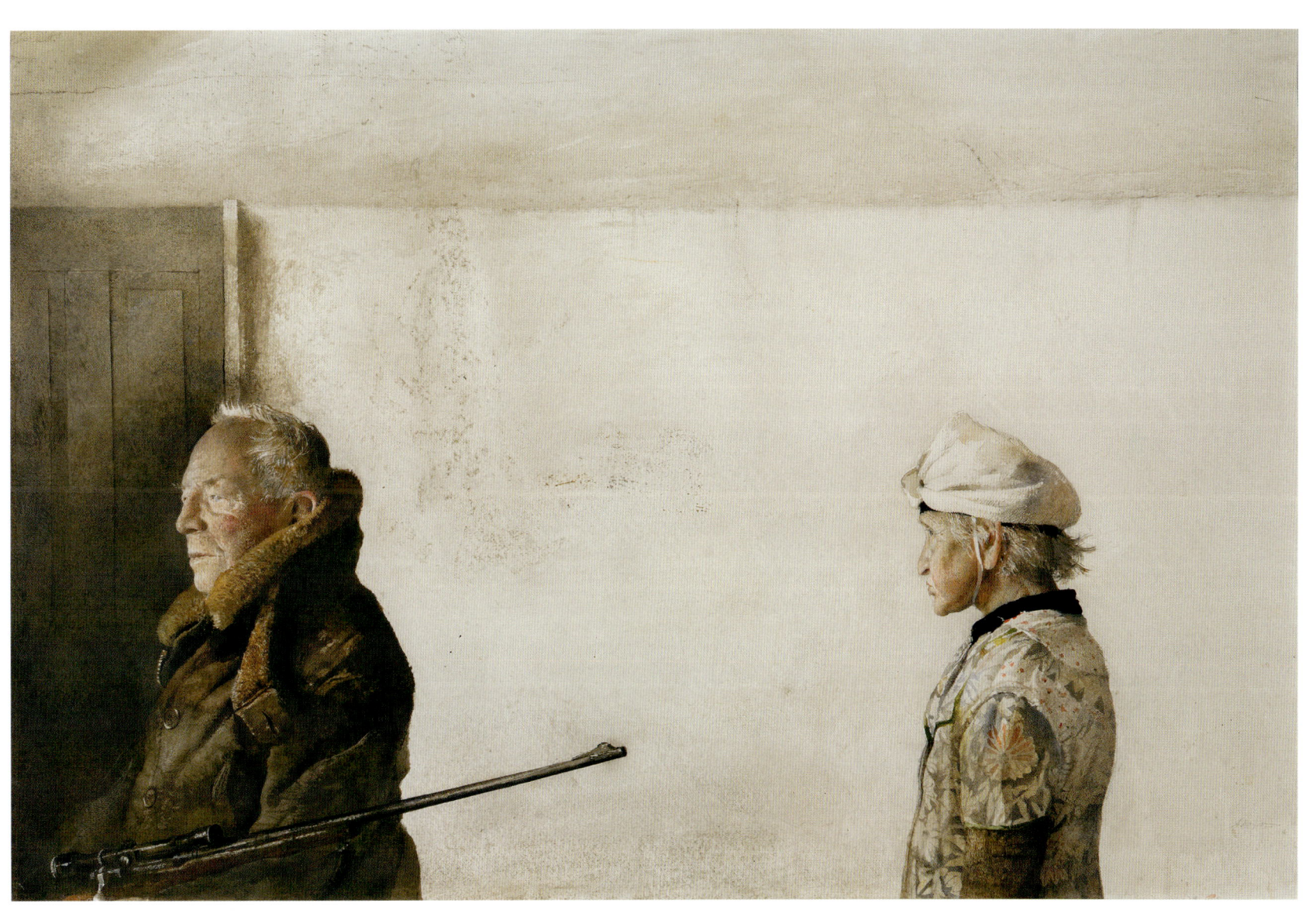

The Kuerners, 1971. Drybrush watercolor on paper, 26 ½ × 40 ⅛ inches

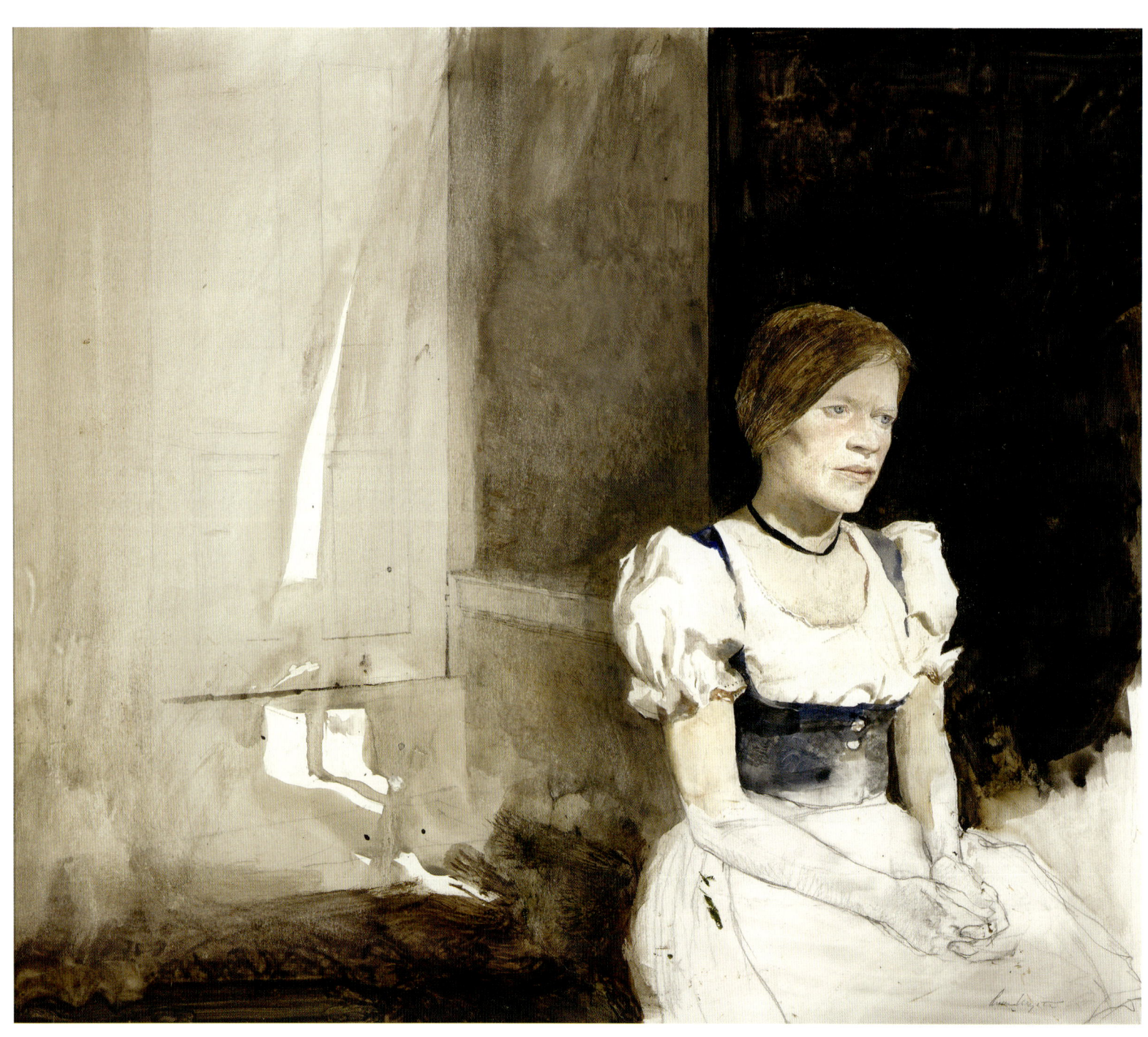

Peasant Dress, 1972. Watercolor and pencil on paper, 19 ½ × 23 inches

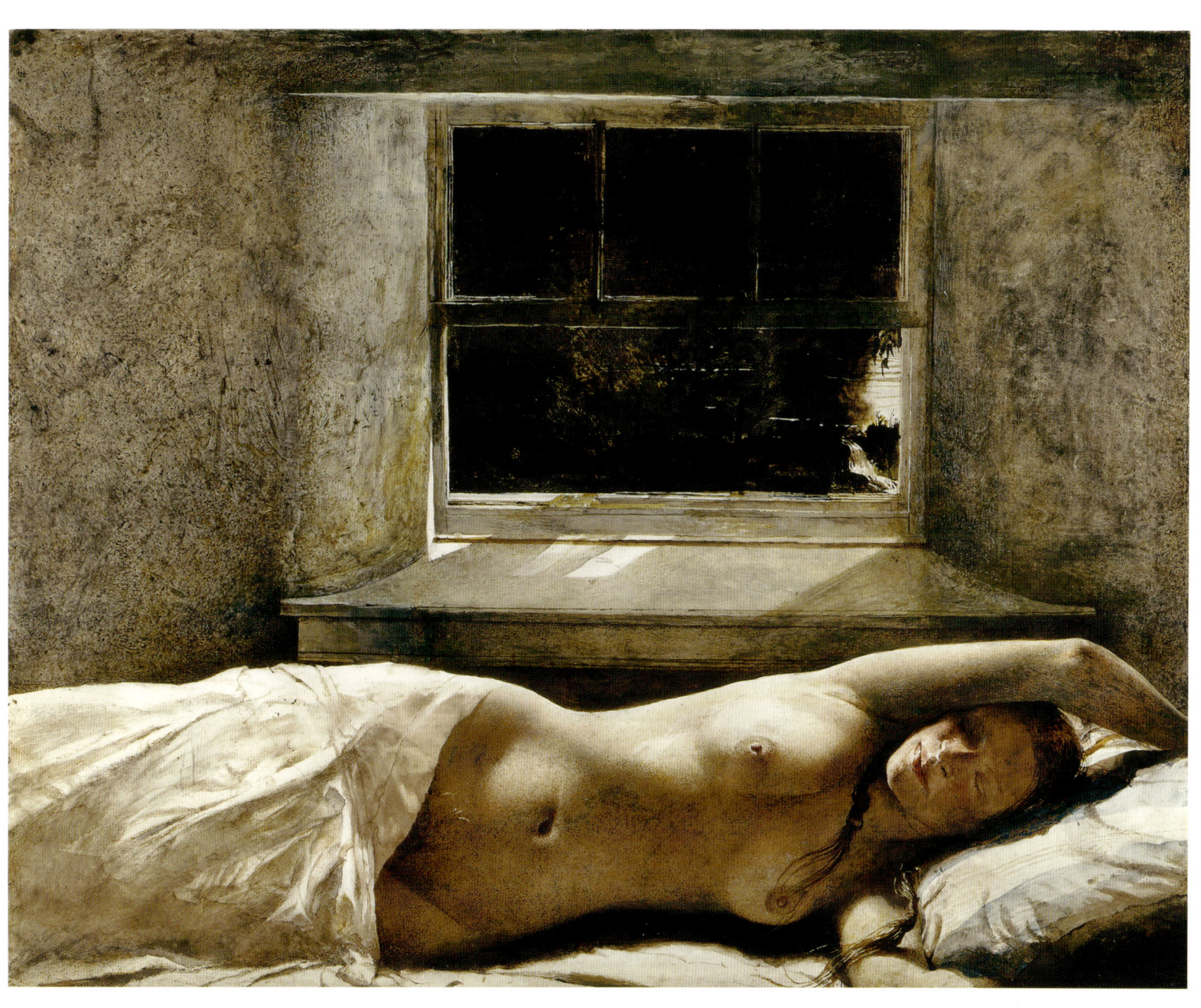

Overflow, 1978. Drybrush watercolor on paper, 23 × 29 inches

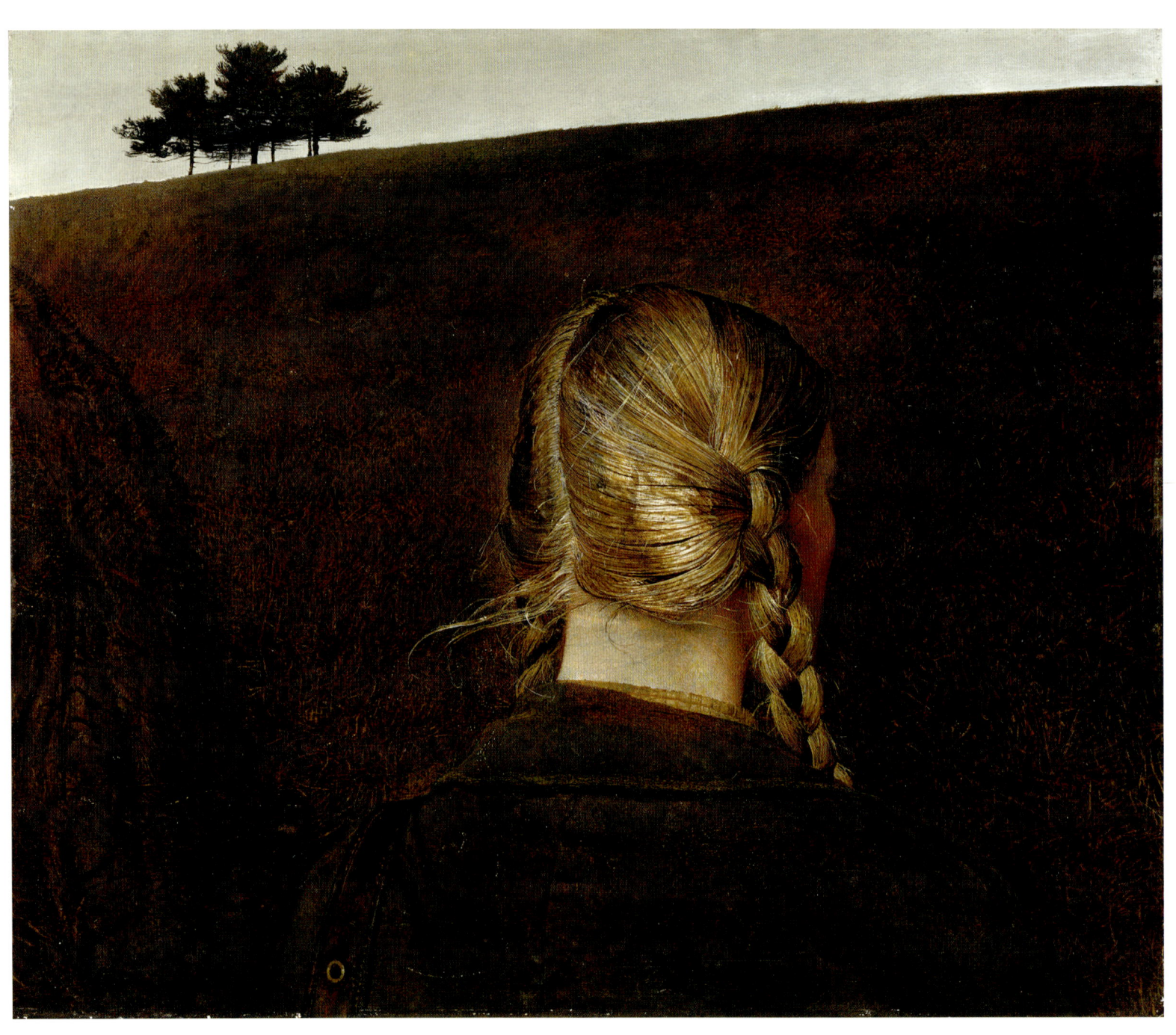

Farm Road, 1979. Egg tempera on panel, 21 × 25 ¼ inches

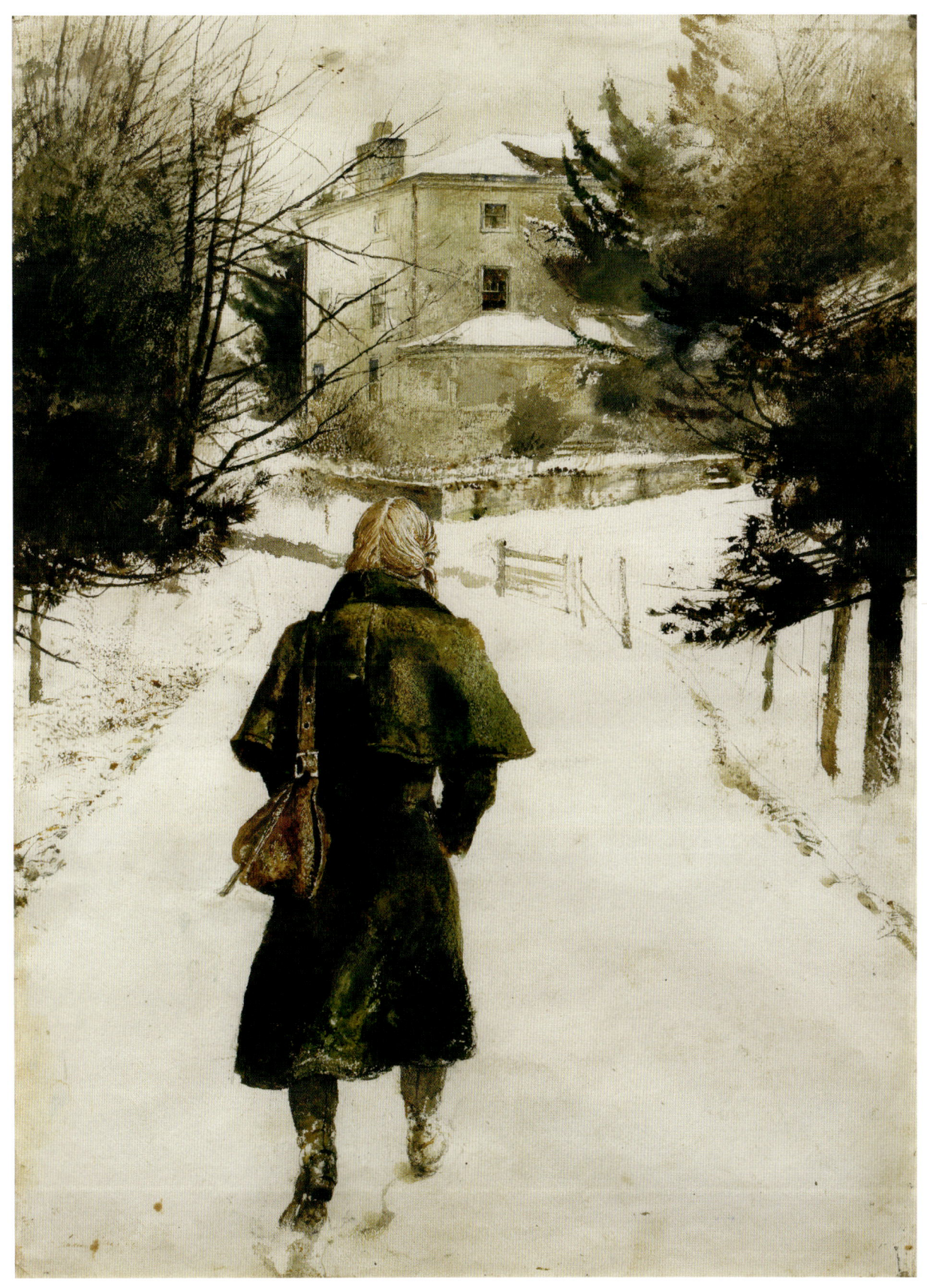

Loden Coat, 1978. Watercolor on paper, 30 × 22 inches

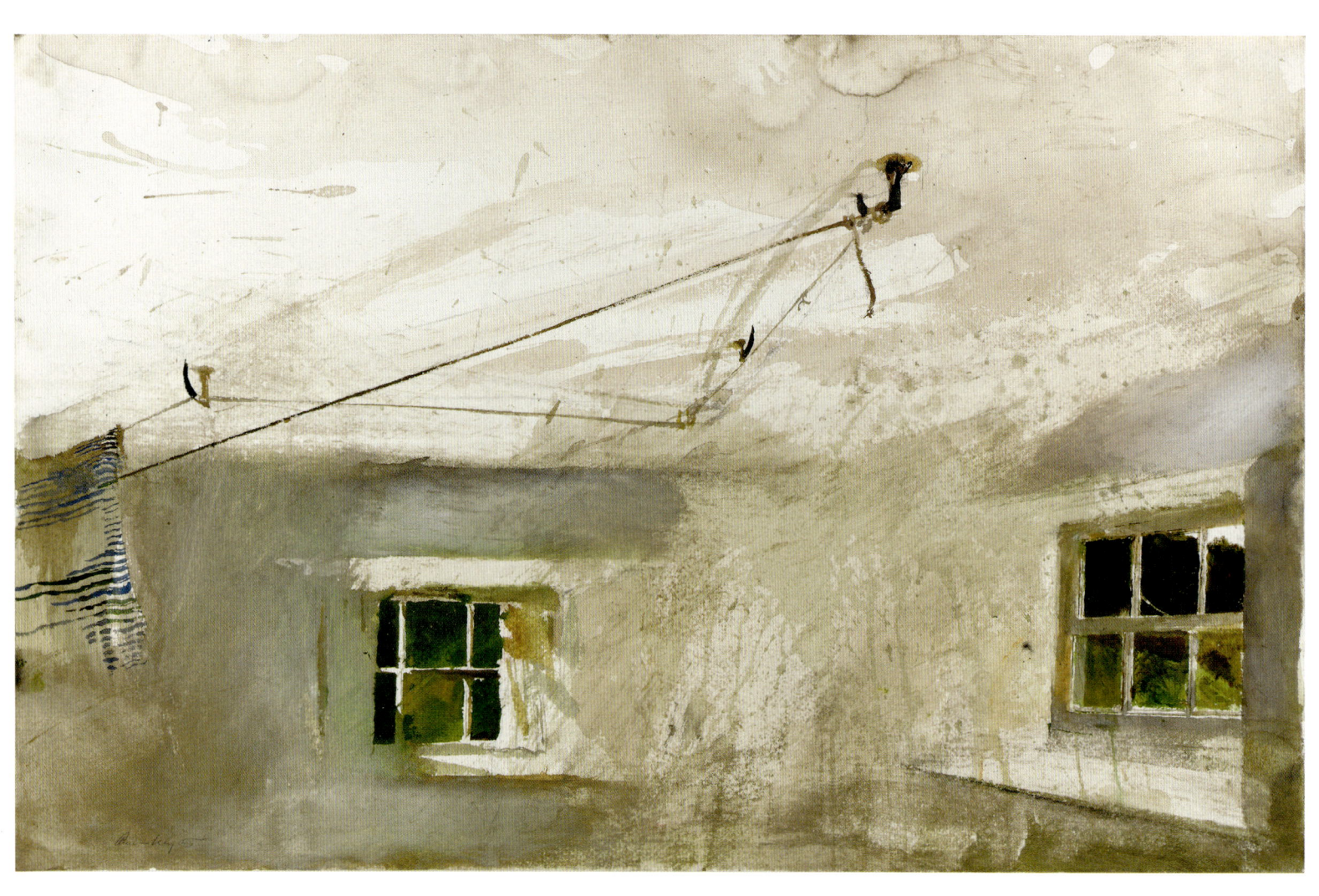

Spare Room – 2nd version, 1973. Watercolor on paper, 19 × 30 inches

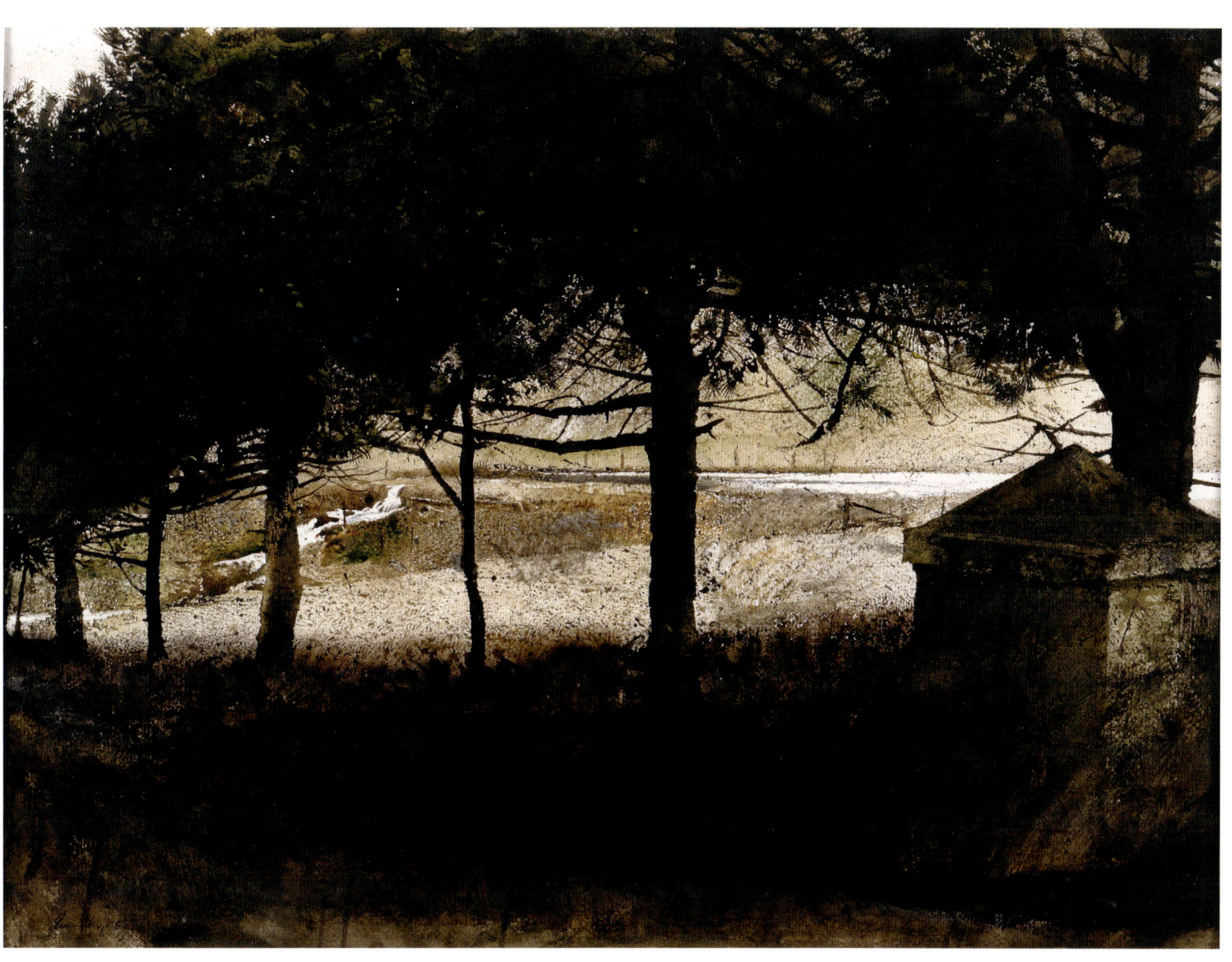

Where the German Lives, 1973. Watercolor on paper, 21 ½ × 29 ½ inches

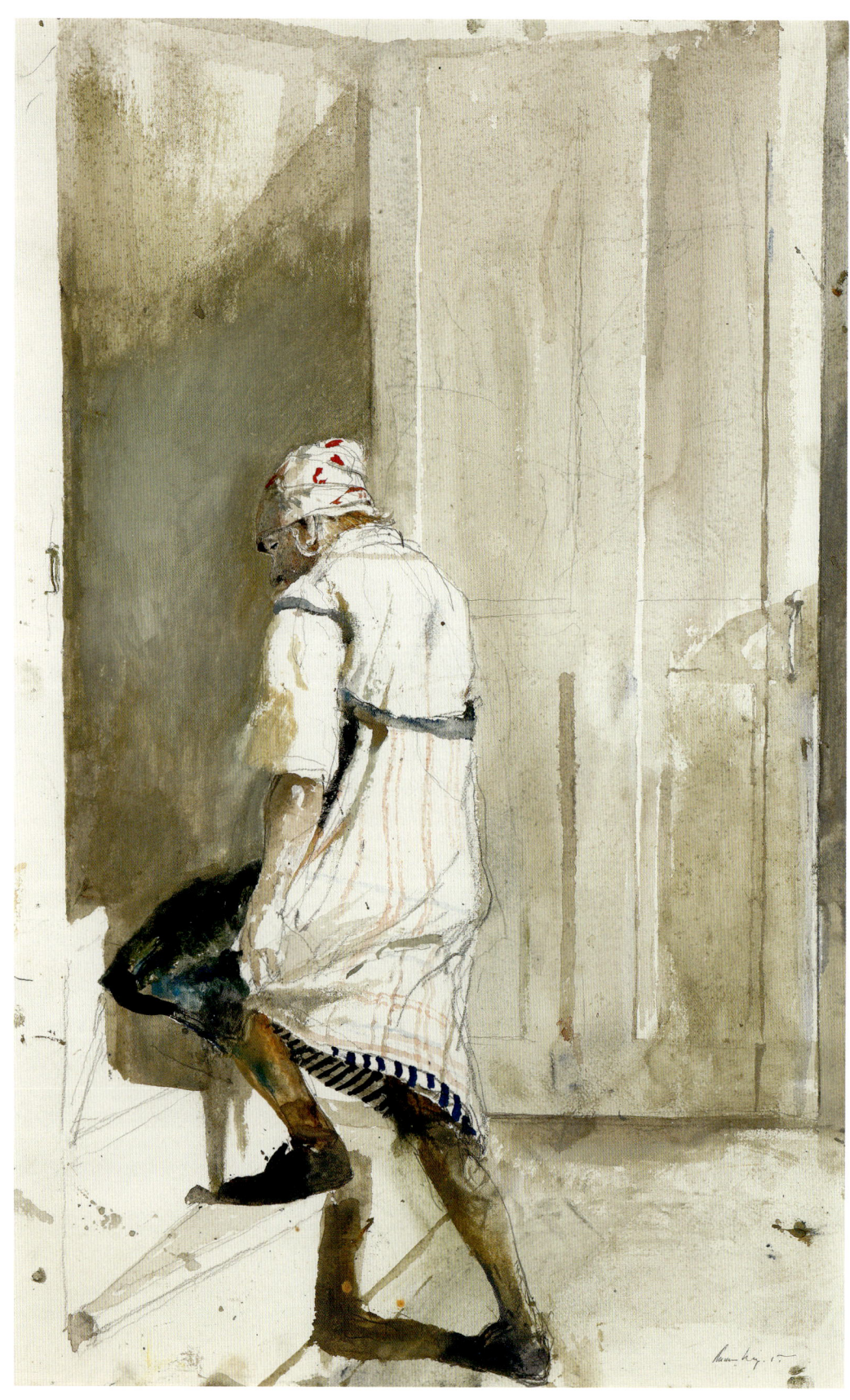

Anna Climbing the Stairs, 1975. Watercolor on paper, 29 ½ × 18 ½ inches

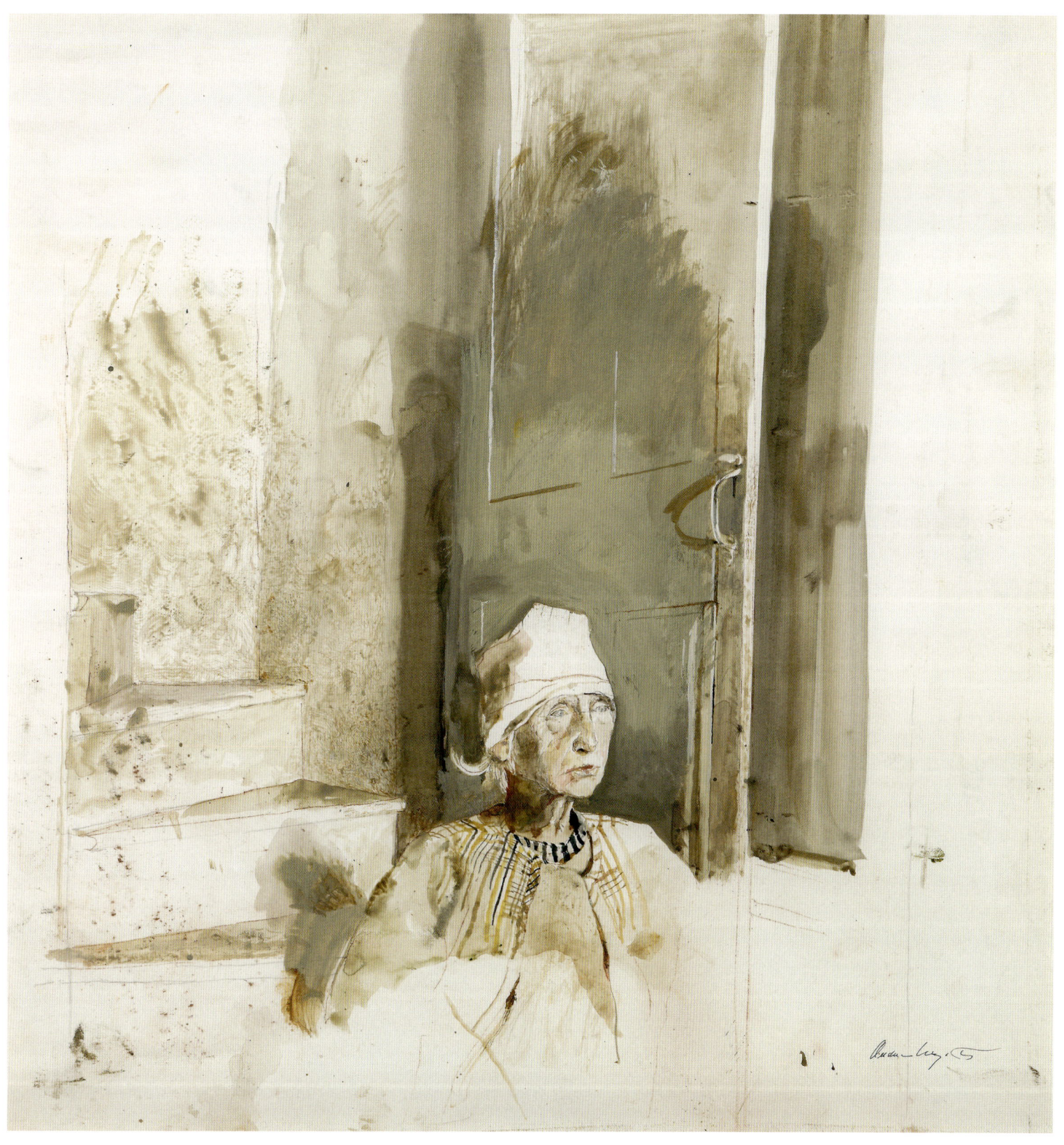

Dust Cap, 1975. Drybrush watercolor on paper, 23 ¼ × 23 inches

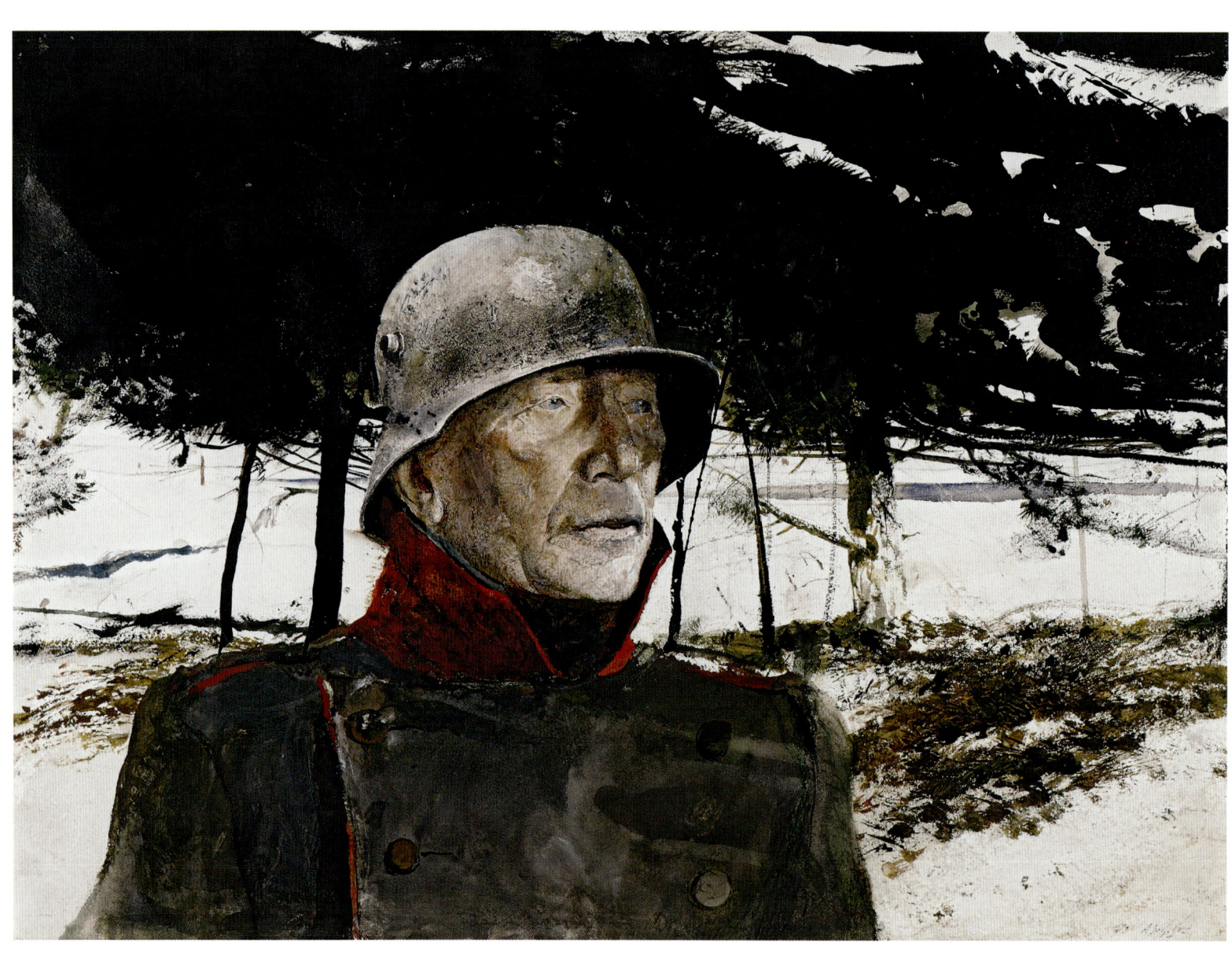

The German, 1975. Watercolor on paper, 21 × 29 inches

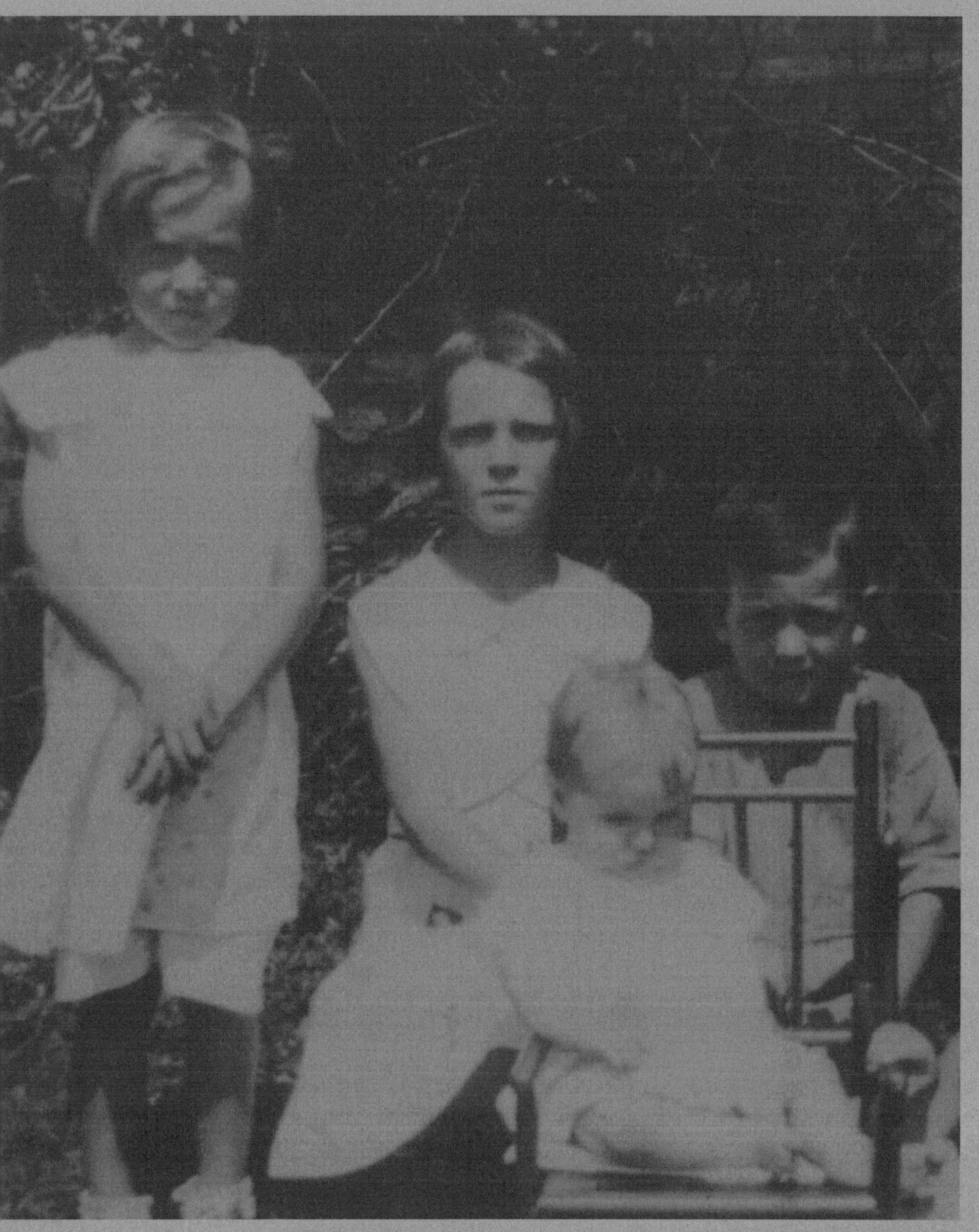

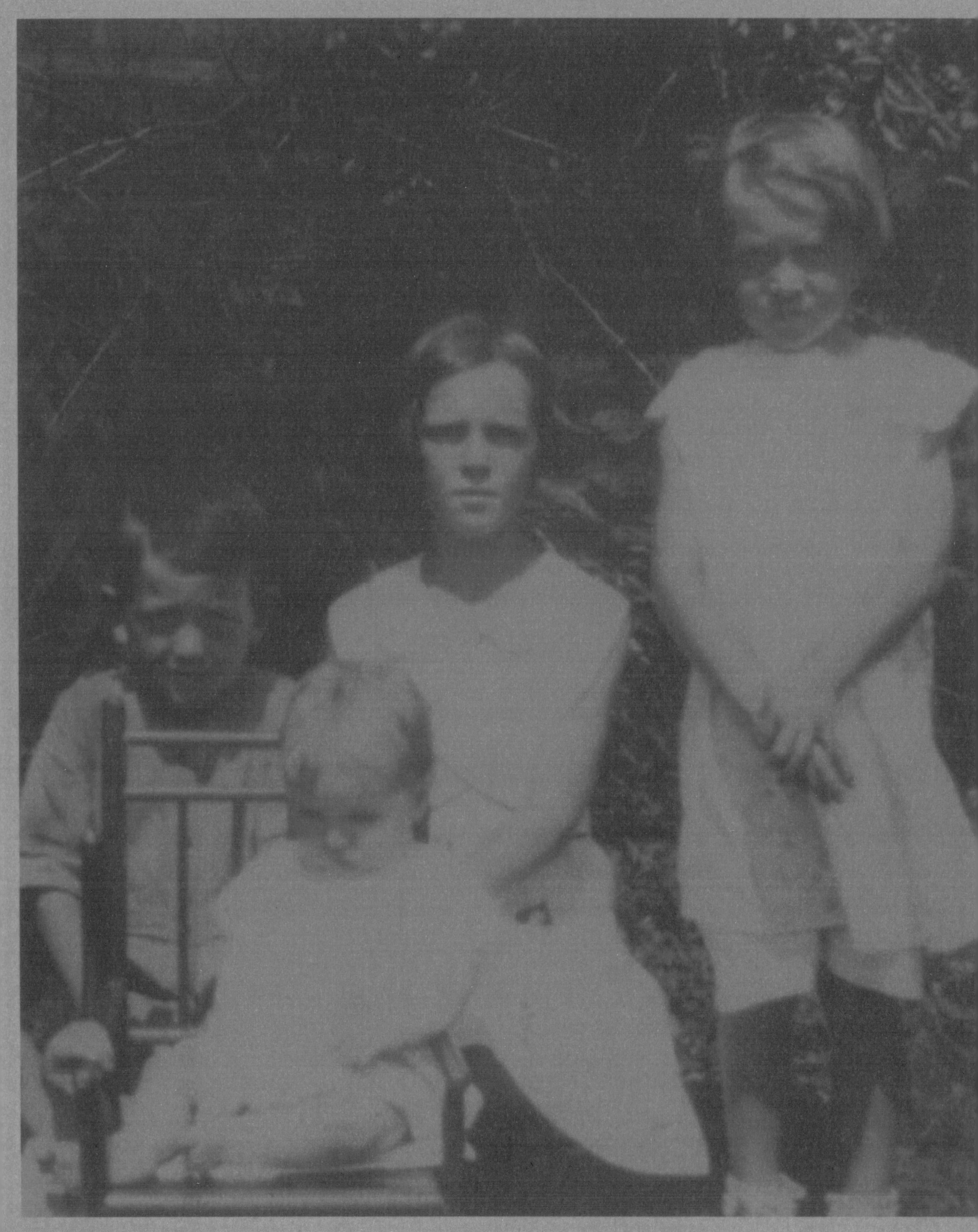

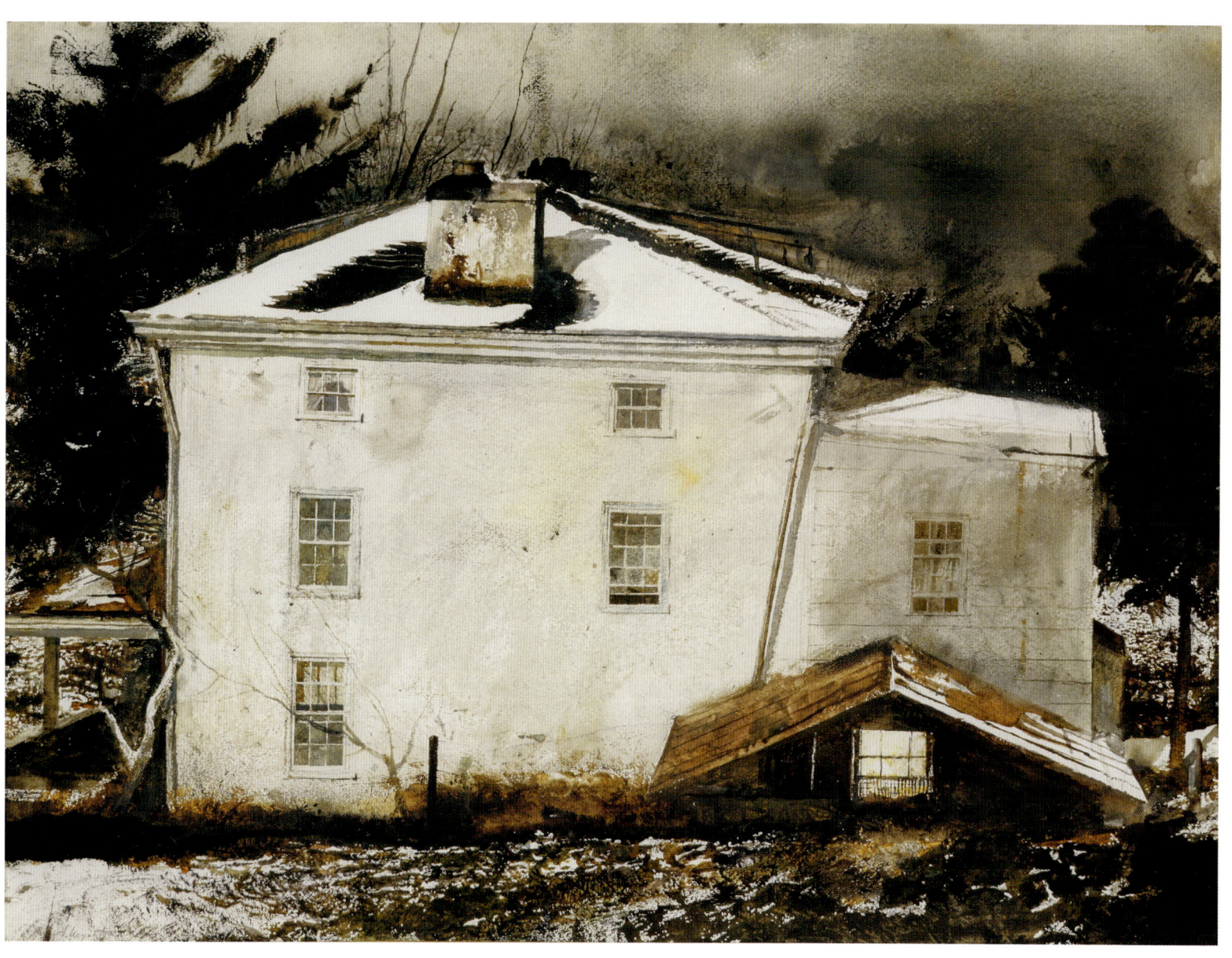

Lamplight, 1975. Watercolor on paper, 21 ½ × 29 ½ inches

Wolf Moon, 1975. Watercolor on paper, 40 ⅛ × 29 inches

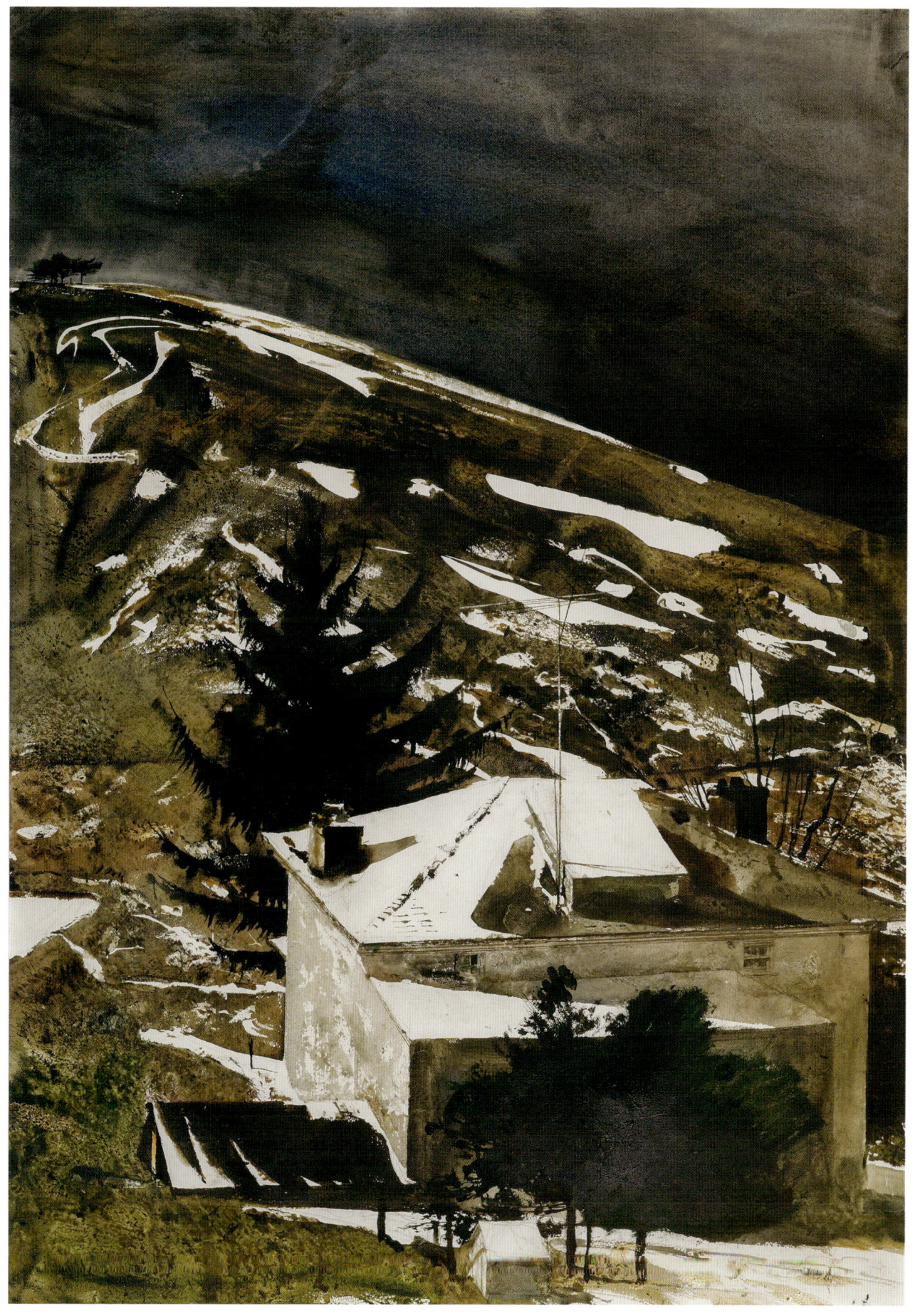

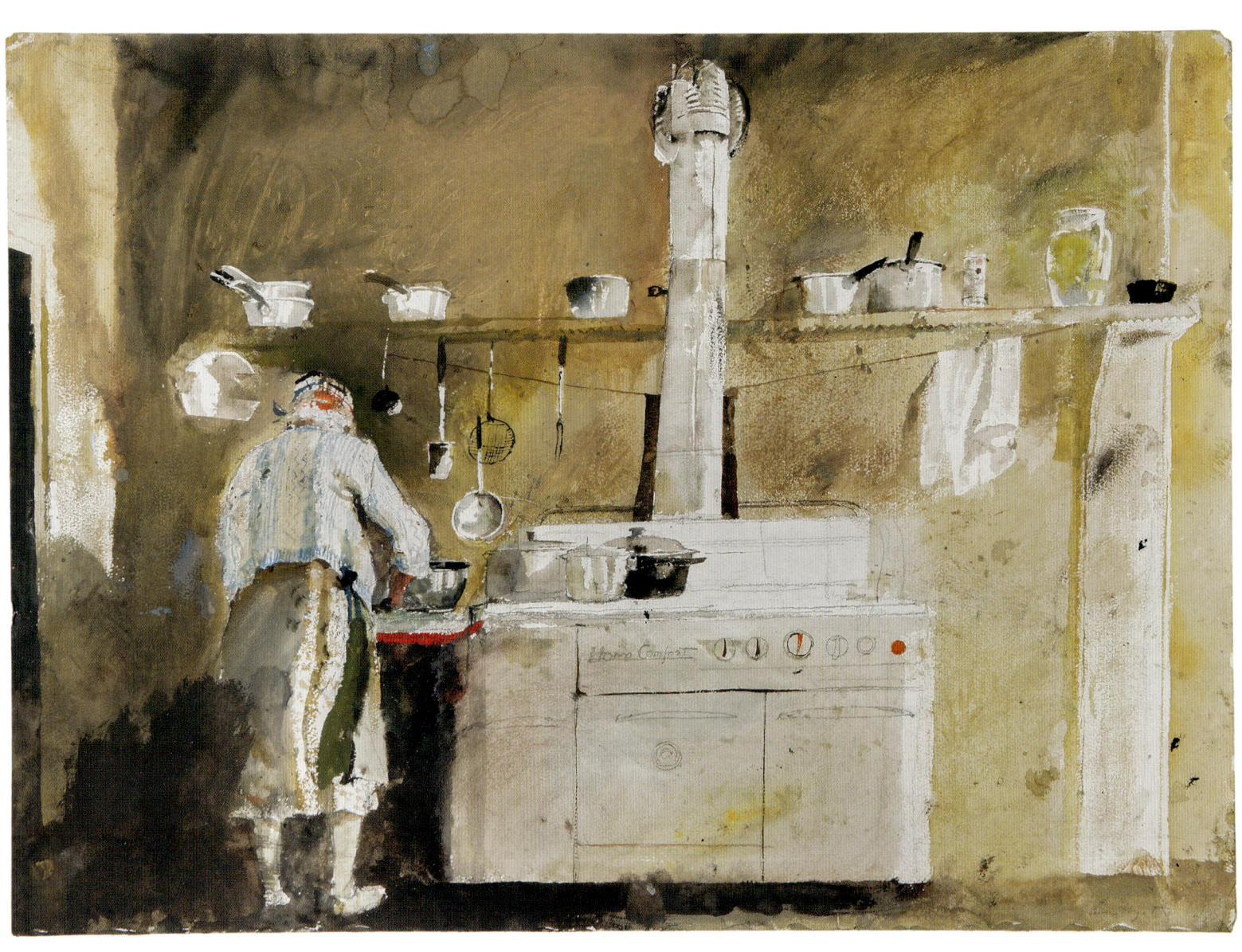

Home Comfort, 1976. Watercolor on paper, 21 ¾ × 30 inches

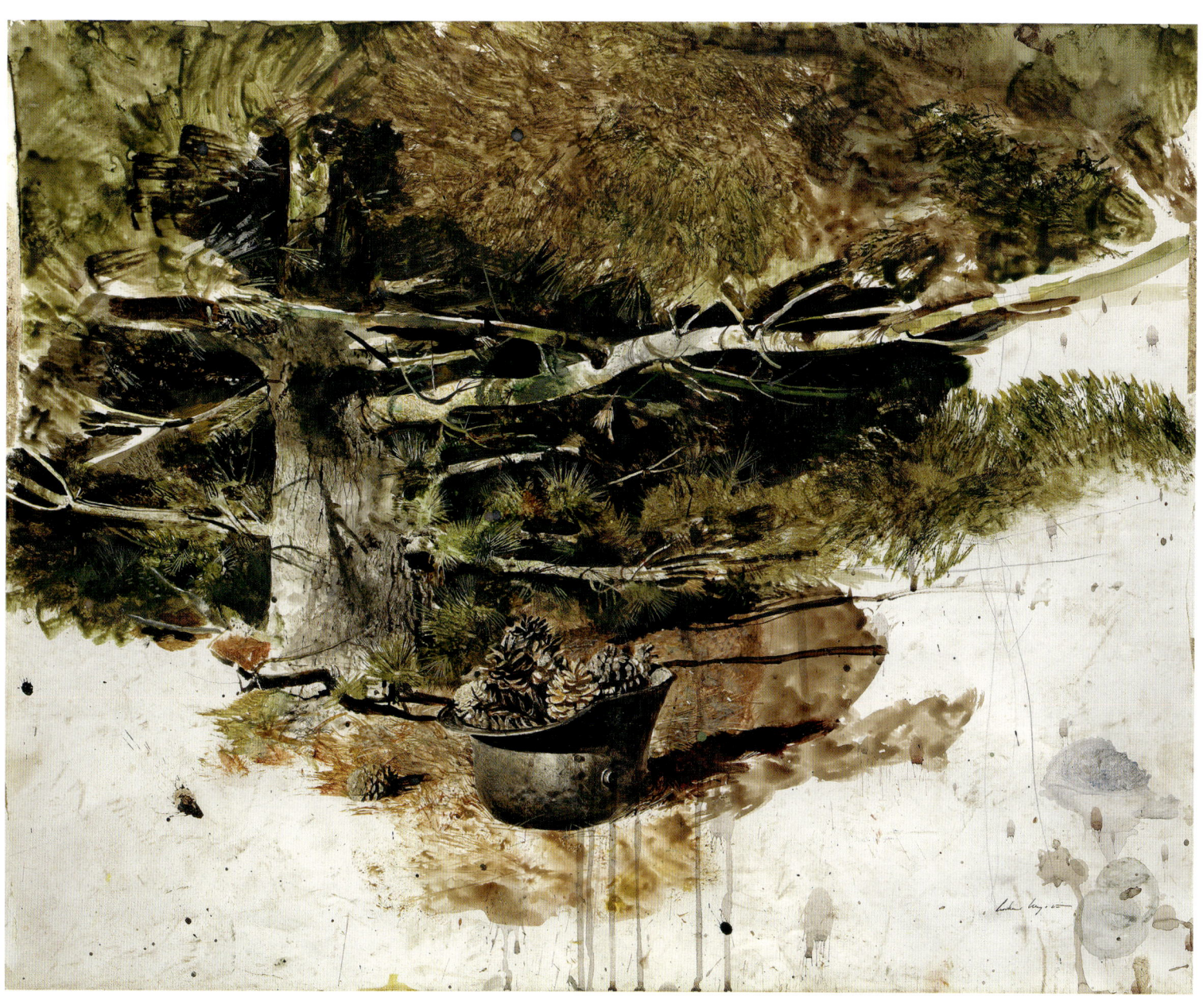

Steel Helmet, Study for Pine Baron, 1976. Drybrush watercolor on paper, 23 × 28 ½ inches

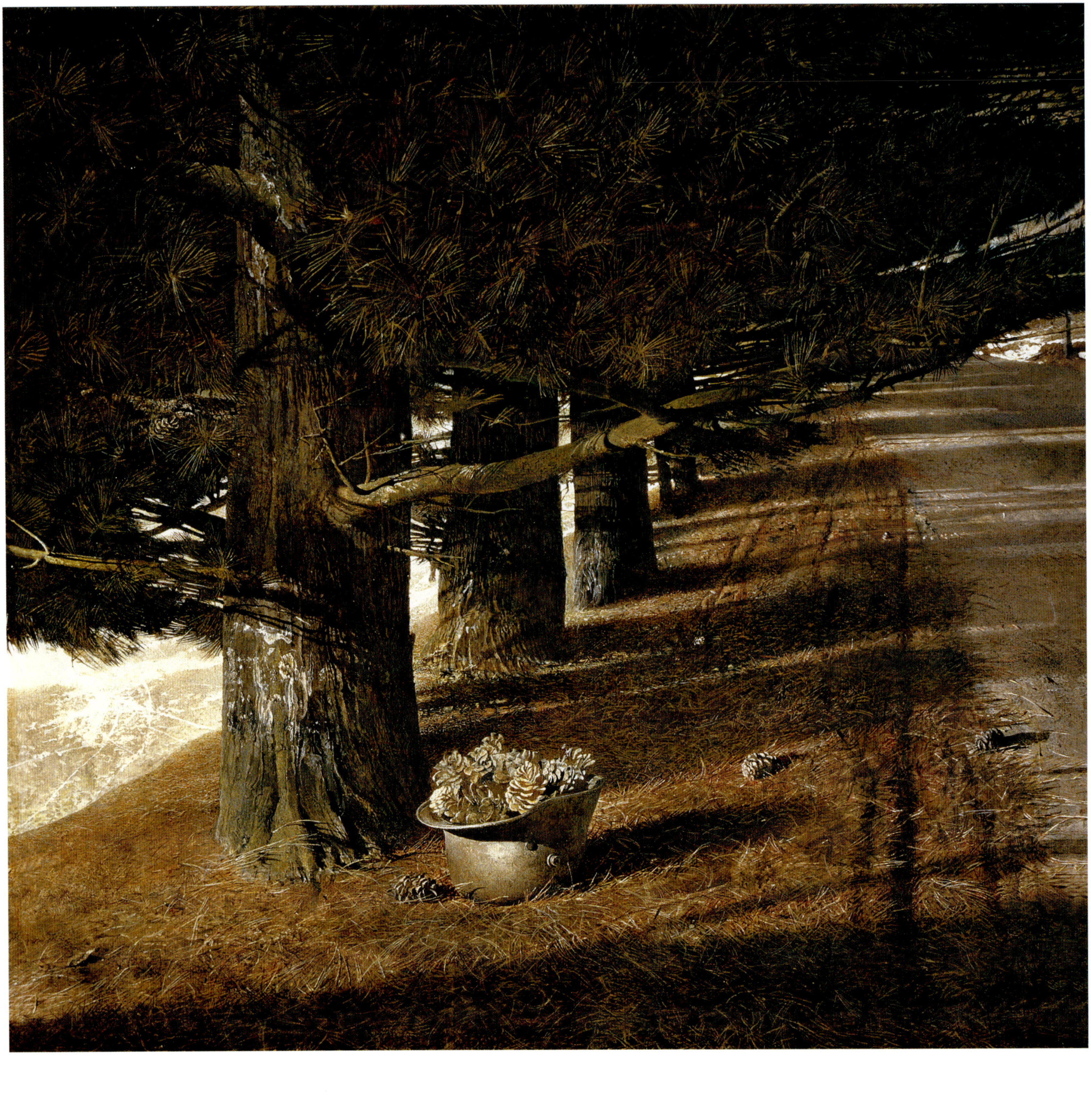

Pine Baron, 1976. Egg tempera on panel, 31 ⅜ × 33 ¼ inches

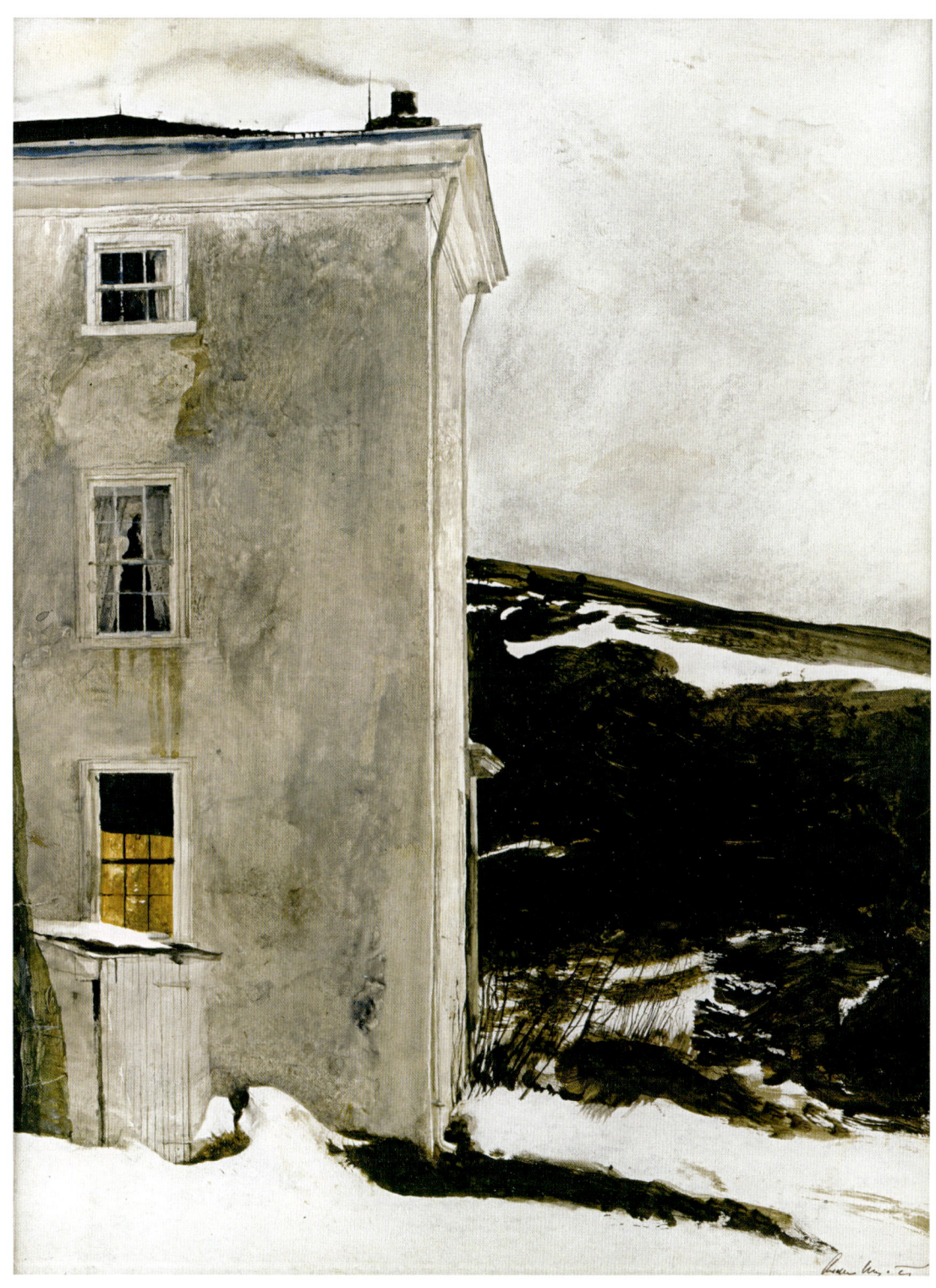

Dusk, 1978. Watercolor on paper, 23 ⅞ × 17 ⅞ inches

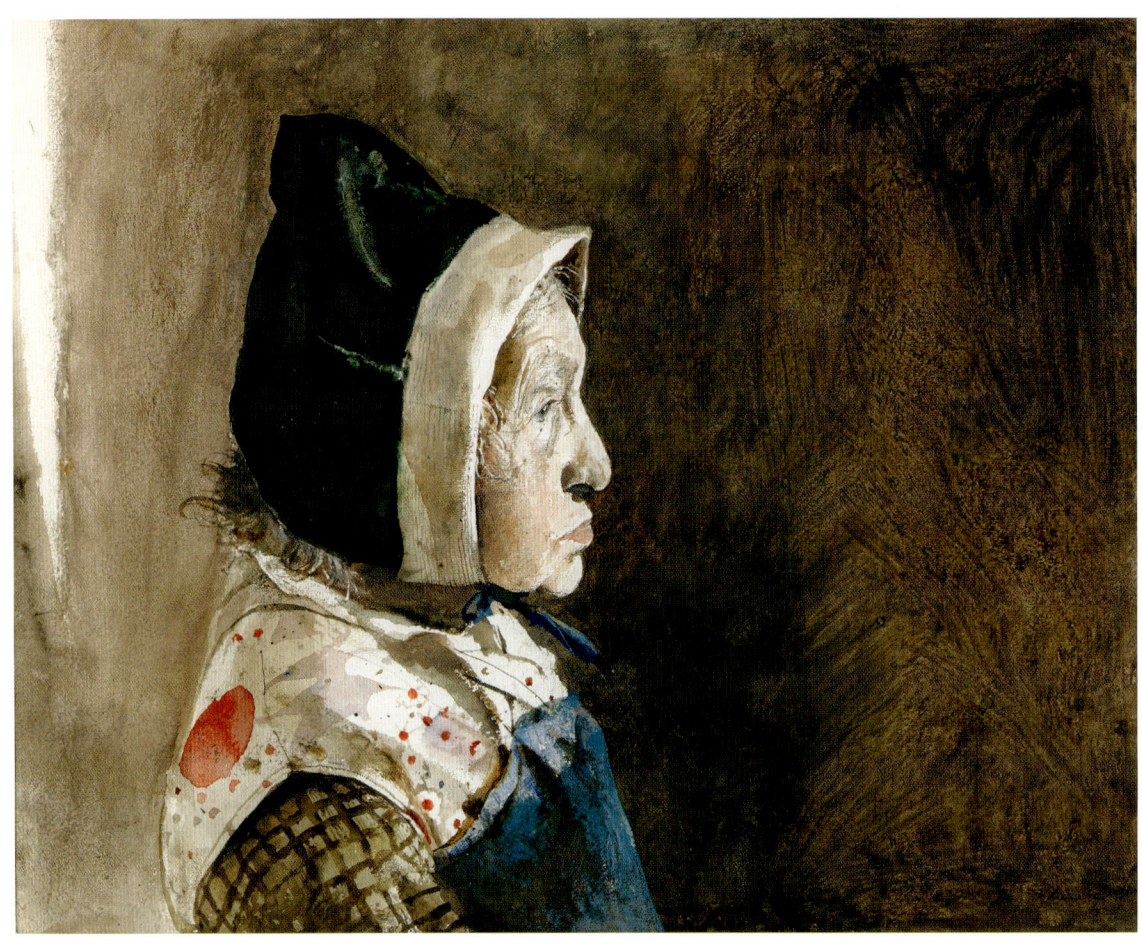

Night Cap, 1978. Watercolor on paper, 18 ¾ × 23 ¾ inches

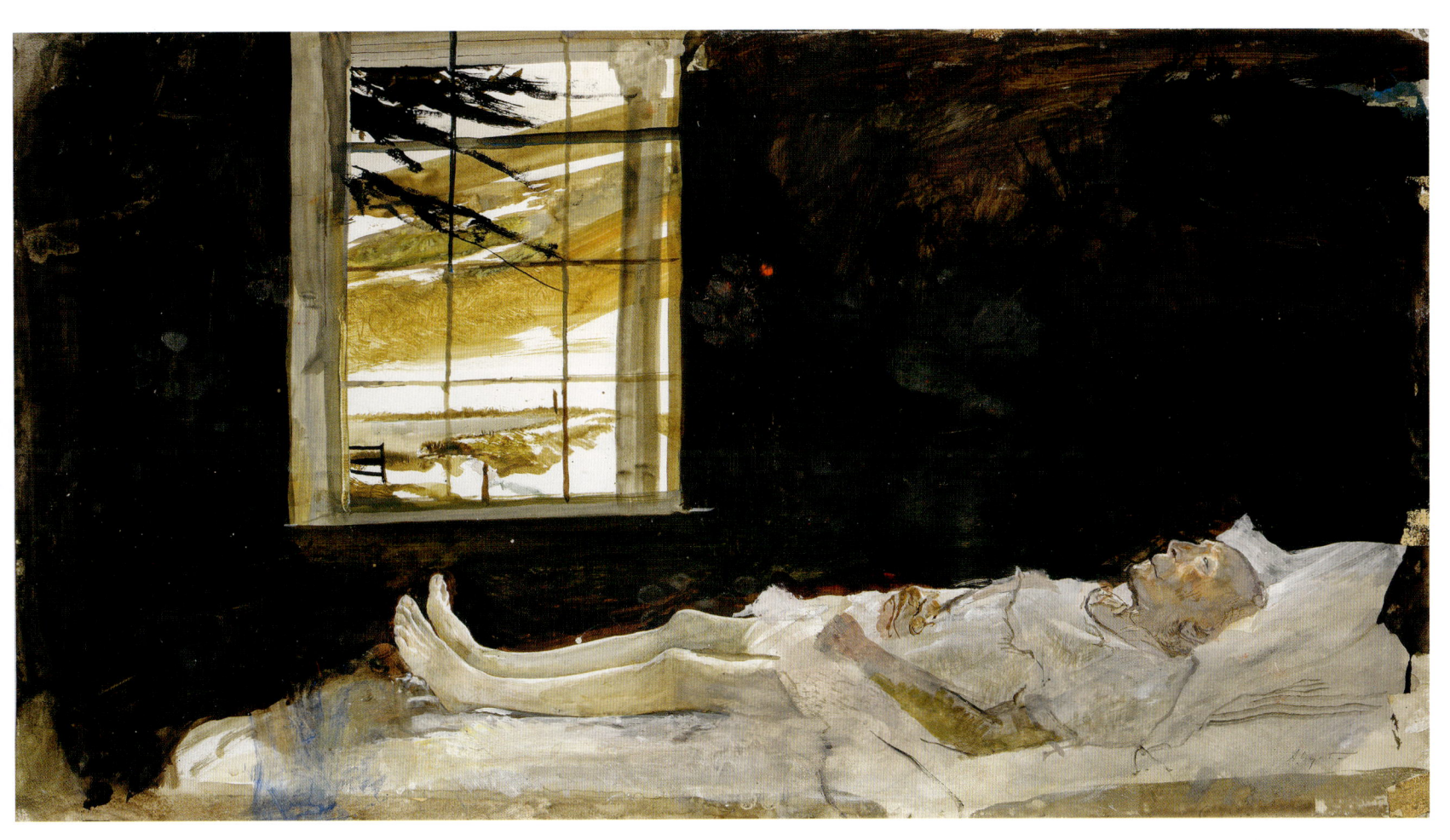

Spring Study, 1978. Watercolor on paper, 21 × 39 ½ inches

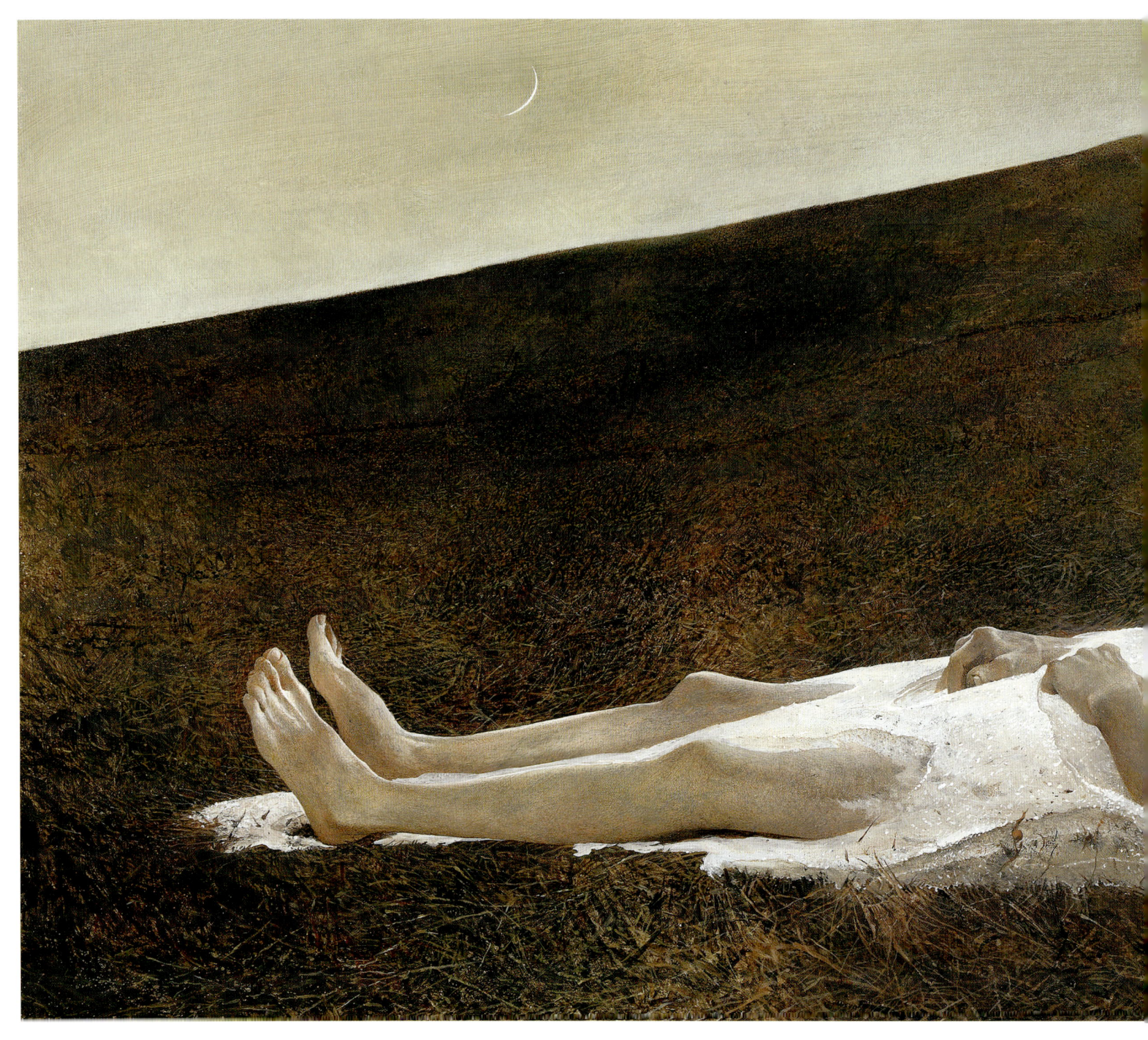

Spring, 1978. Egg tempera on panel, 24 × 48 inches

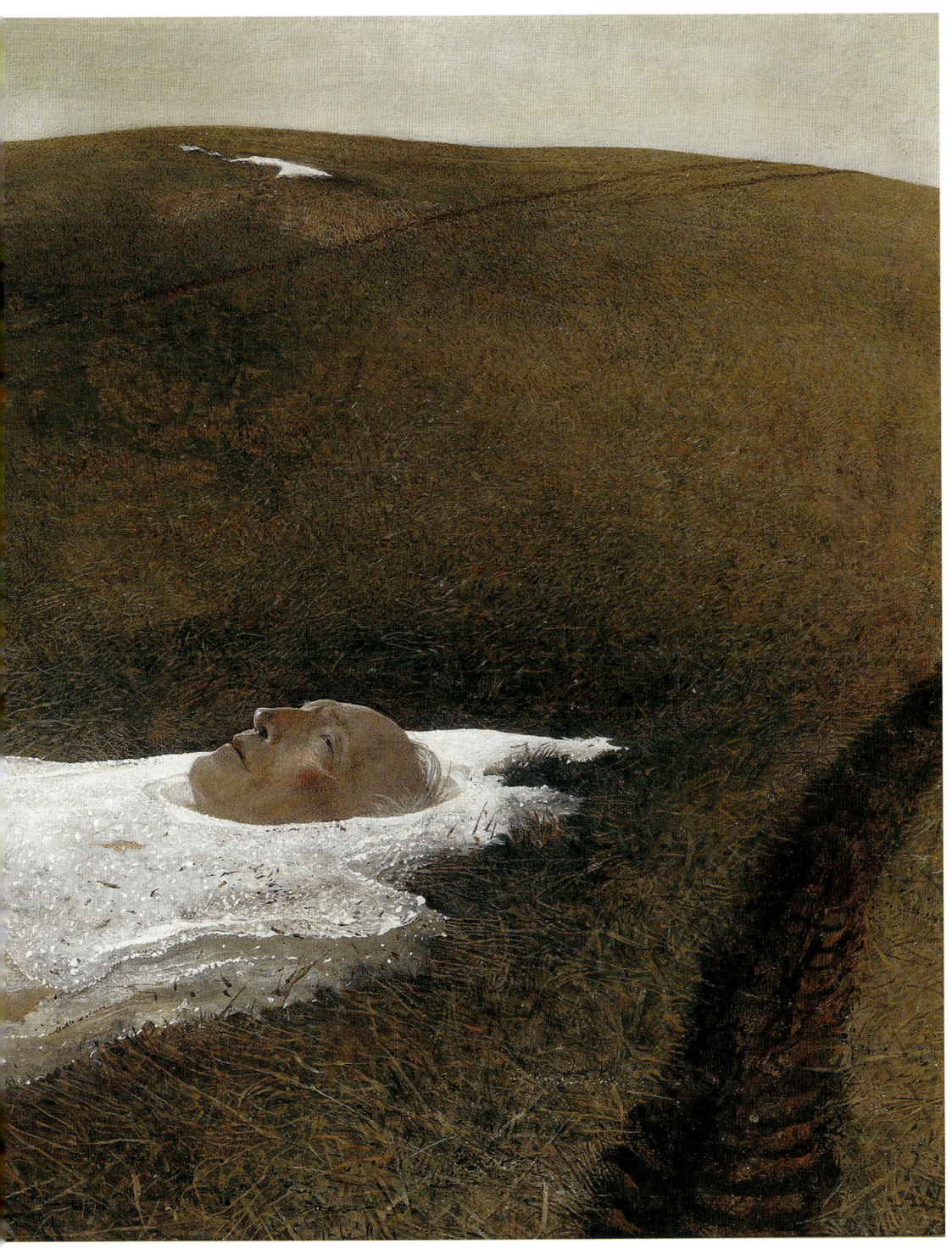

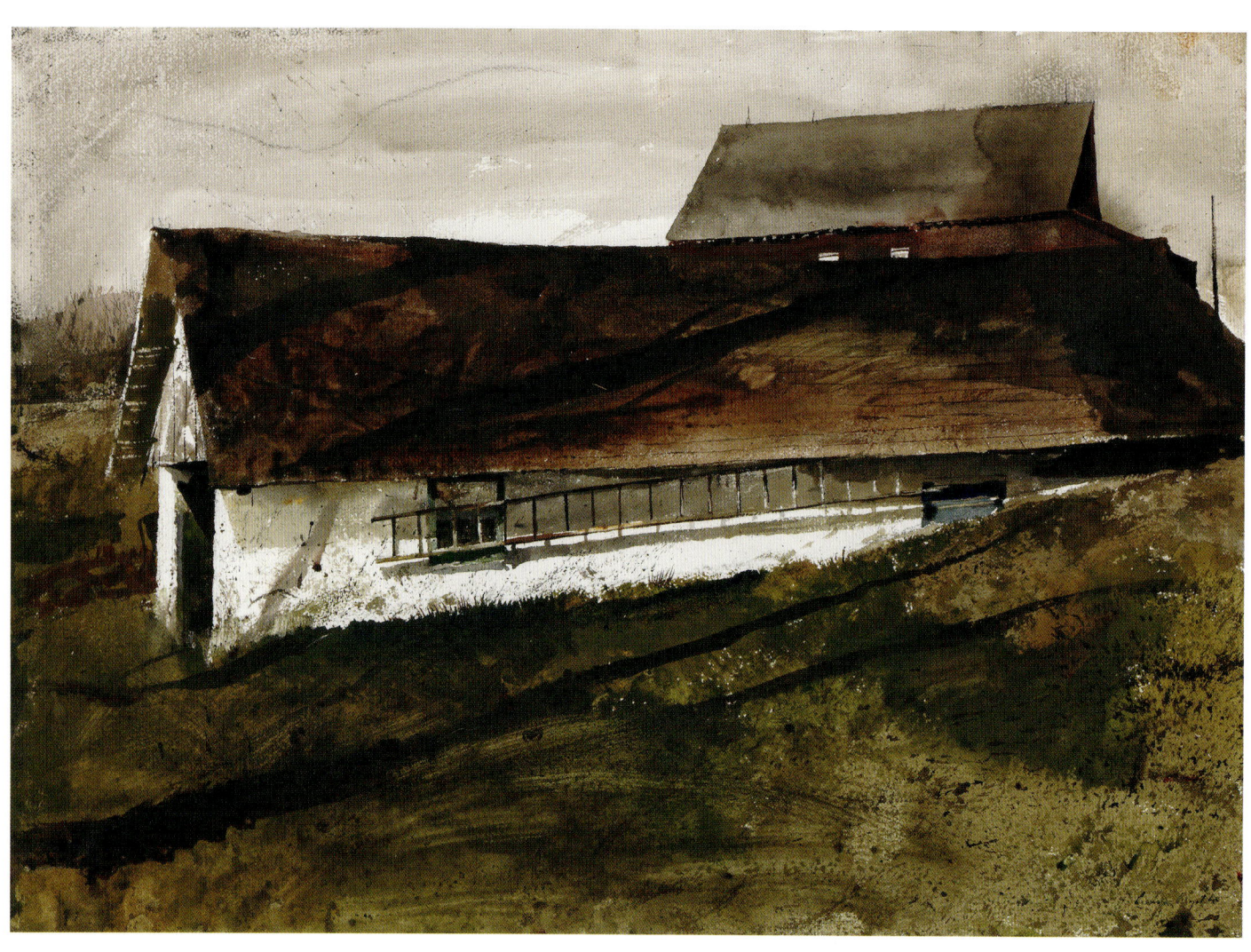

Roof Ladder, 1979. Watercolor on paper, 21 ½ × 29 ¾ inches

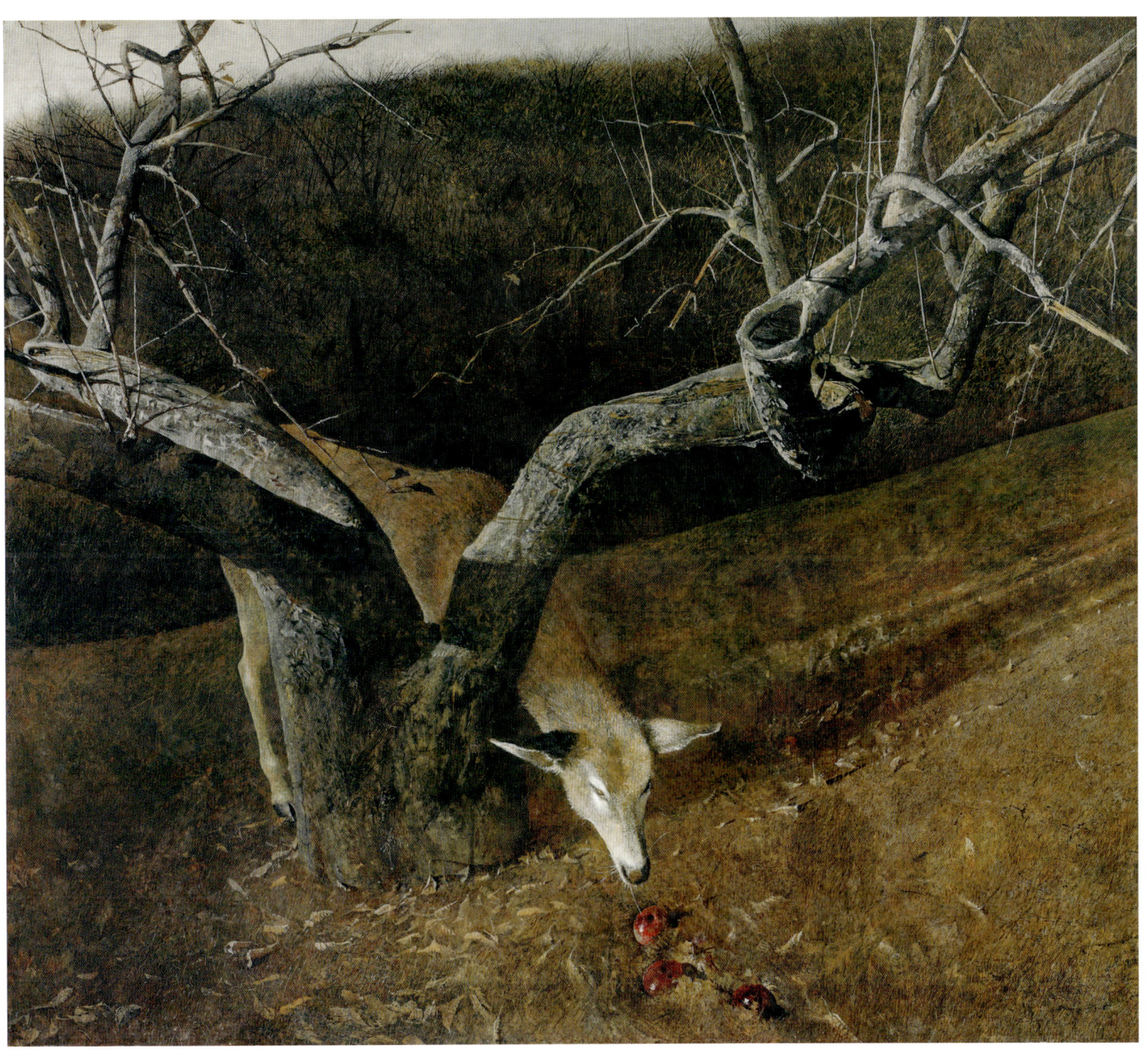

Jacklight, 1980. Egg tempera on panel, 43 ½ × 49 ¾ inches

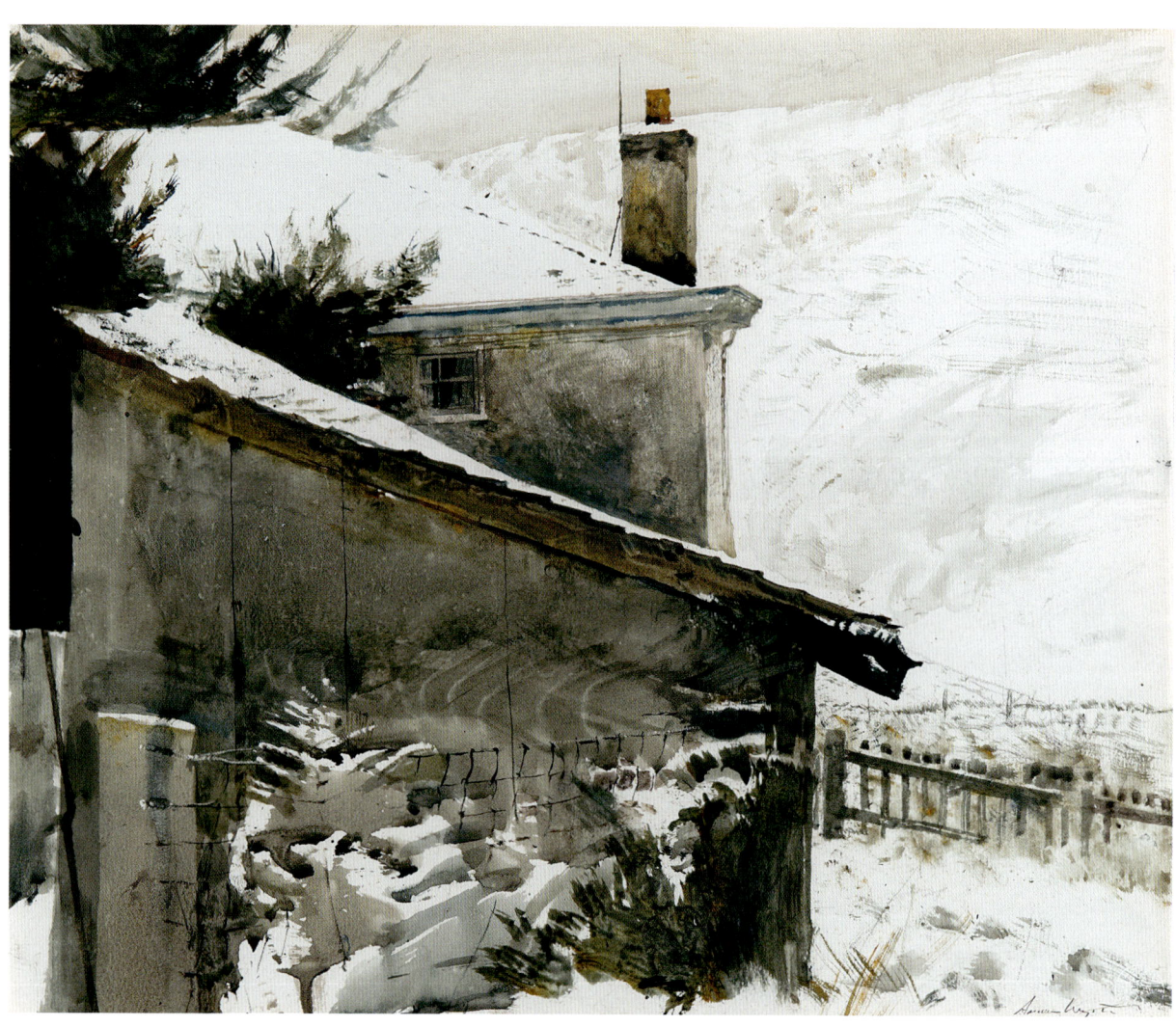

Snow Fence, 1980. Watercolor on paper, 16 × 19 inches

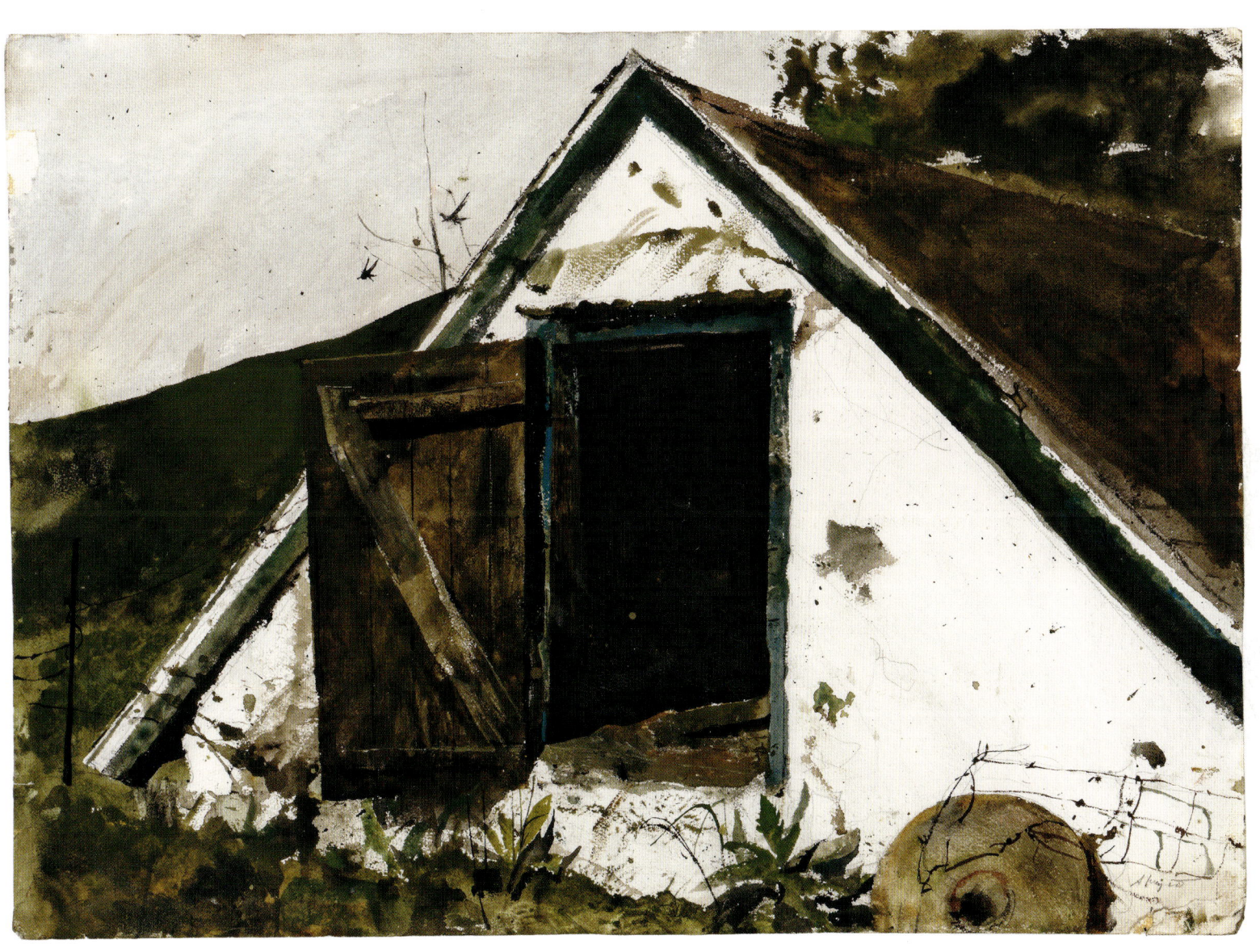

Grindstone – 1st version, 1981. Watercolor on paper, 21 ¾ × 29 ⅞ inches

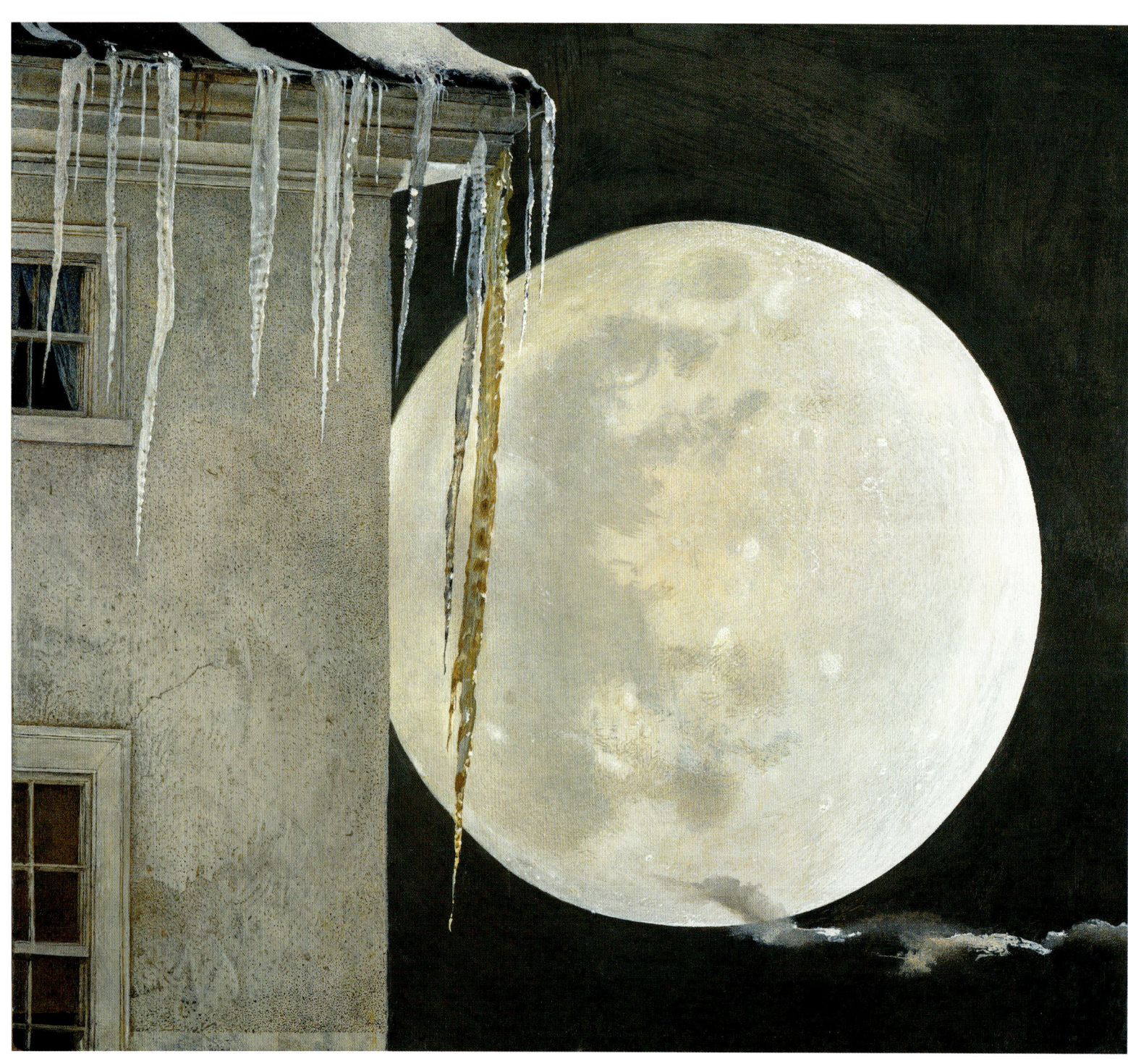

Moon Madness, 1982. Egg tempera on panel, 18 × 20 inches

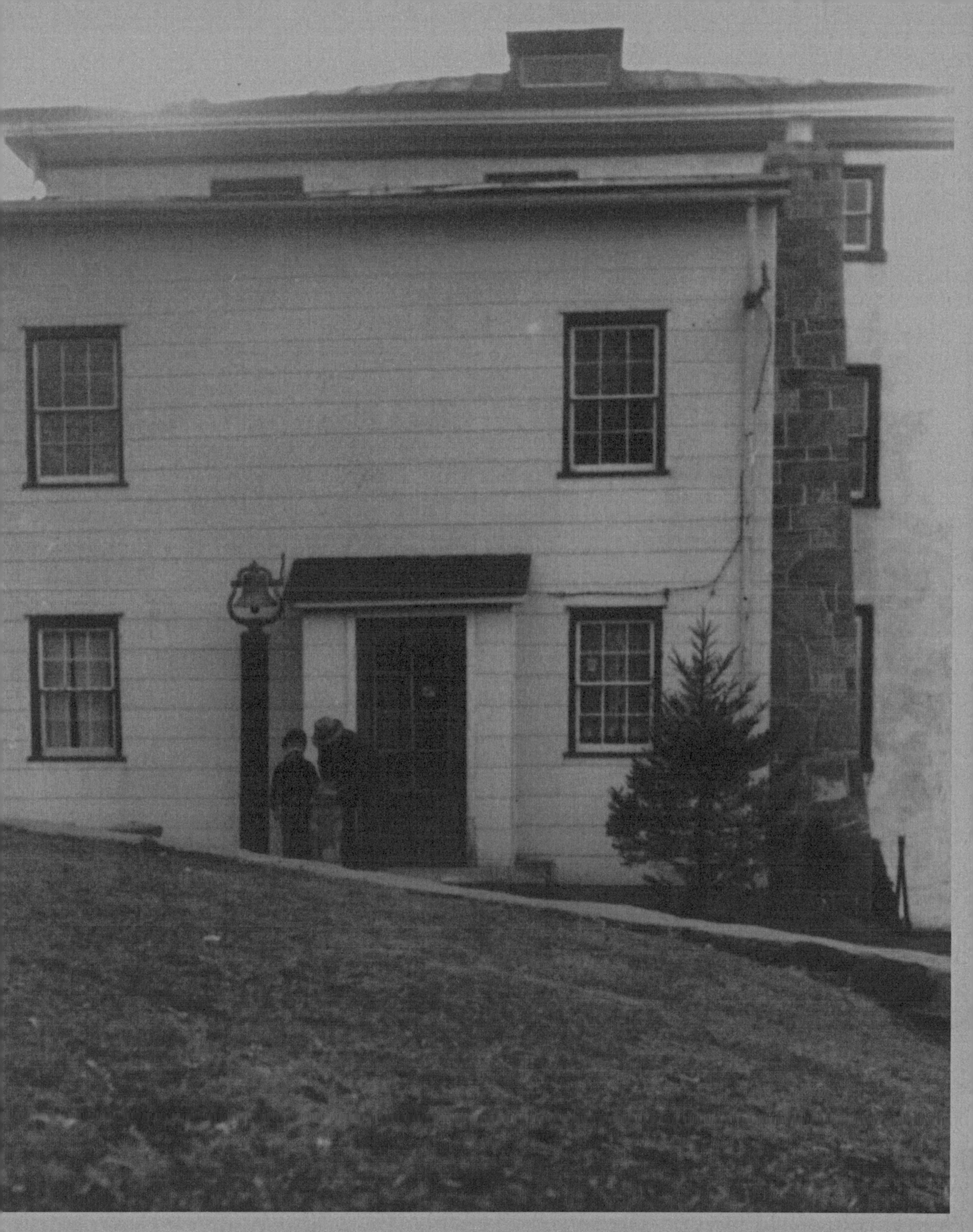

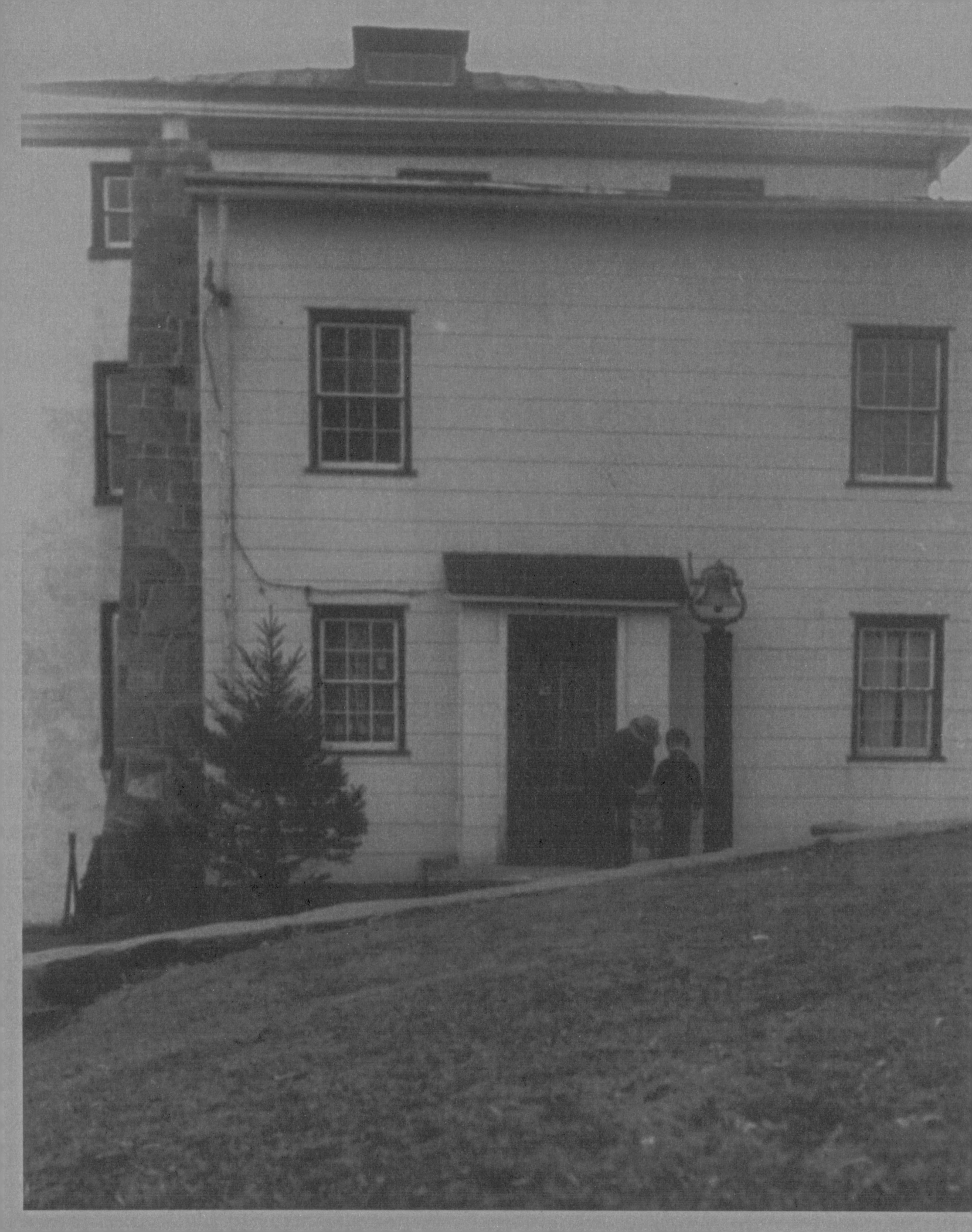

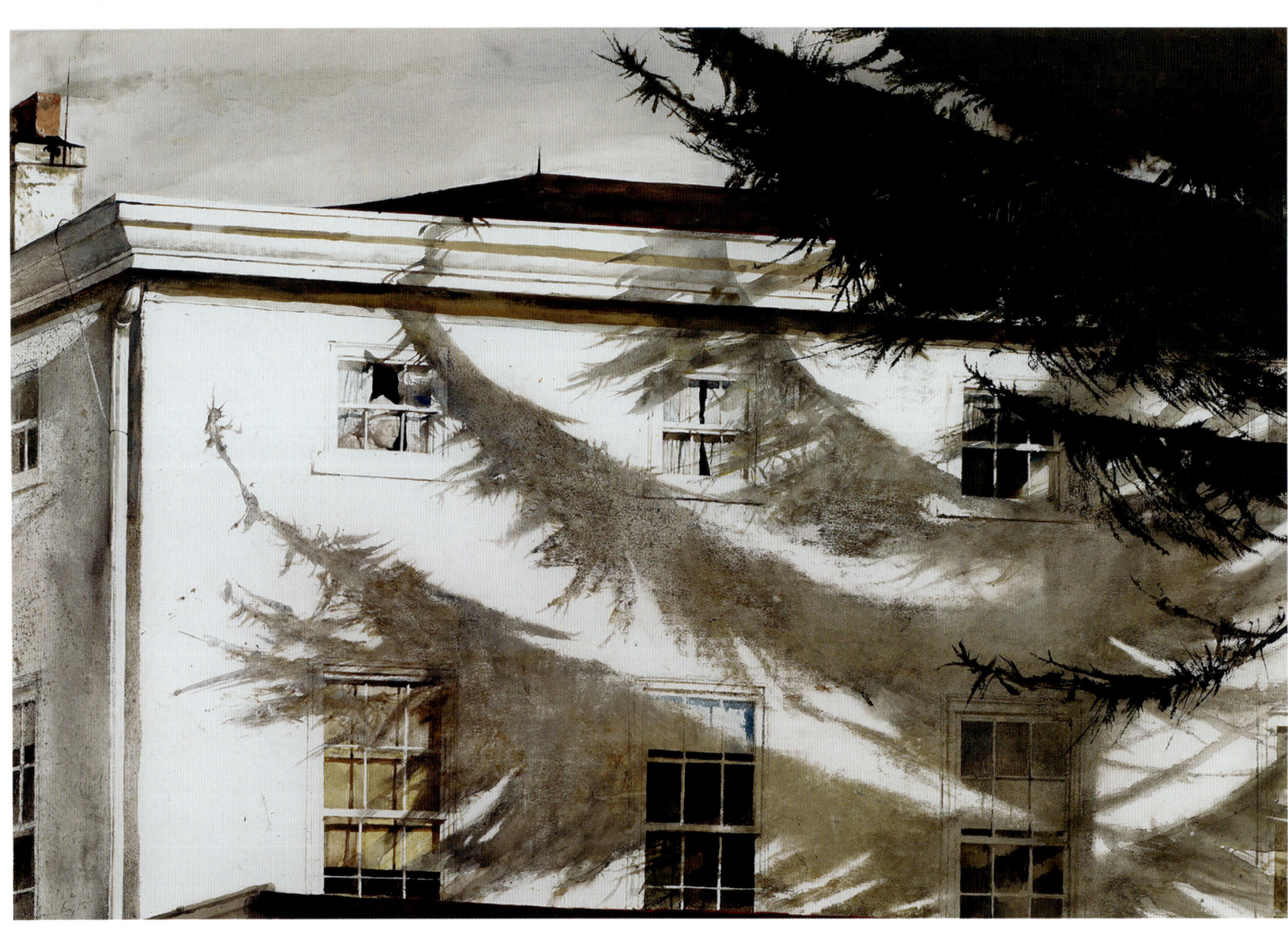

Tree House, 1982. Watercolor on paper, 27 × 40 inches

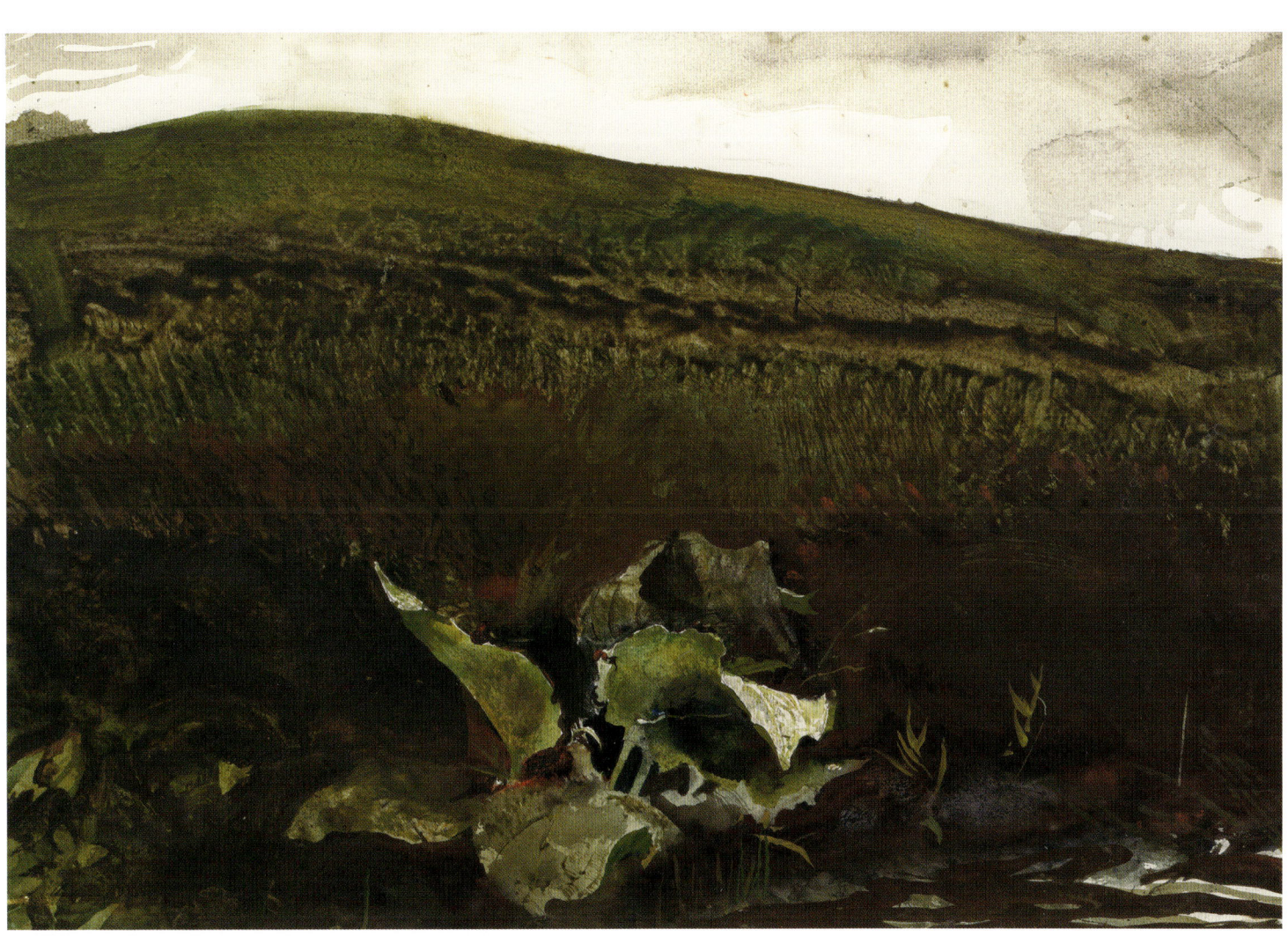

Spring on Kuerners Hill, 1984. Watercolor on paper, 18 ¾ × 26 ⅝ inches

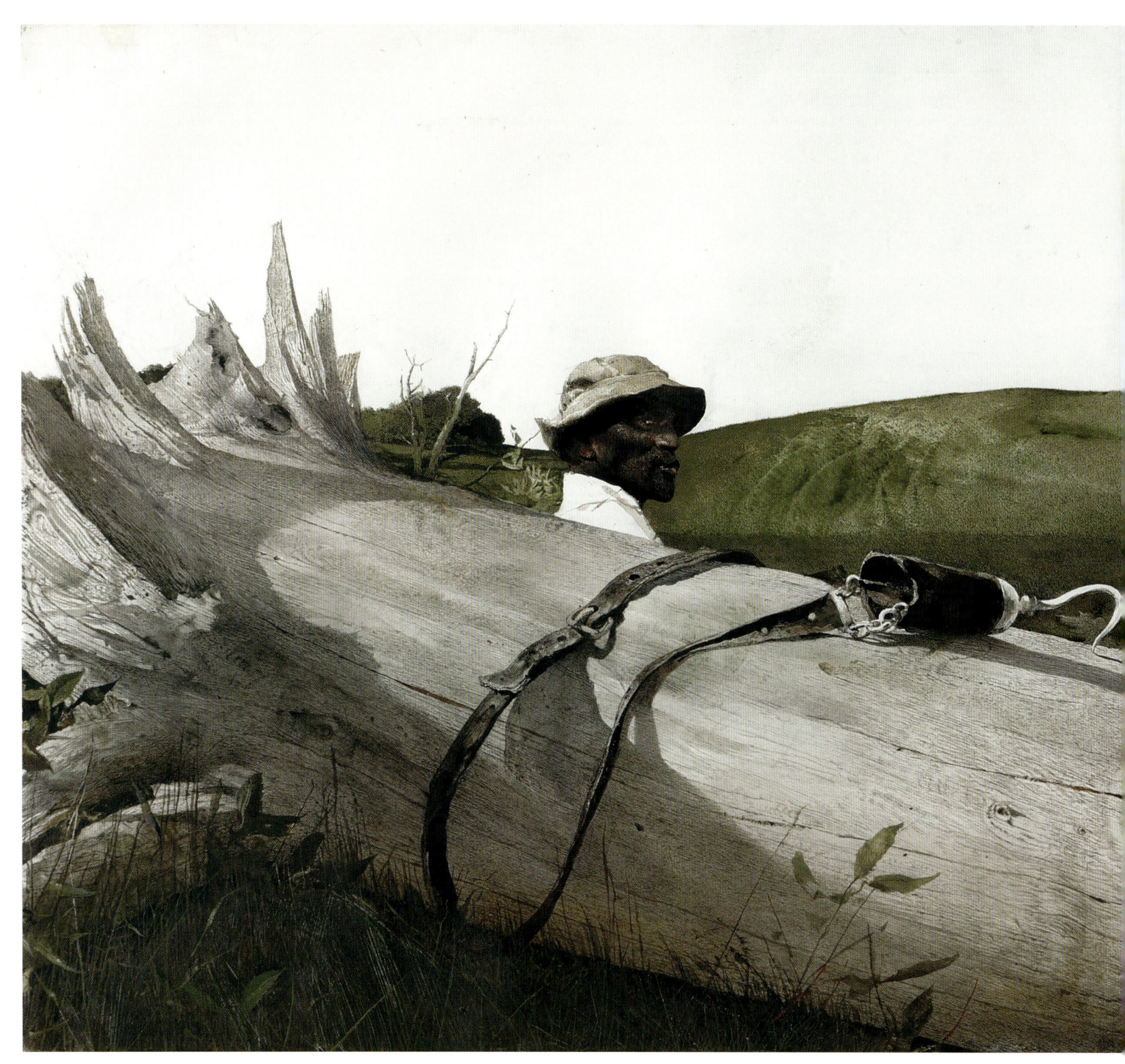

Field Hand, 1985. Drybrush watercolor on paper, 21 ¾ × 39 ⅞ inches

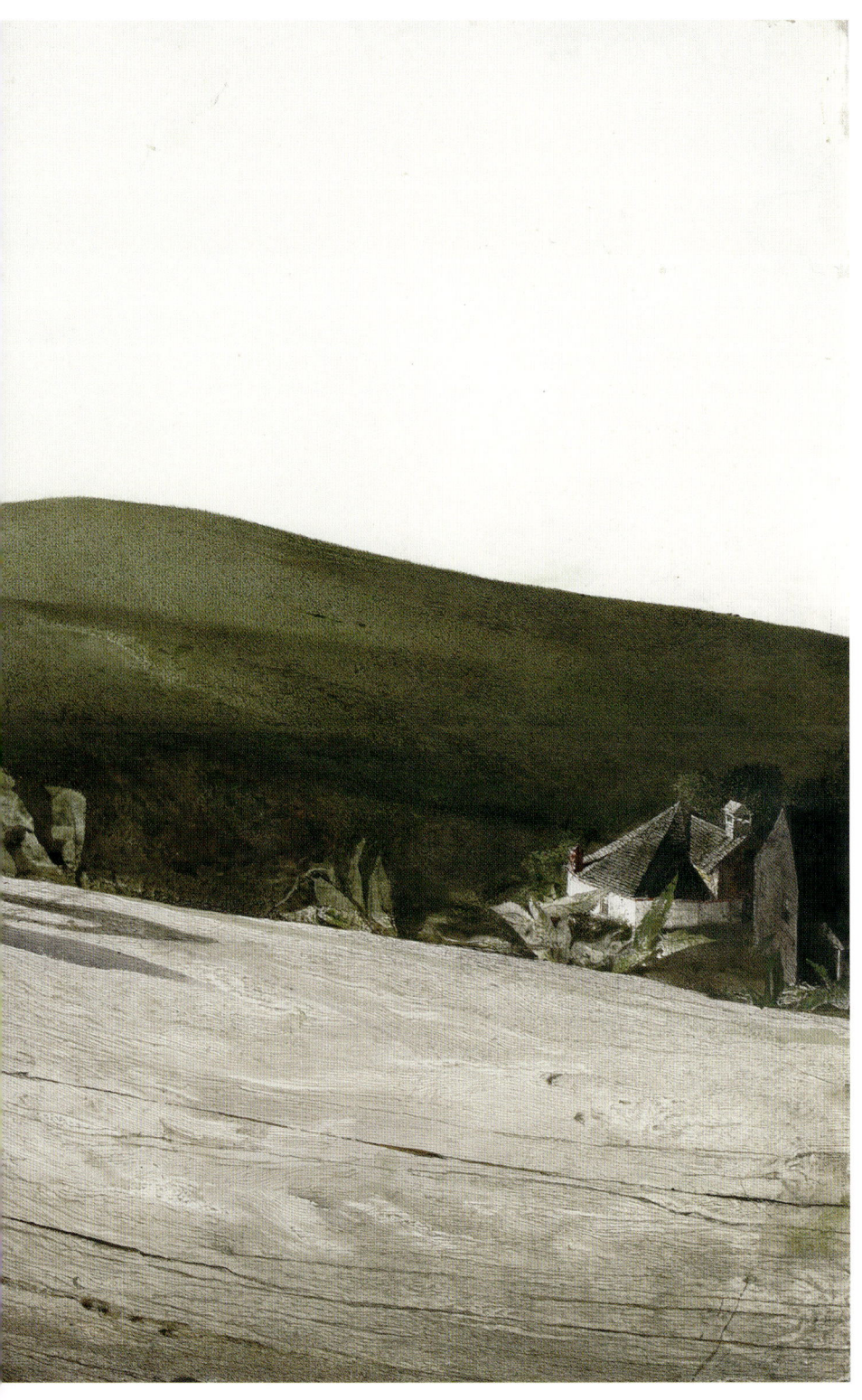

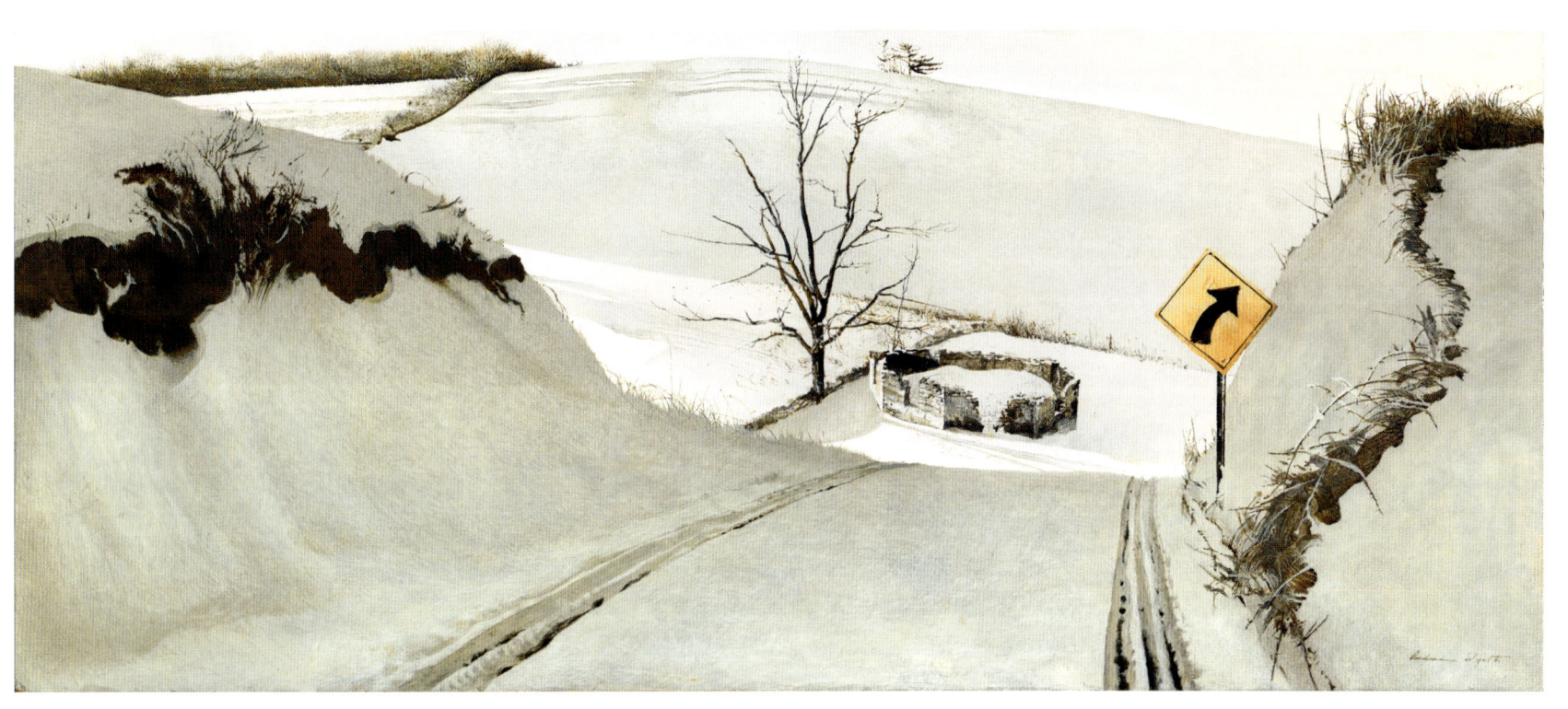

Ring Road, 1985. Egg tempera on panel, 16 ⅞ × 39 ¼ inches

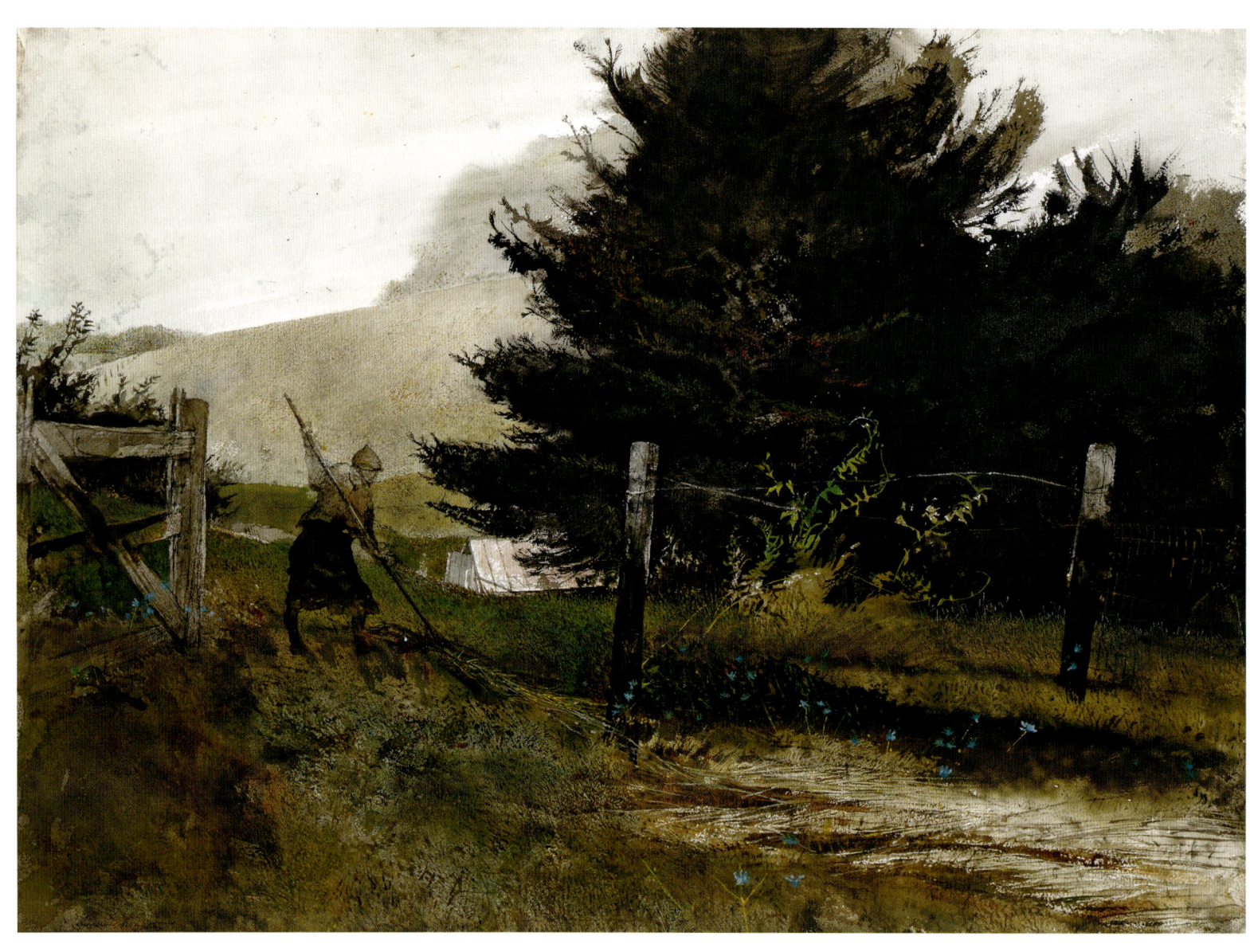

Cornflowers, 1986. Watercolor on paper, 21 ¾ × 29 ⅞ inches

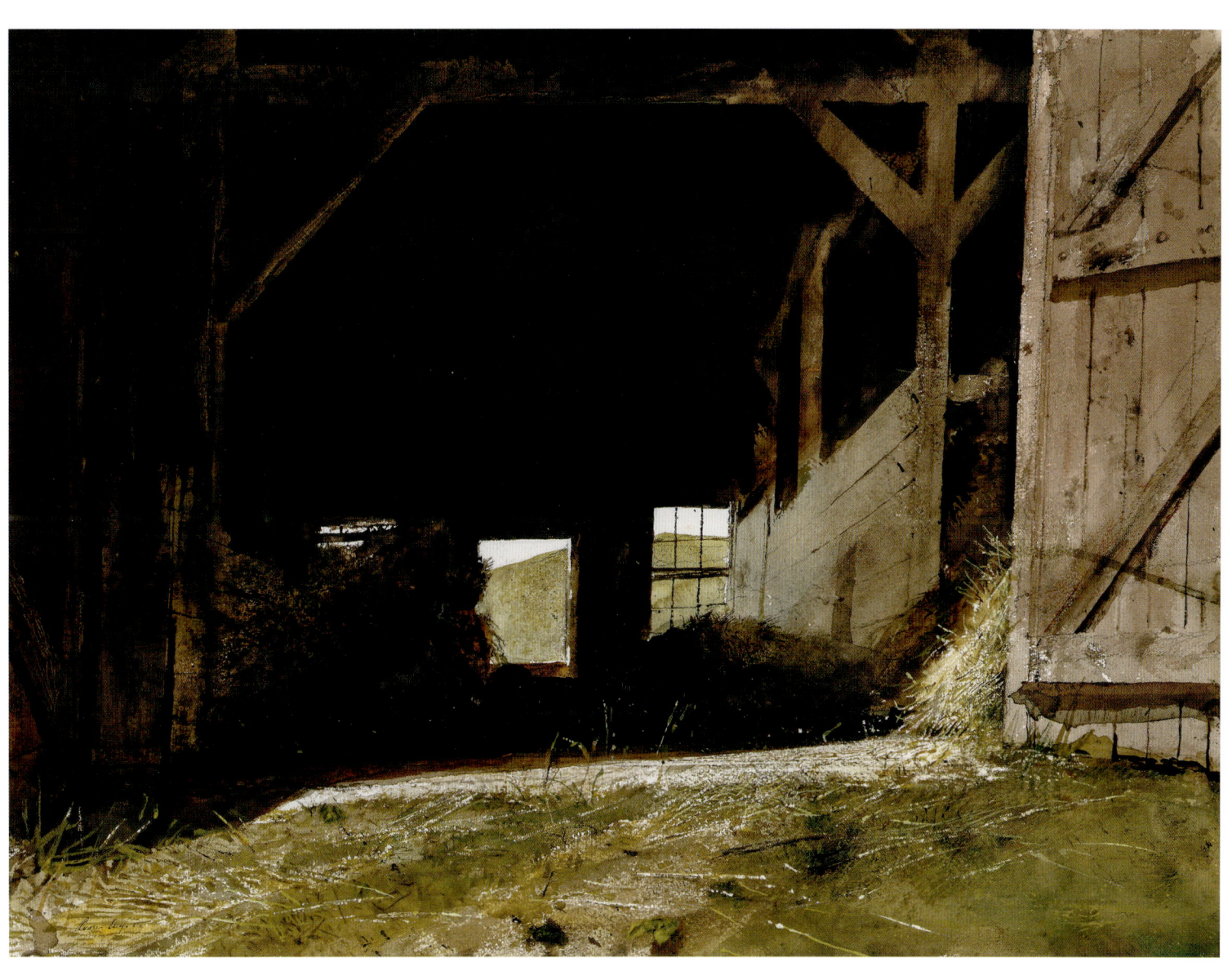

Haymow, 1988. Watercolor on paper, 21 × 28 ⅜ inches

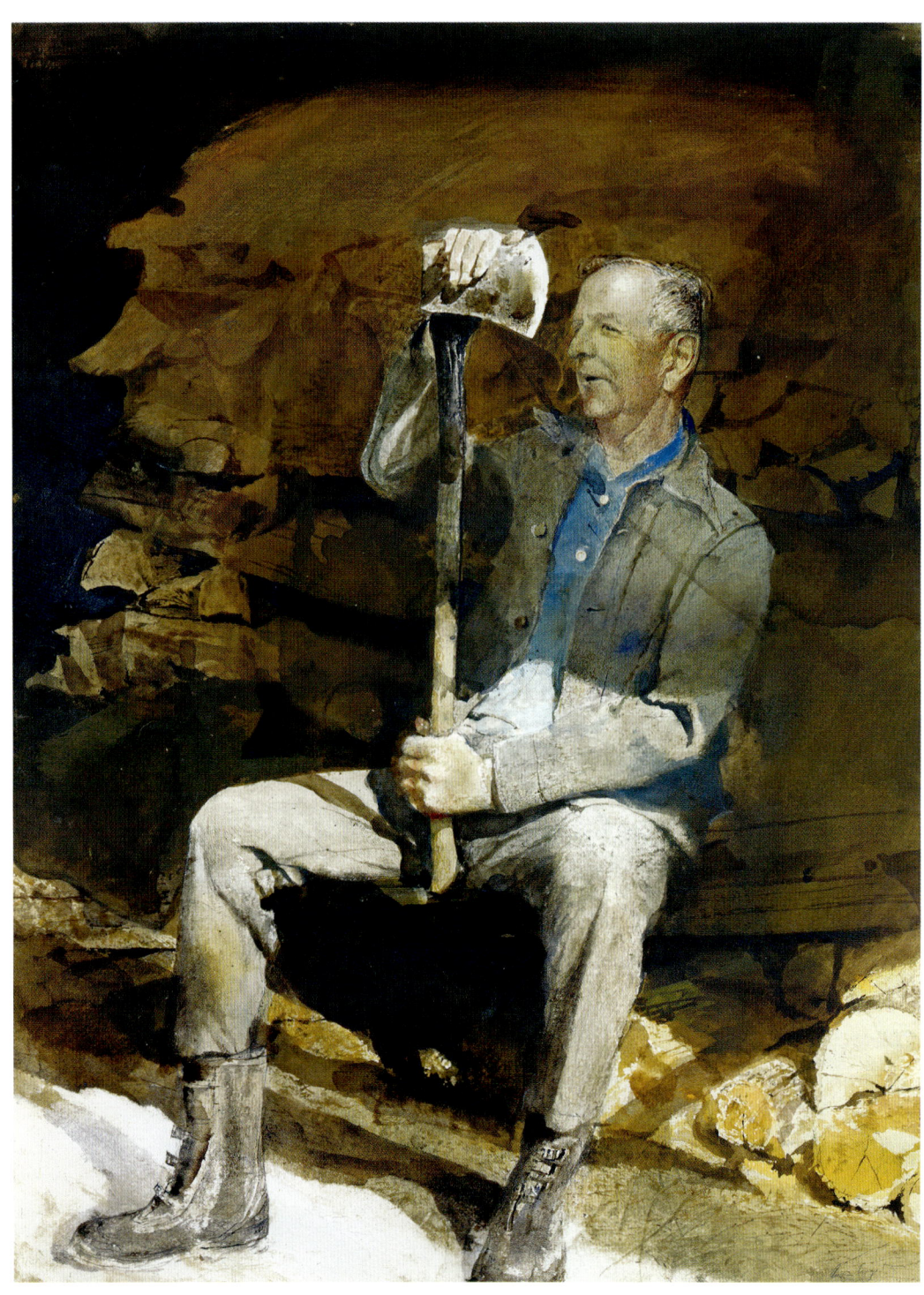

Razor Sharp, 1988. Watercolor on paper, 29 ¼ × 21 ¾ inches

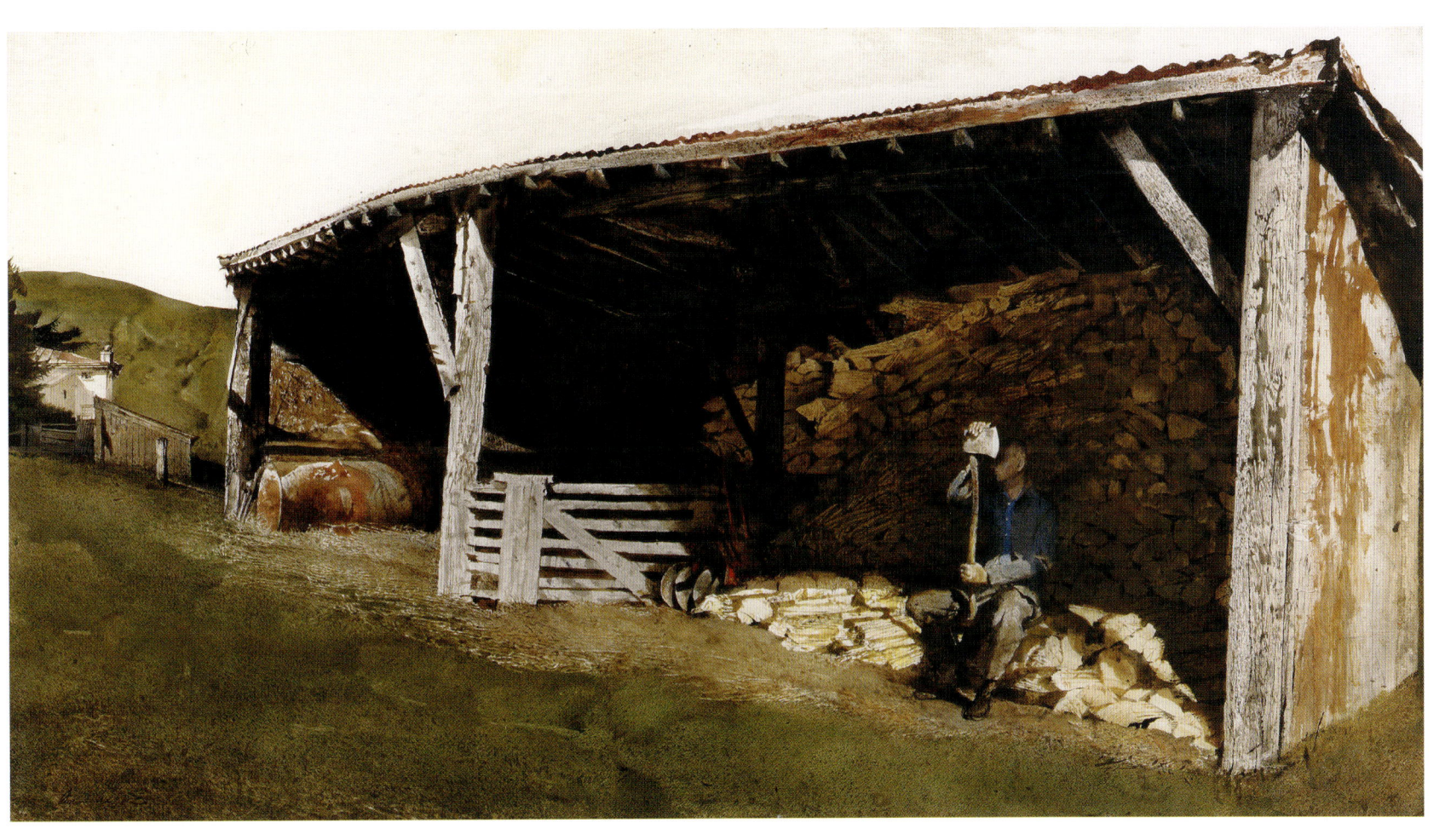

Working Farm, 1988. Drybrush watercolor on paper, 21 ⅞ × 39 ⅞ inches

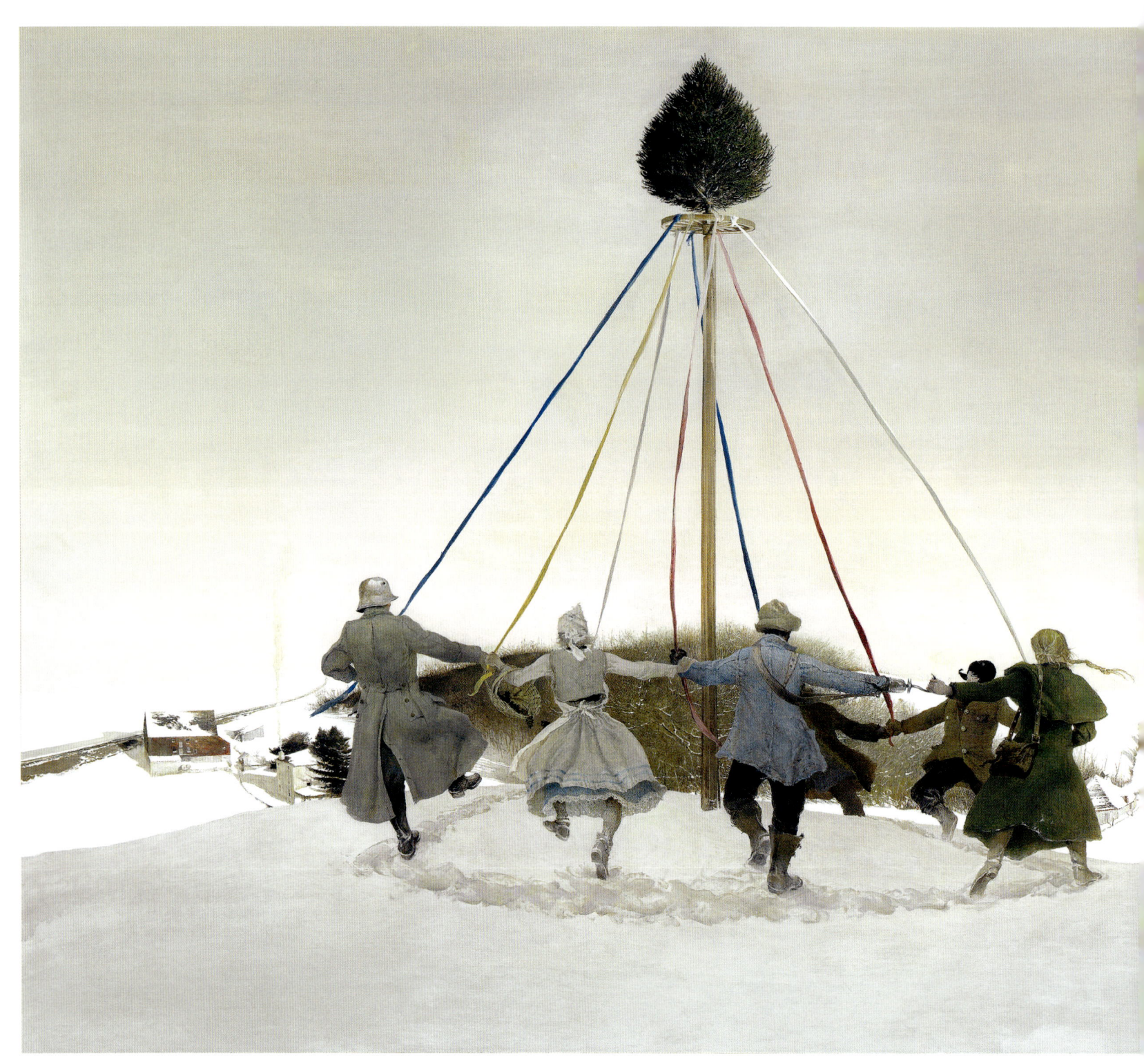

Snow Hill, 1989. Egg tempera on panel, 48 × 72 inches

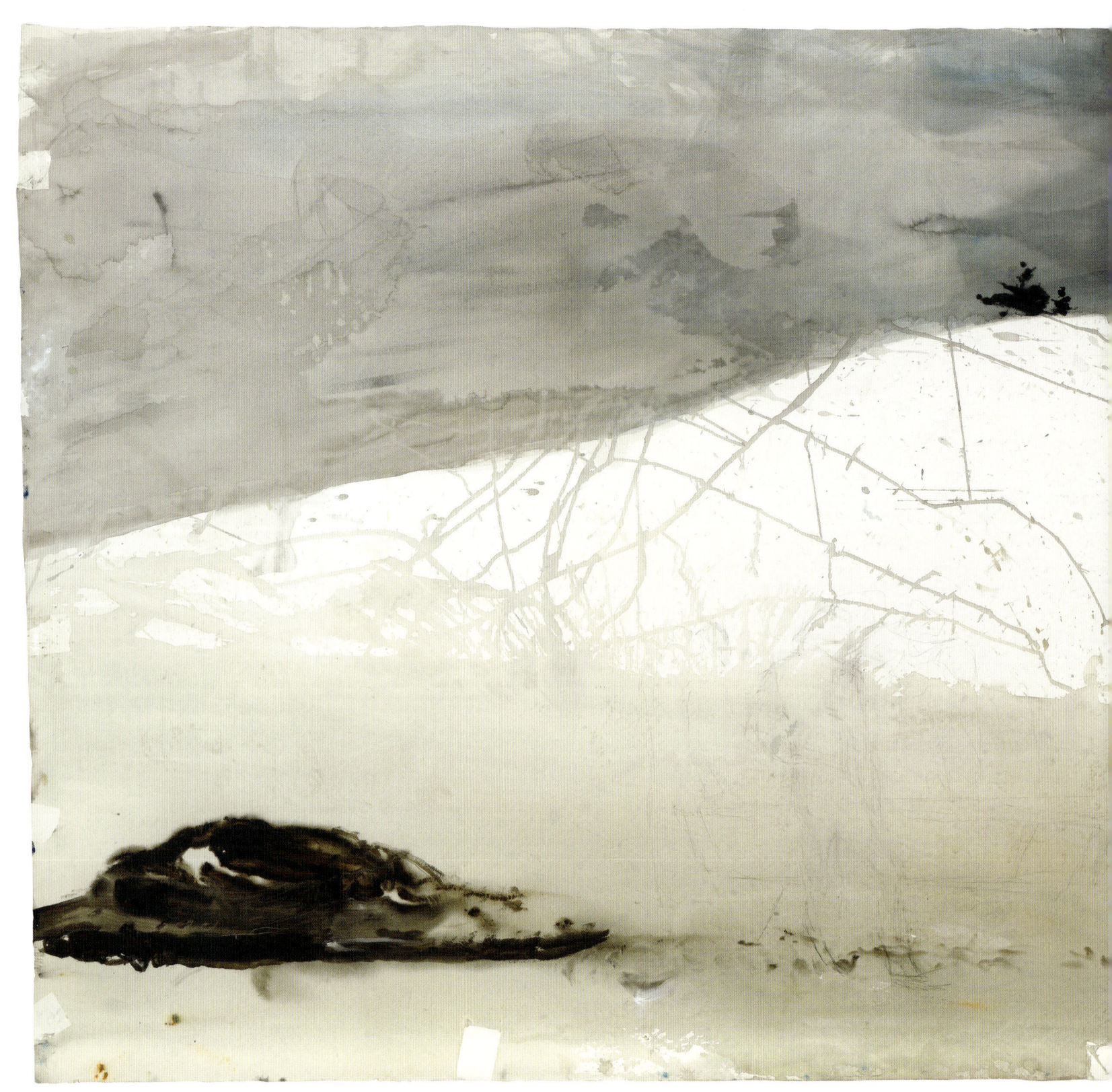

Funeral Group (Kuerner's Hill I), c. 1991. Watercolor on paper, 51 × 70 ¼ inches

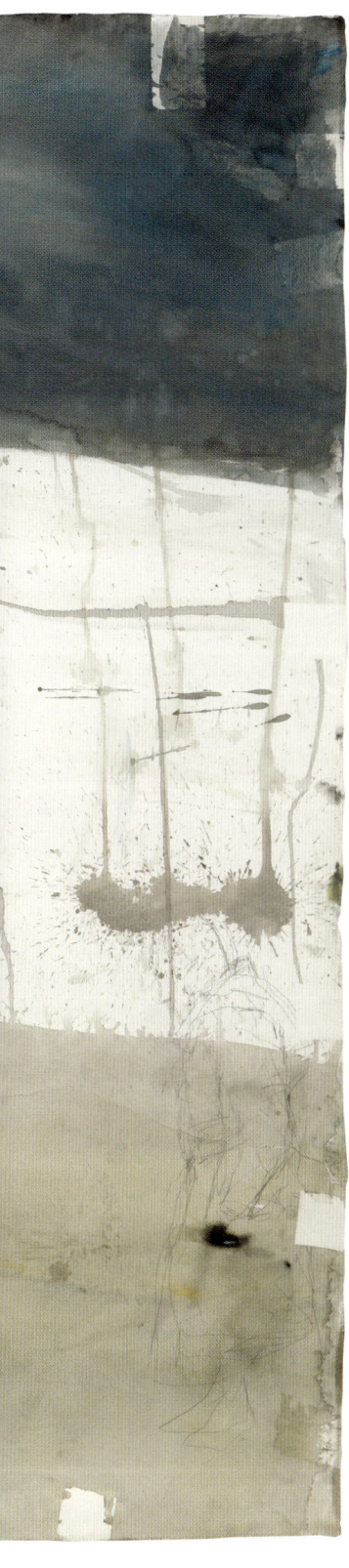

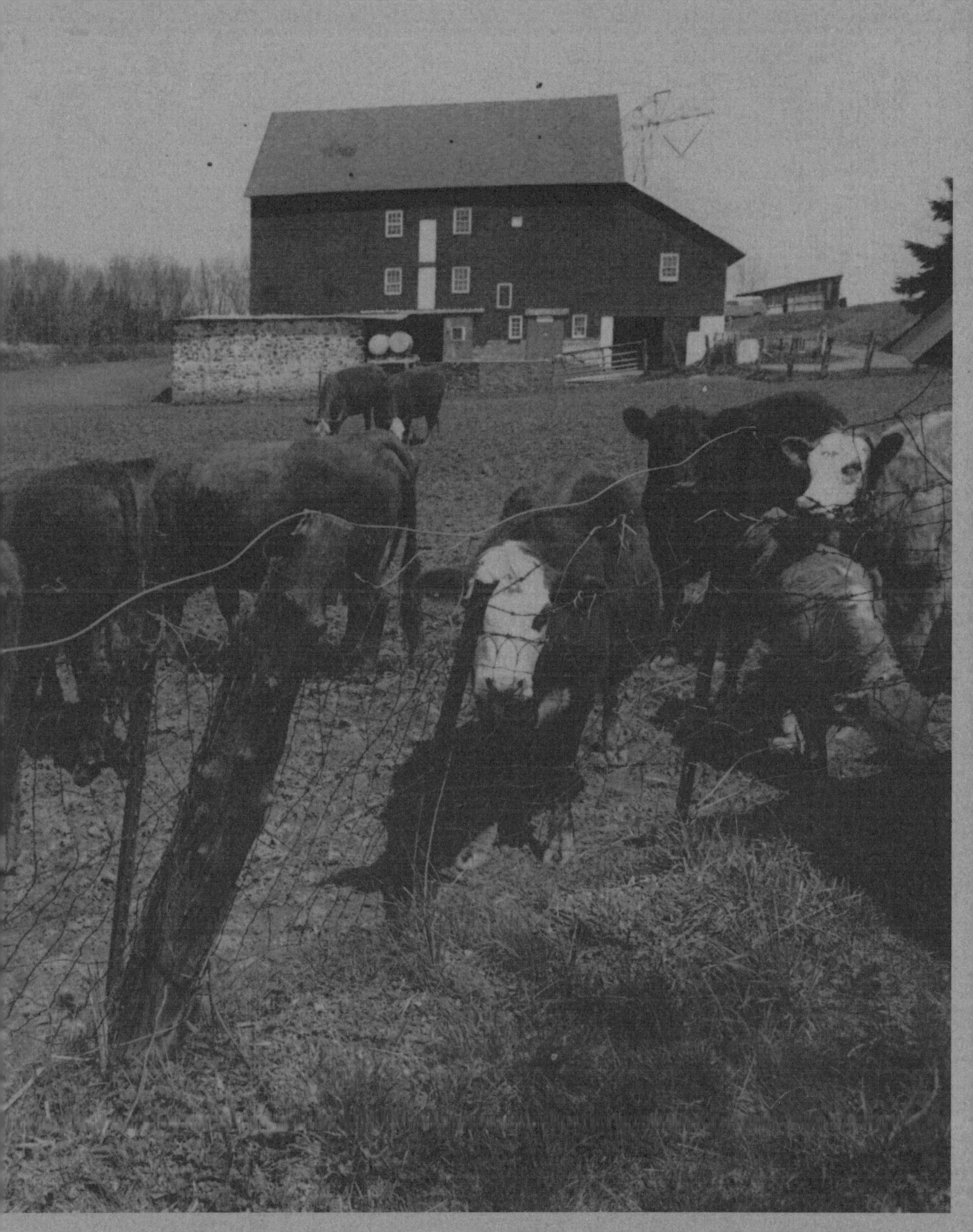

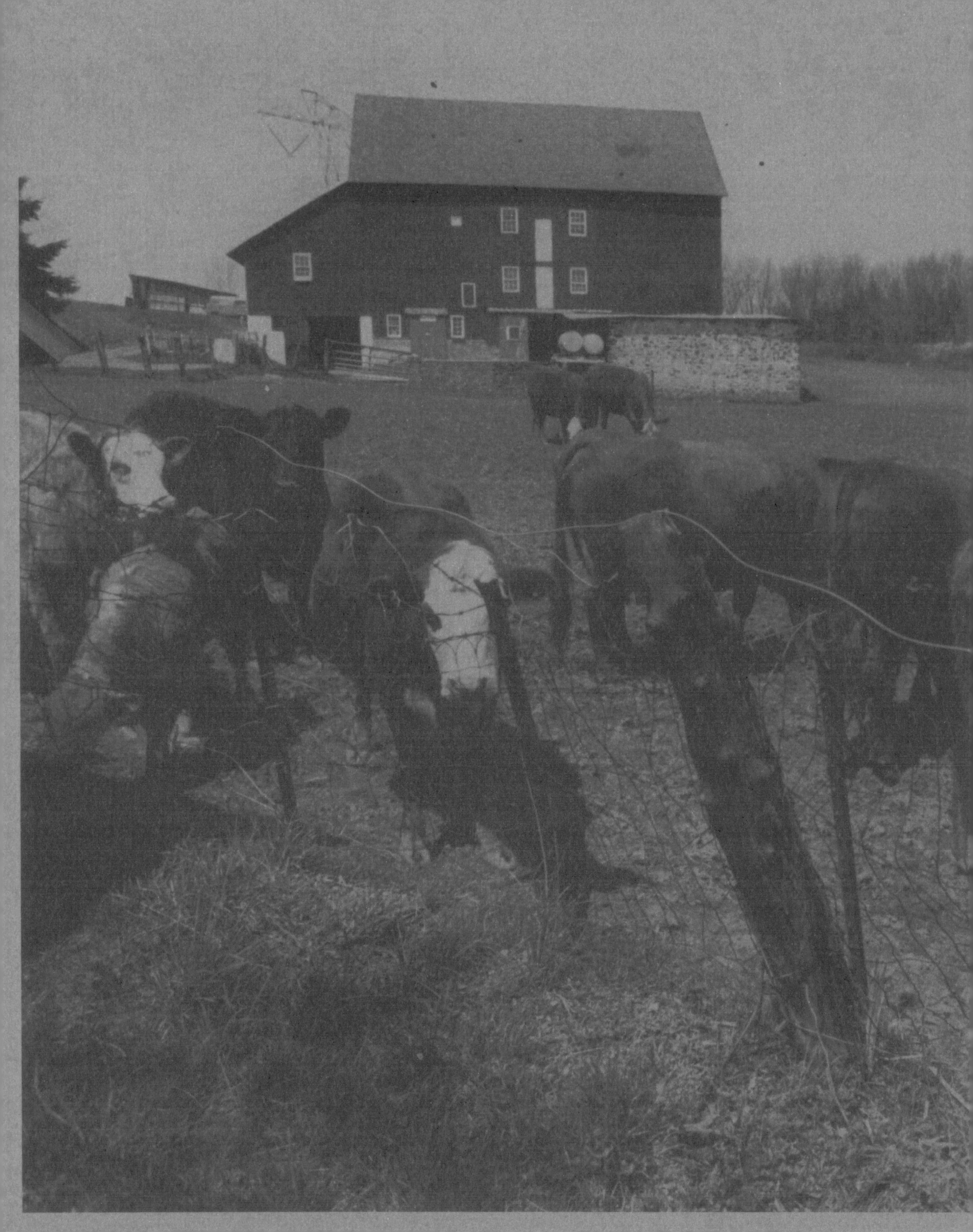

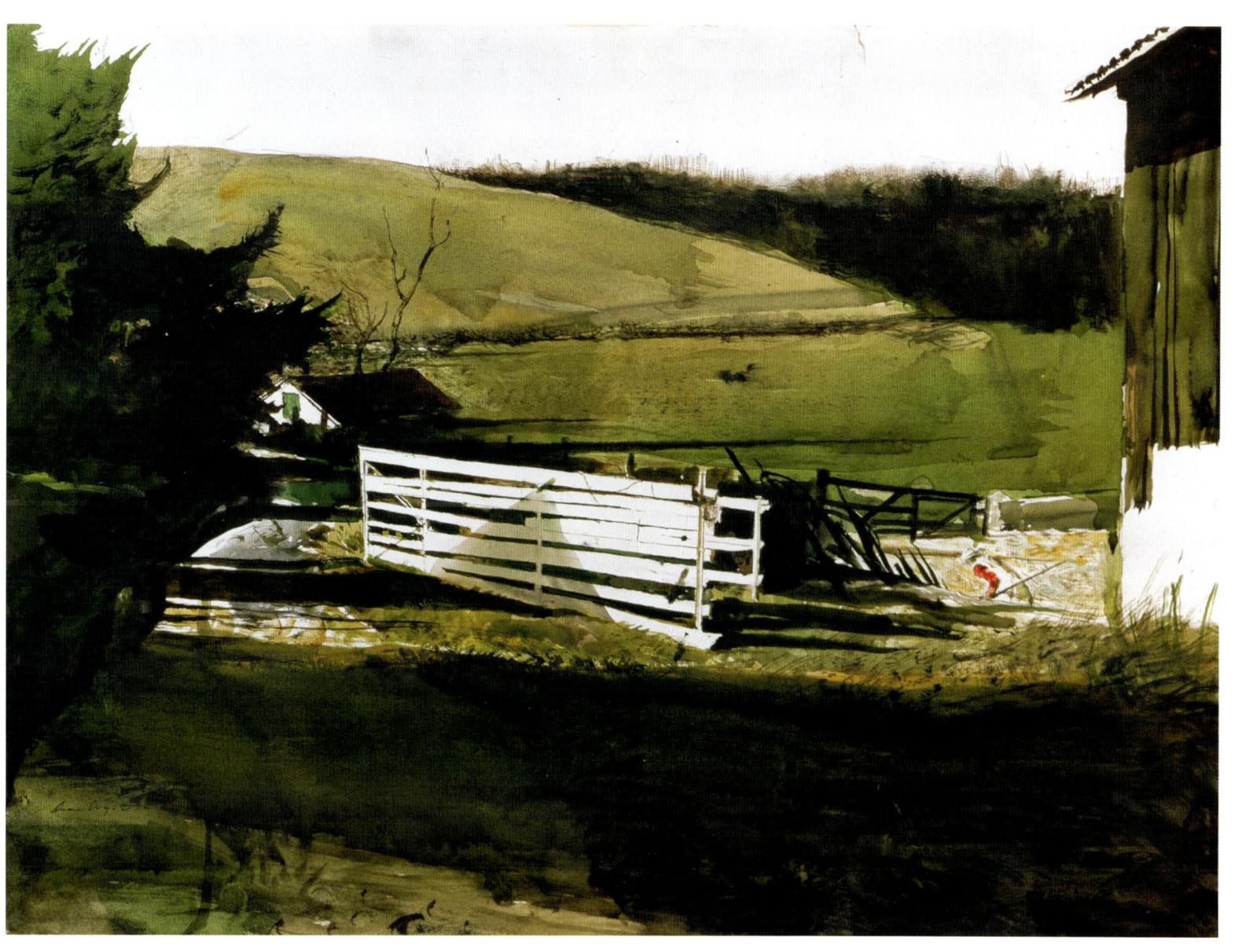

Barnyard, 1991. Watercolor on paper, 18 ⅞ × 25 ⅞ inches

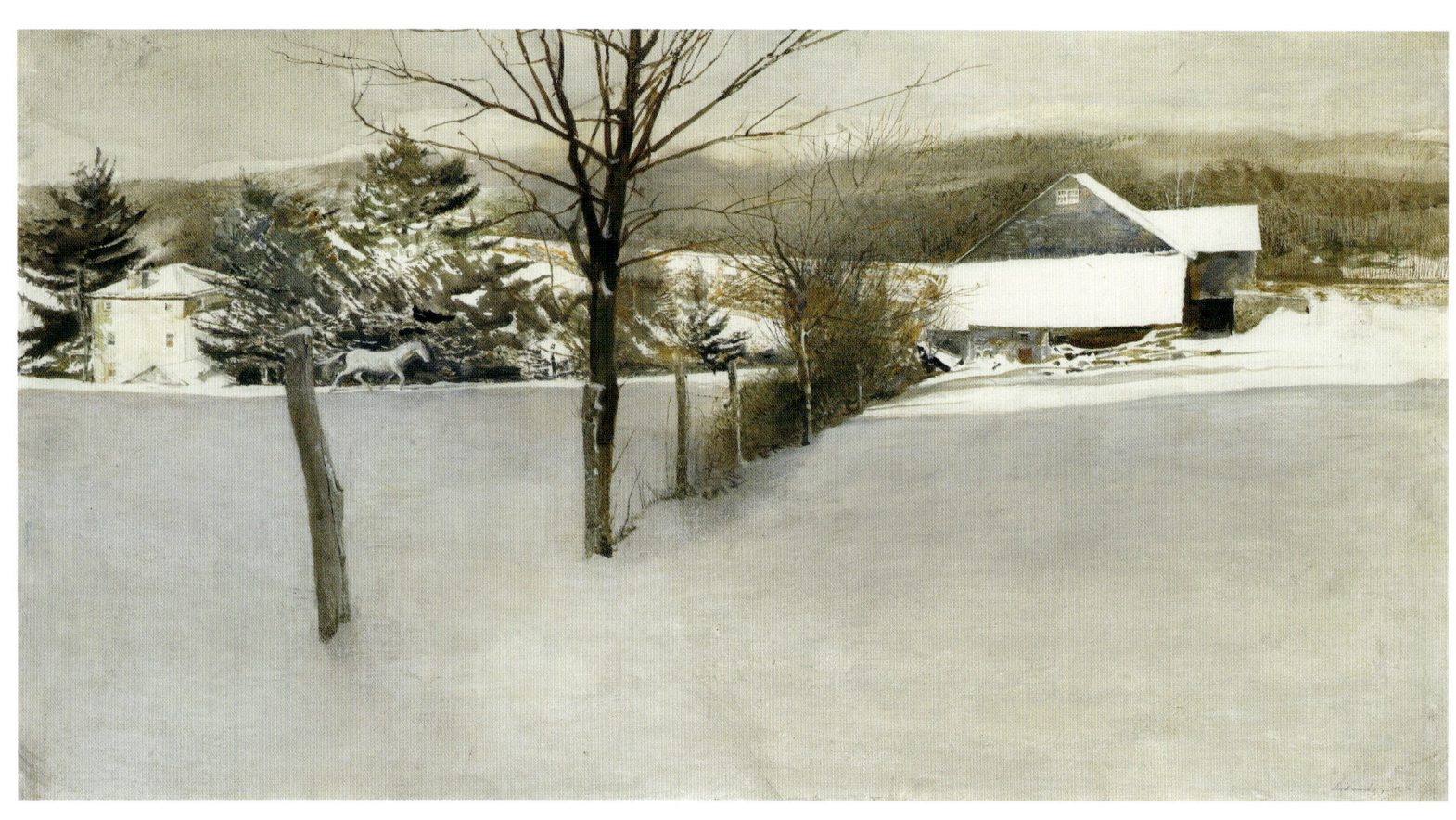

Free Rein, 1994. Drybrush watercolor on paper, 29 ½ × 39 ¼ inches

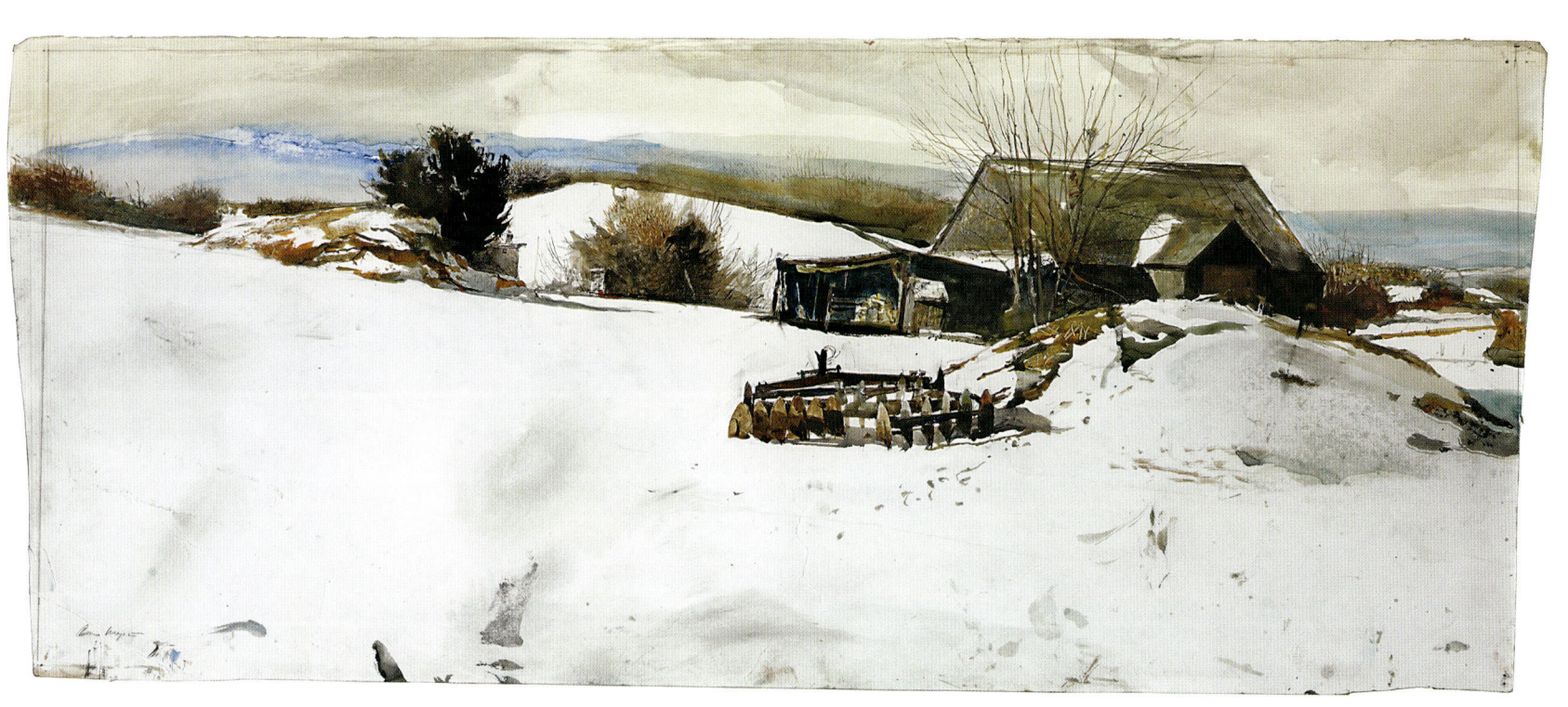

Disk Harrow, 1996. Watercolor on paper, 17 ½ × 43 inches

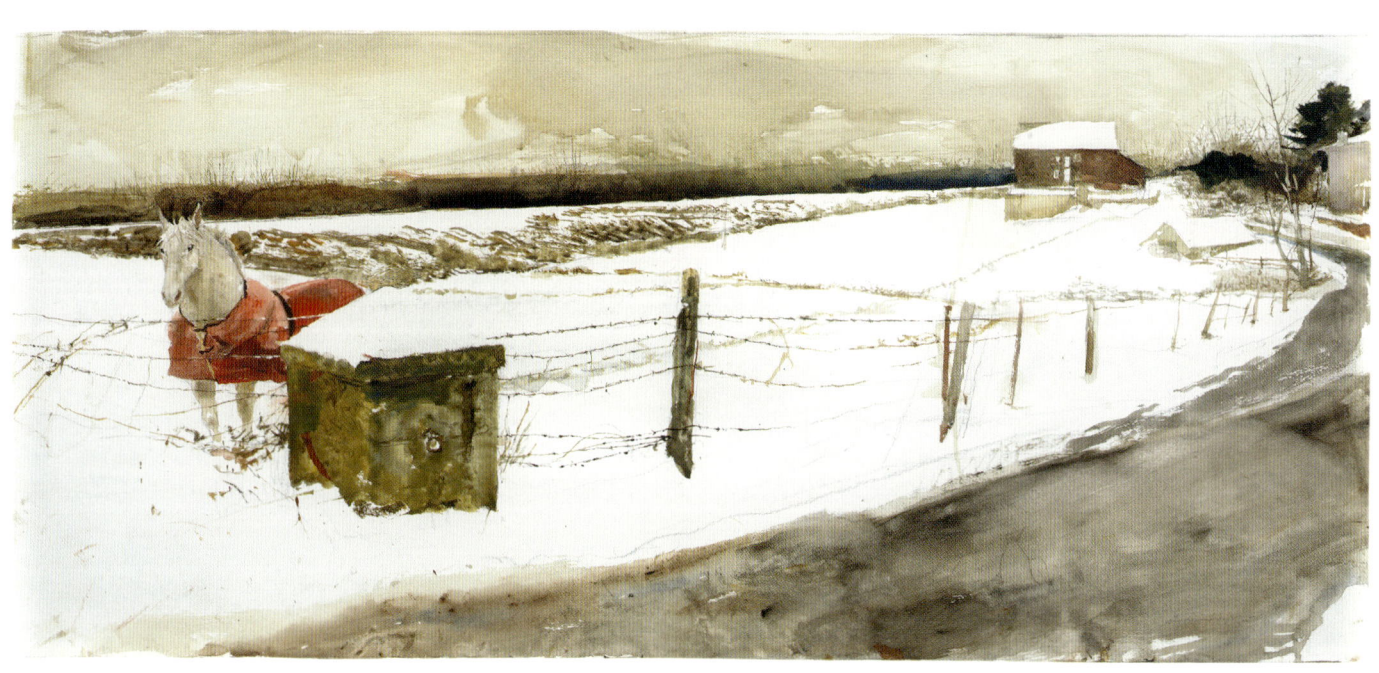

Fenced In, 2001. Watercolor on paper, 17 ¾ × 39 ¼ inches

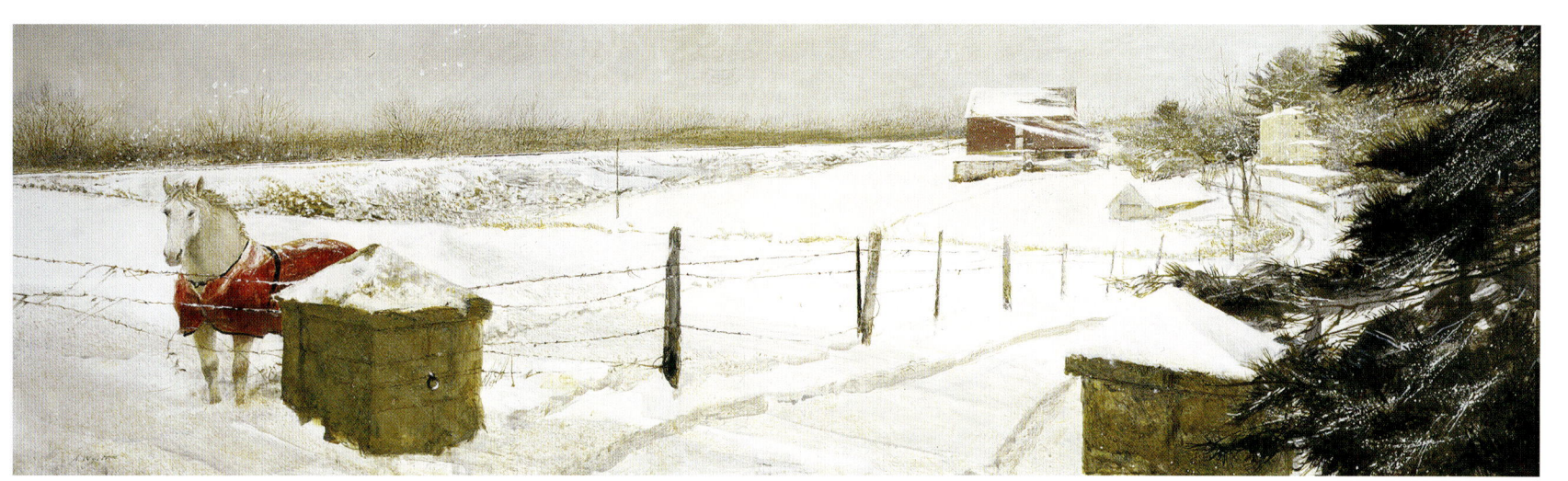

Karlanna, 2001. Egg tempera on panel, 14 ½ × 47 ¾ inches

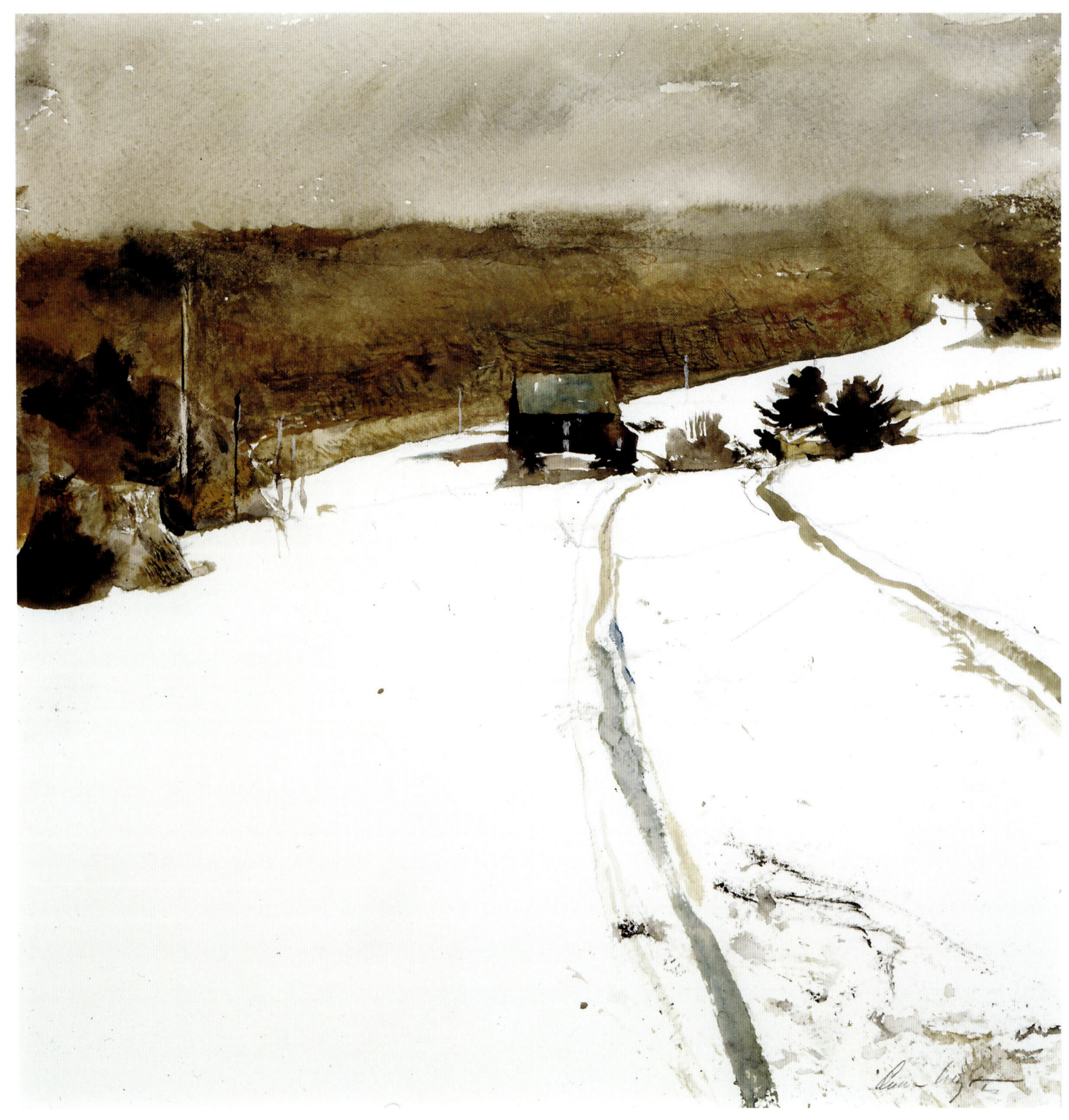

Stump, 1995. Watercolor on paper, 10 ¾ × 10 ⅞ inches

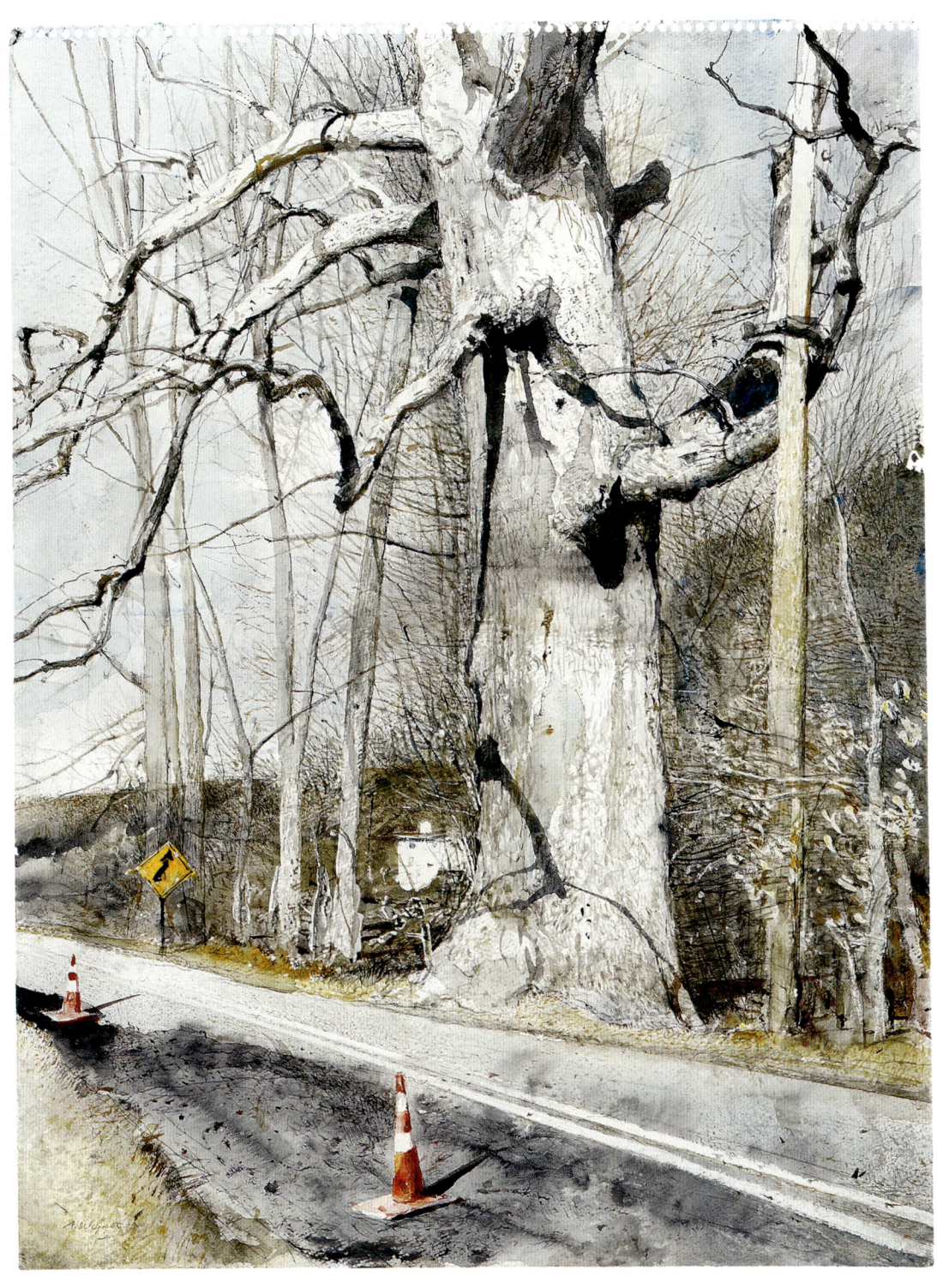

Walking Stick, 2002. Watercolor on paper, 23 ⅞ × 18 inches

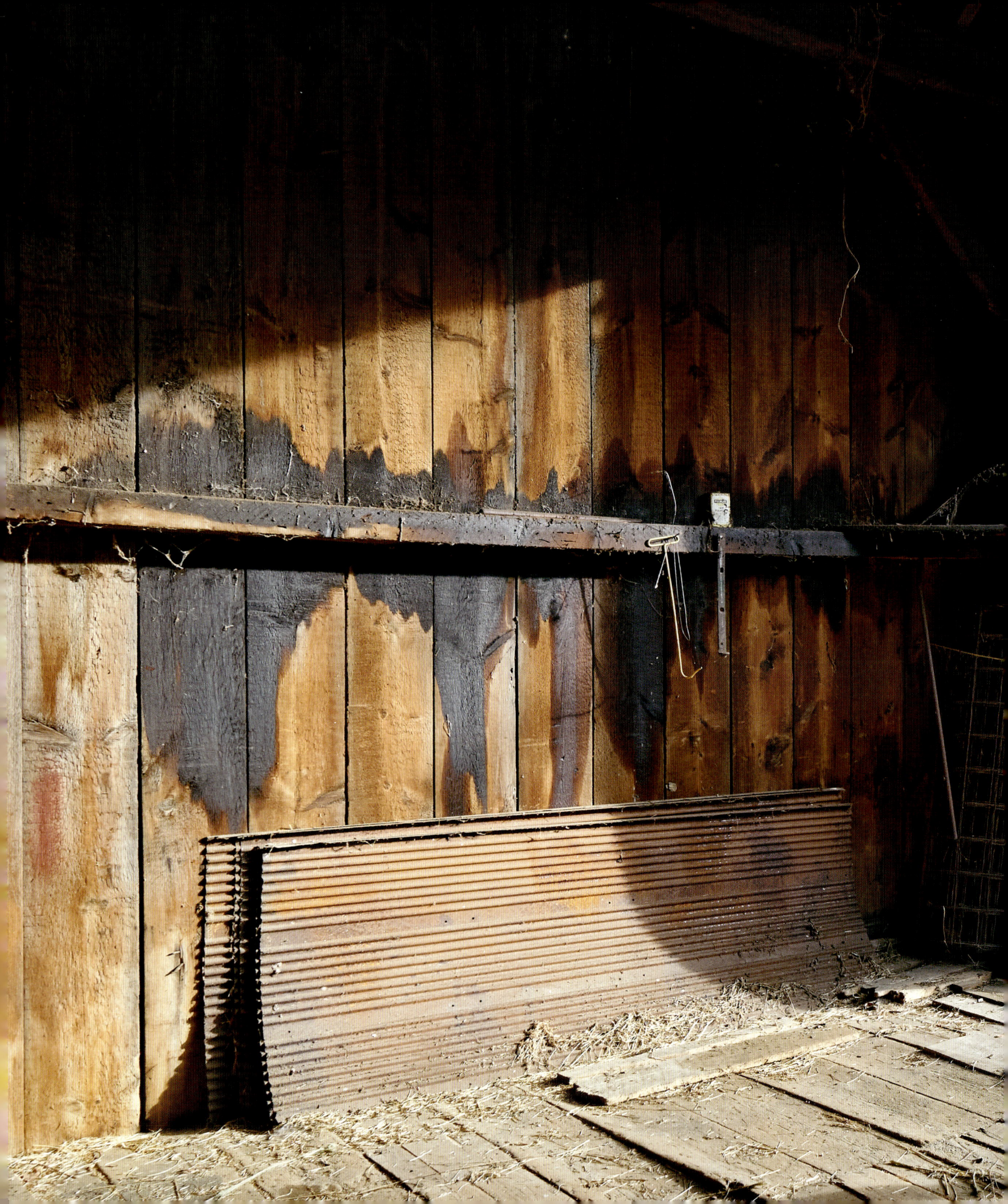

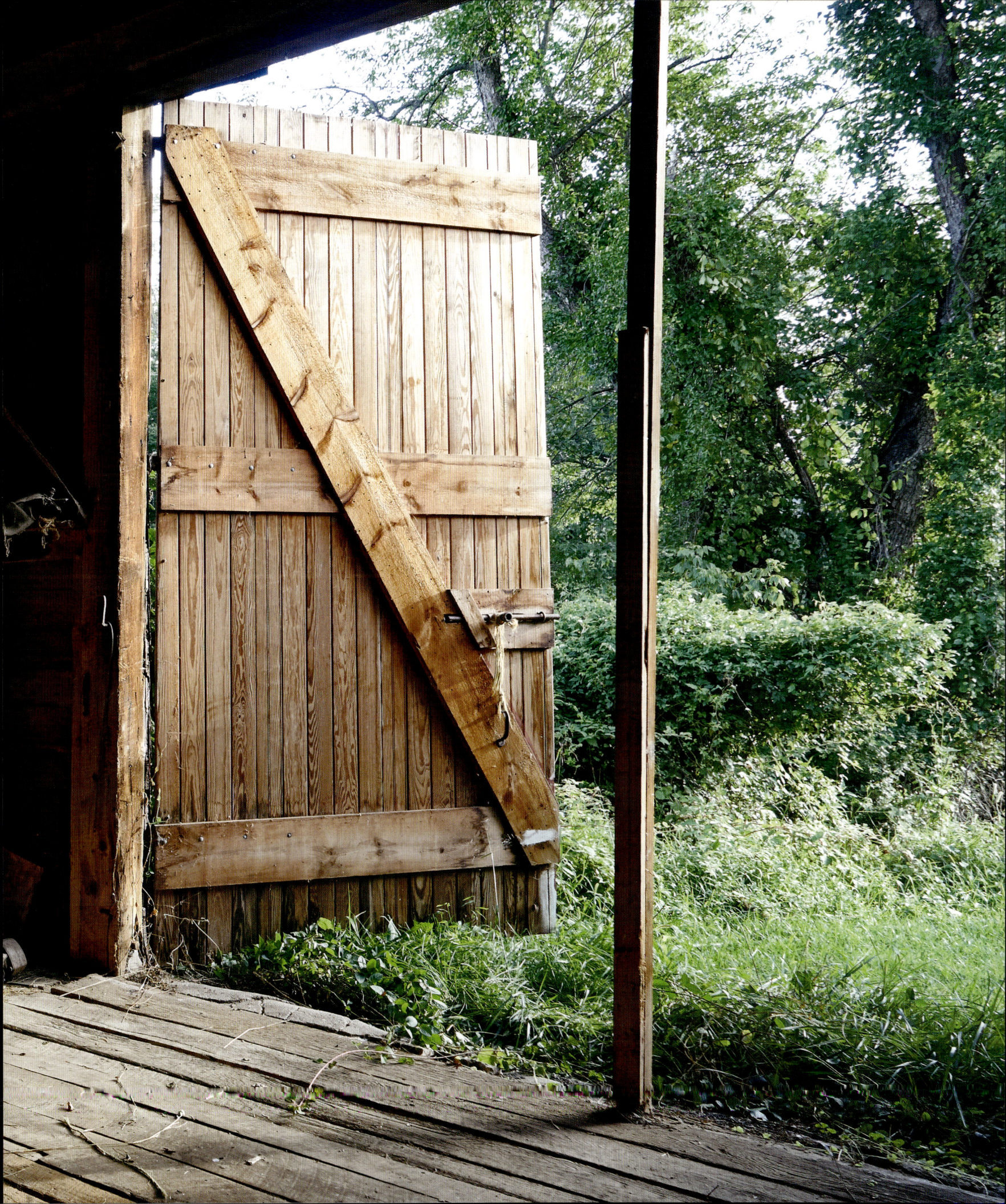

LIST OF ILLUSTRATIONS

All works are listed chronologically and appear at each venue except where noted. Works identified with a (*) are reproduced in the catalogue only.

Chestnut Tree, 1933
Oil on canvas, 30 × 33 in.
Brandywine Museum of Art, Anonymous gift, 2017
Page 51

*Green Hill, 1934
Watercolor on paper, 15 × 21 in.
Wyeth Foundation for American Art, B0070
Page 52

Haying at Kuerners, 1934
Watercolor on paper, 22 × 30 in.
Wyeth Foundation for American Art, B0017
Page 53

*Spring Landscape at Kuerners, 1935
Oil on canvas, 32 × 40 in.
Private collection
Page 54

Untitled, 1935
Ink wash on paper, 15 ¾ × 20 ½ in.
Wyeth Foundation for American Art, B0444
Jacksonville and Winston-Salem only
Page 55

Black Hunter, 1938
Egg tempera on panel, 32 × 40 in.
Wyeth Foundation for American Art, B0004
Page 56

*Winter Morning, 1944
Drybrush watercolor on paper, 25 ½ × 38 ⅜ in.
Private collection
Page 57

Woodshed Study, 1944
Ink wash, watercolor, and pencil on paper, 16 × 20 ¾ in.
Wyeth Foundation for American Art, B0493
Jacksonville and Winston-Salem only
Page 58

Woodshed, 1944
Egg tempera on panel, 31 ½ × 56 ¾ in.
Brandywine Museum of Art, bequest of C. Porter Schutt, 1995
Chadds Ford only
Page 59

*Young Buck, 1944
Watercolor on paper, 29 × 22 ¾ in.
Private collection
Page 60

*Untitled, 1946
Watercolor on paper, 21 ½ × 29 ½ in.
Wyeth Foundation for American Art, B0235
Page 62

End of Winter, Study for Winter, 1946, 1946
Watercolor on paper, 20 ¾ × 28 ¾ in.
The Trout Gallery at Dickinson College, Carlisle, Pennsylvania. Dickinson College Fine Arts Collection, gift of Mildred Sawyer, 1972.2.1
Page 63

*Winter, 1946, 1946
Egg tempera on panel, 31 ⅜ × 48 in.
North Carolina Museum of Art, Raleigh. Purchased with funds from the State of North Carolina, 72.1.1
Page 64

Karl, 1948
Egg tempera on panel, 30 ½ × 23 ½ in.
Albuquerque Museum. Gift of Hope Aldrich, PC2023.29.1
Page 67

*Trodden Weed, 1951
Egg tempera on panel, 20 × 18 ¼ in.
The Phyllis and Jamie Wyeth Collection
Page 68

*Snow Flurries, 1953
Egg tempera on panel, 37 ½ × 48 in.
National Gallery of Art, Washington, D.C. Gift of Dr. Margaret I. Handy, 1977.57.1
Page 69

*Cider and Pork, 1956
Watercolor on paper, 21 ¾ × 29 ¼ in.
Private collection
Page 70

Farm Pond, Study for Brown Swiss, 1957
Watercolor on paper, 13 ¼ × 21 ⅞ in.
Reynolda House Museum of American Art, Winston-Salem, North Carolina. Gift of Barbara B. Millhouse. Reynolda House is an affiliate of Wake Forest University.
Page 71

*Brown Swiss, 1957
Egg tempera on panel, 30 × 60 ⅛ in.
Private collection
Pages 72–73

Rope and Chains, Study for Brown Swiss, 1957
Pencil on paper, 17 ¾ × 23 ½ in.
Wyeth Foundation for American Art, B0857
Page 74

Chimney Smoke, 1957
Watercolor on paper, 21 ⅝ × 29 ¾ in.
Private collection
Page 75

First Snow, Study for Groundhog Day, 1959
Drybrush watercolor on paper, 13 ⅜ × 21 ⅛ in.
Delaware Art Museum, Wilmington. Gift of Mr. and Mrs. William E. Phelps, 1964
Chadds Ford and Winston-Salem only
Page 77

Groundhog Day Study, 1959
Watercolor and pencil on paper, 23 × 17 ⅞ in.
Wyeth Foundation for American Art, B0904
Page 78

Wild Dog, Study for Groundhog Day, 1959
Watercolor on paper, 13 ½ × 19 in.
The Phyllis and Jamie Wyeth Collection
Page 79

*Groundhog Day, 1959
Egg tempera on panel, 31 × 31 ¾ in.
Philadelphia Museum of Art. Gift of Henry F. du Pont and Mrs. John Wintersteen, 1959
Page 80

*Below the Kitchen, 1960
Drybrush watercolor on paper, 23 × 17 ¾ in.
Private collection
Page 82

Night Light at Kuerners, 1960
Watercolor on paper, 22 ⅛ × 28 ½ in.
Wyeth Foundation for American Art, B0950
Page 83

Watering Trough, 1960
Watercolor on paper, 21 ½ × 29 in.
Forsyth County Public Library, North Carolina
Winston-Salem only
Page 84

Young Bull Study, 1960
Watercolor on paper, 14 × 16 ½ in.
Wyeth Foundation for American Art, B2645
Page 85

Young Bull, 1960
Drybrush watercolor on paper, 19 ¾ × 41 ¼ in.
Mr. and Mrs. Nicholas Wyeth
Winston-Salem only
Pages 86–87

*The Trophy, 1963
Watercolor on paper, 22 ⅜ × 30 ½ in.
Private collection
Page 88

Milk Room Study, 1964
Watercolor on paper, 28 ¾ × 23 ¾ in.
Wyeth Foundation for American Art, B1826
Jacksonville and Winston-Salem only
Page 89

*Fence Line, 1967
Watercolor on paper, 21 × 30 in.
Private collection
Page 90

Gate Chain – 1st version, 1967
Watercolor on paper, 22 × 29 in.
Wyeth Foundation for American Art, B1584
Chadds Ford and Jacksonville only
Page 91

Spring Fed Study, 1967
Watercolor on paper, 21 ¾ × 29 ⅞ in.
Wyeth Foundation for American Art, B1601
Page 92

*Spring Fed, 1967
Egg tempera on panel, 27 ½ × 39 ½ in.
Private collection
Page 93

Evening at Kuerners, 1970
Drybrush watercolor on paper, 25 ½ × 39 ¾ in.
Mr. and Mrs. Nicholas Wyeth
Pages 94–95

The Porch, 1970
Watercolor on paper, 21 ½ × 29 ¾ in.
Private collection
Page 97

Spillway – 1st version, 1970
Watercolor on paper, 21 ¾ × 30 in.
Wyeth Foundation for American Art, B1544
Page 98

*After Christmas, 1971
Watercolor on paper, 21 ½ × 40 in.
Private collection
Page 99

Anna Kuerner Study, 1971
Pencil on paper, 14 × 16 ¾ in.
Wyeth Foundation for American Art, B1817
Page 100

*Anna Kuerner, 1971
Egg tempera on panel, 13 ½ × 17 in.
Private collection
Page 101

First drawing, 1971
Pencil on paper, 14 × 11 in.
Collection of Frank E. Fowler
Page 102

The Kuerners, 1971
Drybrush watercolor on paper, 26 ½ × 40 ⅛ in.
Wyeth Foundation for American Art
Page 103

*Peasant Dress, 1972
Watercolor and pencil on paper, 19 ½ × 23 in.
Private collection
Page 104

Spare Room – 2nd version, 1973
Watercolor on paper, 19 × 30 in.
Wyeth Foundation for American Art, B1828
Page 108

*Where the German Lives, 1973
Watercolor on paper, 21 ½ × 29 ½ in.
Fukushima Prefectural Museum of Art, Japan
Page 109

Anna Climbing the Stairs, 1975
Watercolor on paper, 29 ½ × 18 ½ in.
Wyeth Foundation for American Art, B2244
Page 110

Dust Cap, 1975
Drybrush watercolor on paper, 23 ¼ × 23 in.
Wyeth Foundation for American Art, B2243r
Jacksonville and Winston-Salem only
Page 111

*Lamplight, 1975
Watercolor on paper, 21 ½ × 29 ½ in.
Private collection
Page 113

The German, 1975
Watercolor on paper, 21 × 29 in.
Wyeth Foundation for American Art
Page 112

Wolf Moon, 1975
Watercolor on paper, 40 ⅛ × 29 in.
Wyeth Foundation for American Art
Page 115

Home Comfort, 1976
Watercolor on paper, 21 ¾ × 30 in.
Wyeth Foundation for American Art, B2430
Page 116

Steel Helmet, Study for Pine Baron, 1976
Drybrush watercolor on paper, 23 × 28 ½ in.
Wyeth Foundation for American Art
Page 117

*Pine Baron, 1976
Egg tempera on panel, 31 ⅜ × 33 ¼ in.
Fukushima Prefectural Museum, Japan
Page 118

Dusk, 1978
Watercolor on paper, 23 ⅞ × 17 ⅞ in.
Greenville County Museum of Art, South Carolina. Purchased with funds from the 2012 Museum Antiques Show, sponsored by TD Bank
Chadds Ford and Winston-Salem only
Page 119

*Overflow, 1978
Drybrush watercolor on paper, 23 × 29 in.
Private collection
Page 105

Loden Coat, 1978
Watercolor on paper, 30 × 22 in.
Collection of Lorinda P. de Roulet
Chadds Ford only
Page 107

Night Cap, 1978
Watercolor on paper, 18 ¾ × 23 ¾ in.
Wyeth Foundation for American Art
Page 120

Spring Study, 1978
Watercolor on paper, 21 × 39 ½ in.
Wyeth Foundation for American Art, B2406
Page 121

Spring, 1978
Egg tempera on panel, 24 × 48 in.
Brandywine Museum of Art. Gift of George A. Weymouth and his son in memory of Mr. and Mrs. George T. Weymouth, 1987
Pages 122–23

*Farm Road, 1979
Egg tempera on panel, 21 × 25 ¼ in.
Private collection
Page 106

Roof Ladder, 1979
Watercolor on paper, 21 ½ × 29 ¾ in.
Wyeth Foundation for American Art, B2472
Page 124

*Jacklight, 1980
Egg tempera on panel, 43 ½ × 49 ¾ in.
Greenville County Museum of Art, South Carolina. Purchased with funds raised through the 2017 Art for Greenville campaign and the 32nd Antiques, Fine Art, and Design Weekend, presented by United Community Bank
Page 125

Snow Fence, 1980
Watercolor on paper, 16 × 19 in.
Karl Novak, Charleston, South Carolina
Page 126

Grindstone – 1st version, 1981
Watercolor on paper, 21 ¾ × 29 ⅞ in.
Wyeth Foundation for American Art, B2747
Page 127

*Moon Madness, 1982
Egg tempera on panel, 18 × 20 in.
Private collection
Page 128

*Tree House, 1982
Watercolor on paper, 27 × 40 in.
Collection of Frank E. Fowler
Page 130

Spring on Kuerners Hill, 1984
Watercolor on paper, 18 ¾ × 26 ⅝ in.
Greenville County Museum of Art, South Carolina. Purchased with funds from the 2012 Museum Antiques Show, sponsored by TD Bank
Chadds Ford and Winston-Salem only
Page 131

Field Hand, 1985
Drybrush watercolor on paper, 21 ¾ × 39 ⅞ in.
National Gallery of Art, Washington, D.C. Gift of Leonard E. B. Andrews
Winston-Salem only
Pages 132–33

*Ring Road, 1985
Egg tempera on panel, 16 ⅞ × 39 ¾ in.
Private collection
Page 135

Cornflowers, 1986
Watercolor on paper, 21 ¾ × 29 ⅞ in.
Wyeth Foundation for American Art
Page 136

Haymow, 1988
Watercolor on paper, 21 × 28 ⅜ in.
Wyeth Foundation for American Art
Page 137

*Razor Sharp, 1988
Watercolor on paper, 29 ¼ × 21 ¾ in.
Asian Museum of Watercolor Art, Haikou City, Hainan Province, China
Page 138

*Working Farm, 1988
Drybrush watercolor on paper, 21 ⅝ × 39 ⅝ in.
Fukushima Prefectural Museum of Art, Japan
Page 139

Snow Hill, 1989
Egg tempera on panel, 48 × 72 in.
Wyeth Foundation for American Art
Pages 140–41

Funeral Group (Kuerner's Hill I), c. 1991
Watercolor on paper, 51 × 70 ¼ in.
The Phyllis and Jamie Wyeth Collection
Pages 142–43

Barnyard, 1991
Watercolor on paper, 18 ⅞ × 25 ⅞ in.
Private collection
Chadds Ford only
Page 145

Free Rein, 1994
Drybrush watercolor on paper, 29 ½ × 39 ¼ in.
Greenville County Museum of Art, South Carolina. Gift of Mary Burnet M. Johnston, Kate Simpson, and Lee Watson
Chadds Ford and Winston-Salem only
Page 146

Disk Harrow, 1996
Watercolor on paper, 17 ½ × 43 in.
Jim and Jocelyn Stewart
Chadds Ford and Winston-Salem only
Page 147

Fenced In, 2001
Watercolor on paper, 17 ¾ × 39 ¼ in.
Greenville County Museum of Art, South Carolina. Purchased with funds from the 2003 Museum Antiques Show, co-sponsored by Cherry, Bekaert & Holland, LLP, and Wachovia Bank
Chadds Ford and Winston-Salem only
Page 148

*Karlanna, 2001
Egg tempera on panel, 14 ½ × 47 ¾ in.
Private collection
Page 149

Stump, 1995
Watercolor on paper, 10 ¾ × 10 ⅞ in.
Private collection
Chadds Ford only
Page 150

*Walking Stick, 2002
Watercolor on paper, 23 ⅞ × 18 in.
Collection of Frank E. Fowler
Page 151

Karen Baumgartner is Collection Manager at the Andrew & Betsy Wyeth Study Center at the Brandywine Museum of Art. Under the employ of the Wyeths, she cared for their art collection and archives from 1999 until 2022. During this time, Baumgartner also contributed scholarship to multiple exhibitions and publications, most notably *Andrew Wyeth: People and Places* (2017), *Andrew Wyeth: In Retrospect* (2017), and *Andrew Wyeth: Life and Death* (2021). In 2022, she joined the Brandywine Museum of Art in its new arrangement with the Wyeth Foundation for American Art, and the following year she curated the exhibition *Abstract Flash: Unseen Andrew Wyeth* at the museum, where she continues to compile research for the artist's eventual catalogue raisonné.

William L. Coleman, Ph.D., is Wyeth Foundation Curator and Director of the Andrew & Betsy Wyeth Study Center at the Brandywine Museum of Art, with additional responsibilities at the Farnsworth Art Museum in Rockland, ME. He writes and teaches on the art of the United States, with a particular research focus on the histories of landscape painting. Coleman was previously Director of Collections & Exhibitions at The Olana Partnership, NY, and Associate Curator of American Art at the Newark Museum of Art, NJ, and he held long-term fellowships from Washington University in St. Louis, the National Endowment for the Humanities, and the Smithsonian Institution. Recent projects include essays for collection catalogues of the Palmer Museum of Art, PA, and the Frances Lehman Loeb Art Center, NY, as well as the exhibitions *Every Leaf & Twig: Andrew Wyeth's Botanical Imagination* (2024) and *Terraforming: Olana's Historic Photography Collection Unearthed*, with artist David Hartt (2023).

Allison C. Slaby is Curator at Reynolda House Museum of American Art in Winston-Salem, NC, where she has been on staff since 2005 and has curated more than thirty exhibitions, including *Chrome Dreams and Infinite Reflections: American Photorealism* (2022) and *Grant Wood and the American Farm* (2016). Coinciding with the latter, she published "Grant Wood's Agrarian Landscapes: Myth, Memory, and Control" in *Formations of Identity: Society, Politics and Landscape*, published by Cambridge Scholars. A graduate of Vassar College in Poughkeepsie, NY, Slaby received her master's degree in art history, specializing in American art, from the University of Massachusetts Amherst in 2002. Previously, she held positions at the Mead Art Museum at Amherst College; the Rose Art Museum at Brandeis University; Harvard University; and at Dumbarton Oaks Research Library in Washington, D.C.

James Welling is a Lecturer with the Status of Professor in the Visual Arts program at Princeton University. From 1995 to 2016 he was a professor in the Department of Art and Area Head of Photography at the University of California, Los Angeles. Welling's photographs are in the collections of the Carnegie Museum of Art, Pittsburgh, PA; Buffalo AKG Art Museum, NY; The Art Institute of Chicago; Centre Pompidou, Paris; Museum moderner Kunst Stiftung Ludwig Wien, Vienna; Kunstmuseum Bielefeld, Germany; Stedelijk Museum voor Actuele Kunst, Ghent, Belgium; Victoria and Albert Museum, London; and the Tate Modern, London. Images from his series *Wyeth* are in the collections of the Wadsworth Atheneum Museum of Art, Hartford, CT; Whitney Museum of American Art, New York; Hammer Museum, Los Angeles; the Brandywine Museum of Art, Chadds Ford, PA; and the Farnsworth Art Museum, Rockland, ME. *Things Beyond Resemblance: James Welling Photographs* was published by the Brandywine Museum of Art in 2015.

Andrew Wyeth working at Kuerner Farm, 1975

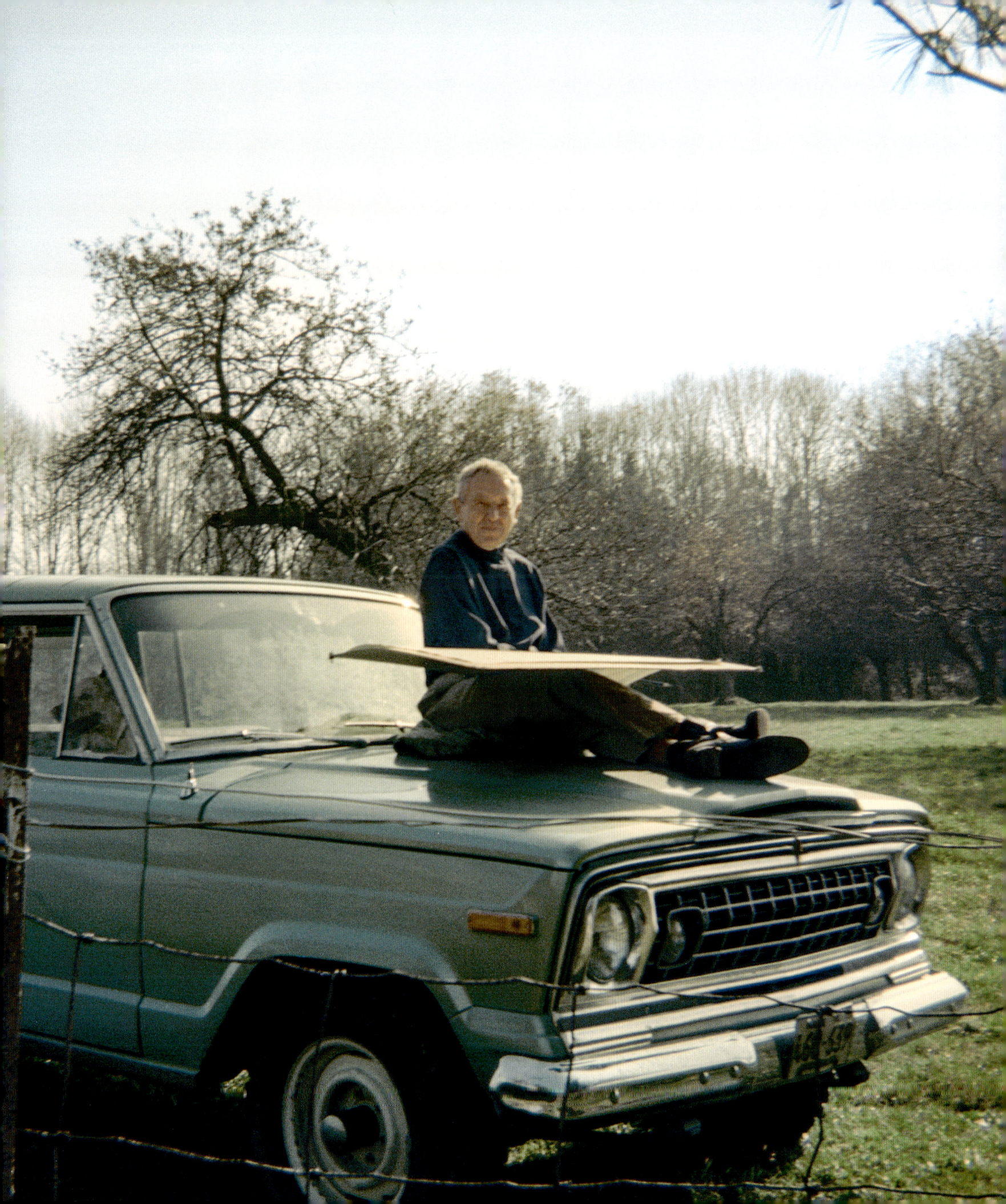

Published on the occasion of the exhibition *Andrew Wyeth at Kuerner Farm: The Eye of the Earth*, organized by the Brandywine Museum of Art, Chadds Ford, PA, and Reynolda House Museum of American Art, Winston-Salem, NC, in association with the Wyeth Foundation for American Art

Exhibition Itinerary
Reynolda House Museum of American Art, Winston-Salem, NC: February 13–May 25, 2025
Brandywine Museum of Art, Chadds Ford, PA: June 21–September 28, 2025
Cummer Museum, Jacksonville, FL: November 7, 2025–February 15, 2026

Generous support for the exhibition is provided by Wells Fargo.

WELLS FARGO

First published in the United States of America in 2025 by

Rizzoli Electa
A Division of Rizzoli International Publications, Inc.
49 West 27th Street
New York, NY 10001
www.rizzoliusa.com

in association with

Brandywine Museum of Art
1 Hoffman's Mill Road
Chadds Ford, PA 19317
www.brandywine.org

and

Reynolda House Museum of American Art
2250 Reynolda Road
Winston-Salem, NC 27106
www.reynolda.org

For the Brandywine Museum of Art:
Editor: William L. Coleman
Managing Editor: Todd Bradway

For Rizzoli Electa:
Publisher: Charles Miers
Associate Publisher: Margaret Rennolds Chace
Editor: Jason Best
Production Manager: Alyn Evans

Design: Robin Brunelle

ISBN: 978-0-8478-4573-6
Library of Congress Control Number: 2024942526

Printed in Hong Kong
2025 2026 2027 2028 / 10 9 8 7 6 5 4 3 2 1

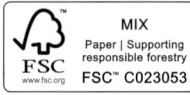

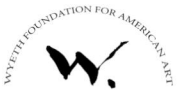

The mission of the Wyeth Foundation for American Art is to support excellence in exhibitions and publications on the historic art of the United States, with a particular commitment to the multigenerational creative legacy of the Wyeth family of artists. Founded by Andrew & Betsy Wyeth with participation from leaders in a variety of fields, it holds the copyright to Andrew Wyeth's work and owns the definitive collection of his art, including some seven thousand paintings and drawings as well as archives and historic properties that are available to researchers. The art collection is entrusted to the management of the Brandywine Museum of Art in Chadds Ford, PA, and shared with the public in galleries there, at the Farnsworth Art Museum in Rockland, ME, and in exhibitions nationwide.

Cover and page 2: Andrew Wyeth, *Loden Coat*, 1978 (detail, p. 107)
Back cover: Andrew Wyeth, *Evening at Kuerners*, 1978 (detail, pp. 94–95)

Photography by Joshua McHugh
Page 4: Farmhouse at Kuerner Farm, 2024
Page 9: Kuerner farmhouse, 2024
Pages 10–11: Kuerner Farm, 2024
Pages 22–23: View from the porch of the Kuerner farmhouse, 2024
Pages 32–33: Attic of the Kuerner farmhouse, 2024
Pages 38–39: Barn at Kuerner Farm, 2024
Pages 48–49: Interior of the barn at Kuerner Farm, 2024
Pages 152–53: Interior of the barn at Kuerner Farm, 2024

Vellum inserts
Pages 16/17: Karl Kuerner in his World War I German soldier's uniform, c. 1916
Pages 32/33: Anna Kuerner, n.d.
Pages 48/49: The Kuerner children, from left to right, Elizabeth, Lydia, Clara, and Karl Jr., 1941
Pages 64/65: Karl Kuerner, 1968
Pages 96/97: Andrew Wyeth at Kuerner's Hill, 1987 (detail). Photograph by Theo Westenberger
Pages 112/113: The Kuerner children, from left to right, Clara, Louise, Elizabeth, and Karl Jr., c. 1934
Pages 128/129: Karl Kuerner and Karl Jr. at the back door of the Kuerner farmhouse, c. 1935
Pages 144/145: Kuerner Farm, n.d.